Dutch
African American Liberators

Dutch Children of African American Liberators

Race, Military Policy and Identity in World War II and Beyond

MIEKE KIRKELS *and* CHRIS DICKON

Afterword by SEBASTIAAN VONK

McFarland & Company, Inc., Publishers

Jefferson, North Carolina

OTHER WORKS BY CHRIS DICKON

Americans at War in Foreign Forces:
A History, 1914–1945 (McFarland, 2014)

The Foreign Burial of American War Dead:
A History (McFarland, 2011)

LIBRARY OF CONGRESS CATALOGUING-IN-PUBLICATION DATA

Names: Kirkels, Mieke, author. | Dickon, Chris, author.
Title: Dutch children of African American liberators : race, military policy
    and identity in World War II and beyond / Mieke Kirkels and Chris Dickon ;
    afterword by Sebastiaan Vonk.
Other titles: Kinderen van zwarte bevrijders. English
Description: Jefferson, North Carolina : McFarland & Company, Inc., Publishers,
    2020 | Includes bibliographical references and index.
Identifiers: LCCN 2020035804 | ISBN 9781476676937 (paperback :
    acid free paper) ∞
    ISBN 9781476641140 (ebook)
Subjects: LCSH: Racially mixed children—Netherlands—Limburg. | Blacks—
    Netherlands—Limburg—History. | World War, 1939-1945—African
    Americans. | Limburg (Netherlands)—Race relations. | Children of military
    personnel—Netherlands—History. | African American soldiers—Family
    relationships—Netherlands—History.
Classification: LCC DJ92.B53 K5713 2020 | DDC
    305.8/059607303931049248—dc23
LC record available at https://lccn.loc.gov/2020035804

BRITISH LIBRARY CATALOGUING DATA ARE AVAILABLE

ISBN (print) 978-1-4766-7693-7
ISBN (ebook) 978-1-4766-4114-0

Front cover image of Robert Joosten and his mother Annie (courtesy Robert Joosten)

Printed in the United States of America

McFarland & Company, Inc., Publishers
    Box 611, Jefferson, North Carolina 28640
    www.mcfarlandpub.com

To Huub Schepers,
1945–2016

Table of Contents

Preface

This book is an American version of the book *Kinderen van zwarte bevrijders* (*Children of black liberators*) by Mieke Kirkels, first published in the Netherlands in 2017 and here revised with coauthor Chris Dickon. It focuses on the lives of 12 biracial Dutch citizens born in the aftermath of World War II. *Kinderen* also presented the powerful and largely unknown story of the continuing American dilemma of racism, as told from the perspective of a small but vital nation across an ocean, several thousand miles away.

Written for both an American and a largely bilingual Dutch readership, this edition expands upon the original book's contexts of American and Dutch history, highlighting the evolution of racism in the U.S. military, and featuring similar stories about the postwar children of African American soldiers in other parts of Europe—including the United Kingdom, Germany and Austria—giving broader scope to stories from the Netherlands. It relates the very human stories of those who have always lived just outside of their own society, without the full knowledge of who they were, and in the shadows of racism. They are now in their seventies and two are deceased.

Kinderen was the fourth in a series of books by Mieke Kirkels about Americans of World War II and the people of the Dutch province of Limburg. The first, *From Farmland to Soldier's Cemetery* (as published in the Netherlands in English), coauthored with Jo Purnot, was the product of an oral history project that was supported by the Dutch Ministry of Health, Welfare and Sport, to capture the experiences of Dutch citizens and Americans who had constructed, taken apart, and reconstructed the great American cemetery at Margraten, under the harsh duress of weather and the relentless press of the dead of war. The cemetery is now the final resting place of more than 8,000[1] Americans, each grave and each of the 1,722 names of the missing on its memorial wall adopted by a Dutch or Belgian family. Its history will help to structure the narrative of this book.

1

The first Americans to turn the earth of the new cemetery were Black members of U.S. Army Quartermaster Service units. One of them was led by Jefferson Wiggins, at the time a young man from a family of sharecroppers in the American South. His contribution to the oral history project led to *Van Alabama naar Margraten* (*From Alabama to Margraten*), an oral history biography of Wiggins in which Kirkels traced his life from his childhood in Alabama, through the war, and to his return to Margraten as a distinguished American educator and honored guest in 2009. Published only in the Netherlands in 2014, it opened up for that audience the larger story of the African American contribution to the liberation of the country from German tyranny.

Kinderen van zwarte bevrijders (by Mieke Kirkels, Vantilt Publishers, 2017) cover image is of Robert Joosten and his mother, Annie (courtesy Robert Joosten).

Van Alabama also played a role in letting the aging, biracial adult children of African American soldiers and Dutch women know that, although they may have been isolated in their lives, they were not alone. A small community of them was brought together by Kirkels as the basis for *Kinderen*, and their stories were also told in other Dutch media. That book, and this one, precede the next project to be undertaken by Kirkels and historian Sebastiaan Vonk in Limburg: researching the biographies of 172 African American soldiers buried at Margraten. A reading of this book will suggest why it is important that their stories be told, and an explanation of the project is told in the Afterword.

Kirkels' work with the history of the Margraten Cemetery was a subject of Chris Dickon's book *The Foreign Burial of American War Dead*, published in 2011 by McFarland. Since that time, the authors have assisted each other with various projects in the United States and Europe. With this book, Kirkels' work on the subject of the role of Black Americans in World War II Netherlands is brought to an American and English-speaking readership and placed more expansively in the context of American racial history.

The stories told of the lives of 12 Dutch citizens will set us out on a long journey through geography and time. It will start on the docks of a newly liberated Antwerp, Belgium and travel from the Alabama of the deep American South, through rural England, into the sandstone caves of Limburg and the woods and destroyed cities of a defeated Germany. Historically, it will range from the Caribbean based slave trade of the 17th century, to the origins of New York City, American racism from the Revolutionary War to the present day, two world wars, and Germany's effort to rethink its history in the 1950s.

We will dip into three old movies and training films and read through documents about military racial policy that have been forgotten for more than half a century. The last paragraph will be written at a father's gravesite seen for the first time by his 73-year-old child in Orlando, Florida. The driving force of the story will be the needs of its subjects to understand their own lives through the prism of whatever knowledge they can gain of the lives of their African American fathers.

From a letter to Henry Van Landingham, July 4, 1995;

My family told me that during World War II at the end of 1944, you had a relation with Mrs. Nols who was my mother. I was born on 9th September 1945 as a Black baby in a white family.

5 years ago my sister told me your name. At that time I began the search for my real father. Then also started the desire to know how he would look like, if he's married and if he has any children and a lot of these questions.

It hurts to know, that there is somebody out there who is part of you, a father you don't know.

The only thing I want is to meet you.

So I ask you, are you that American soldier my mother had a relation with?

Please forgive me if this letter is going to hurt you and your family. Maybe you are angry if you read this letter, but believe me, I'm asking myself for years this question: Who is my father?

If I know that, then I can forwards with my life.

Els Geijselaers
Berg en Terblijt [Limburg province, Netherlands]

ONE

War Babies

I should have given you away to the circus.—Rosy's mother, Roos

As the years played out, there would be no doubt that Lenie Wetzel, a young woman of Dutch Limburg, and Edward Moody, a biracial young man of New Jersey, had conceived a child in genuine romance. They had met in the first months of the liberation of the Netherlands. It was a turbulent time and the province was partying. The women of Limburg and the men of the U.S. Army had gotten together for the whole range of reasons that men and women had sex, good and bad. Some of the men had been Black, and the couples formed had overcome the strenuous effort especially of the American military command to keep them apart—or to put them out of reach of each other if their relationships became known.

After learning of the pregnancy, Edward and Lenie had gotten married, though it would be a marriage that was not permitted by various military regulations.[1] It was now September 5, 1945, and their child would be born in just a few days, but they would never see each other again. He had been transferred from Heer right after the wedding and she had moved to her uncle's house in Hasselt, Belgium and all she could learn for sure was that he would be returning to America on a troopship from Antwerp, where now she stood searching for him on a quay of the Scheldt river.

Antwerp and the Scheldt had been the most active European source of America's immigrant population for more than a century, largely through the ships of the Red Star Line. A creation of the Pennsylvania Railroad and other interests in 1883, it offered a passage by rail from points deep within Europe, up the Scheldt and across the ocean by ship, then deep into America by rail at the other end of an arduous journey. The enterprise was conducted in collaboration with the social service organizations of immigration and brought nearly three million people to America until 1934.

Lenie Wetzel and Edward Moody among friends in 1945 (courtesy Ed Moody).

Among its passengers had been Albert Einstein, Irving Berlin and the first Jews to escape Nazi Germany in 1933 and 1934.

The Scheldt had been one of the most contested rivers of the war. Its 220 miles took the course from Aisne, France through Ghent, Belgium, then to Antwerp and 80 miles northwest into the Netherlands and the North Sea. Antwerp had been liberated on September 4, 1944, but it would take the Battle of the Scheldt to gain full control of the river and to open the port of Antwerp to British, Canadian and Polish forces two months later.

> At the same time, American forces attempting to reach Aachen, Germany, as part of the larger effort of Operation Market Garden to cross the Rhine on bridges as far north as Arnhem in the Gelderland province, had pushed across the Belgian-Dutch border and into south Limburg. They were able to get only as far as Sittard, north of Maastricht and 25 miles from their goal, but the liberation of the most southern part of Limburg was a result.

With the advance into Germany stalled, south Limburg became a concentrated outpost of American men and the culture they brought with them. When the oil and truck supply lines opened up from Antwerp the harbor in Cherbourg later on, they were mostly driven by the African Americans of the Quartermaster Corps (QMSC). With few exceptions, the

QMSC soldiers formed a separate part of the U.S. Army Including many of those who had not been allowed to fight in the war, but only to perform the tasks of support. In Limburg, however, they were, among others, the gravediggers of the creation of the American cemetery at Margraten, and the drivers of the convoys of the Red Ball Express which moved more than 420,000 tons of supplies along the push from Normandy to the German border.

One of the Quartermaster troops had been Edward Moody in a large truck. Now, one year and one day after the liberation of Antwerp, Lenie walked the docks of the recovering city looking for a troopship that she thought might be taking Edward home, but to no avail. He would be gone from Europe, never to return—though that would not be the end of it.

His son, the baby Ed Moody, Jr., was born on September 14, 1945, in the U.S. Army hospital in Roermond, up against the German border. Legally, he would have been an American citizen[2] and was not registered as a Dutch citizen. He was born into a Limburg now reviving from the harsh privations of years of German occupation since 1940. The province was about to embark on change at breakneck speed. It was on the brink of a new era in its long history.

As it had preceded the difficult years of the Second World War, that recorded history dated back to Roman times, but did not take the actual name of Limburg ("fortification" of the "linden, or lime, tree") until the creation of the Kingdom of the Netherlands (the "lower country") in 1815. The region was to have been called Maastricht, but it soon took on a referential name to the Duchy of Limburg/Limbourg, a state of the Roman Empire. In 1839, the larger Limburg was split into separate, adjacent Belgian and Dutch provinces. Some of Dutch Limburg's mid-century years were spent as a state of the German Confederation until 1867. During that time and into the mid–20th century the social and economic life of the province was mostly defined by coal mining and agriculture. The first coal fields were owned by Augustinian Catholics who used it as fuel for their work and abbey until the late 19th century when technology helped to discover significant underground seams at the time of the Second Industrial Revolution.

At the outset of the 20th century, the Netherlands, belatedly in the view of some, began to take control of coalfields that had become owned by foreign interests, most notably across the common border with Germany which was, in essence, selling Dutch coal to the Dutch. By the 1930s, state owned mining predominated in the region and employed nearly 25,000 people. One of its mines, the Maurits, emerged as the largest in Europe.

The southern region's largest cities all could trace their known origins to various centuries of the Roman Empire and its largest, Maastricht, to a Roman bridge across the Meuse River that would complete a highway from France to Germany. Its name could be translated to "a crossing of the Meuse." By the 20th century, it had served as a strategic center for the trade, culture and wars for the countries, kingdoms and empires from the English Channel to the eastern edge of Germany. In 1992, it would give its name to the Maastricht Treaty, which created the European Union and the international currency, the Euro.

The city of Heerlen shared similar Roman origins, though excavations late in the 20th century would point to settlements dating back to 4000 BC. It would become an urban center of the coal mining industry of the late 19th through mid–20th centuries. The first settlements of Sittard were found to go even further back, and its modern origins to the 9th century. Valkenburg aan de Geul (on the Geul River) and its environs held the mines and marl (chalk) caves that could be traced back to the 1st century AD. The ruins of its centerpiece 12th century Valkenburg Castle would remain a tourist attraction of the 21st century. By 1974, the discovery of oilfields in the north of the country and the development of industrial coals would lead to the closing of all of the mines of South-Limburg.

Roermond, in the middle of Limburg, grew up on both sides of the Roer River and over its history had fallen under the various rules of the Roman Empire, Germany, France, the Habsburgs, the Netherlands and Spain. At various times it had managed to serve as its own, independent political entity, or to reinforce its identity with its own coinage.

As Limburg joined in the formation of the Kingdom of the Netherlands in 1815, the Kingdom, in turn, evolved from agriculture to industrialization along with its neighbor nations and was a full partner in the development of world culture, art and science. Its social, religious and economic beliefs and practices would be strong though never monolithic, and always in dynamic contrast with each other.

The Netherlands also maintained a portfolio left over from its centuries as a navigator of the seas, the settling of the New World and the holder of Empire, especially in the 17th century. During that time, it had pioneered international commerce, created multinational corporations, famously founded New York City as New Amsterdam in 1653, and transported perhaps a million of the enslaved from Africa to North and South America. Enslavement, however, was illegal within its own European borders.

By the time of the advent of World War II, the Dutch kingdom had held only the East Indies (now Indonesia) on the Pacific equator above Australia, and Suriname and the Dutch Antilles just off the north coast of South America. The country managed to remain neutral in World War I and not without controversy,[3] although that would eventually be deemed to have been a stance that had been ultimately helpful to the Allied cause.

It was not able to repeat that position in World War II. The response to a 1939 declaration of neutrality was a German invasion and bombing of Rotterdam in May 1940. Then the exiled Dutch government in London was compelled to declare war against the Japanese after the attack on Pearl Harbor in December 1941. The Japanese wanted the Dutch East Indies for strategic position and its natural resources, and they took it in March of 1942. They were welcomed at first as the bringers of respite from Dutch rule since 1815, but the Japanese occupation inclined quickly toward cruelty, torture and imprisonment.

The German occupation of the Netherlands became equally harsh and deadly to 100,000 of the country's Jewish population, and perhaps most of its Roma and Sinti population of 500.[4] Homosexuals were oppressed, but it is believed that none were killed for that specific reason. The Nazis were eventually met by a strong Dutch underground and resistance movement that did not, however, do much to prevent the inherent bureaucracy and national infrastructure from carrying out the round up and movement of Jews to concentration camps that would eventually send them on to the death camps. Anne Frank may have been the symbol of Jewish resistance against the machinations of the Holocaust, but, like most of the 80,000 Jews of Amsterdam, she was taken by the national railroad first to Westerbork transit camp in the Drenthe province, then sent first to Auschwitz, then to Bergen Belsen in Germany where she died of typhus.

Through it all, the occupied country kept up with the attempted Nazi oppression of its cultural and religious distinctions with a fierce determination to maintain what the Dutch believed to be their strong and particular Dutch identity.[5] As the war and occupation were coming to an end, the Dutch were coming to yet another challenge to the notions of who they were. They were emerging from a war that had impoverished them and would still feature long stretches of regional starvations, some of them aggressively enforced by the Germans. They were in need of what would become the thorough-going support of the forces that had brought them their liberation, but those forces also brought with them difficult new challenges, opportunities and problems for their strong cultures and social traditions. And, in the case of the American led liberation and recovery of their nation, it would bring with it the deep racial dysfunction of American society.

A future for the baby Ed Moody would be emblematic of those challenges and he would live a life into the 21st century that would encompass the best of Dutch society under postwar change. But there were others like him who would not be as fortunate.

Rosy Heuts had been born on July 16, 1945, into a life that would take her to an attempted suicide nearly 40 years later. Her mother, Roos, would not say it directly, but she may have been a child of rape. She had grown up as one of 12 children in a mining family in a portion of Limburg that was well described by its name *Kale Heide*—barren heath, near Brunssum on the German border. At the time of the liberation, Roos worked as a chambermaid at the Grand Hotel in Heerlen. The hotel had served as German headquarters during the occupation and its owners would be led off with shaved heads as collaborators after the war. It would at one time be visited by American Gen. Dwight Eisenhower in planning for the continuing advance into Germany.

Roos had been perhaps too popular with the young men of the region, but of Rosy's father she would only say "A Black American soldier grabbed me in the woods next to our house. I was pregnant right away," and she could provide no name for the man. After Rosy's birth, Roos moved to Amsterdam to earn a living, leaving Rosy behind with an aunt in her first years, and in later years, in Rosy's memory, telling her things like "I should have given you away to the circus," always following similar comments with "but of course I didn't."

Rosy Heuts and Ed Moody were just two of an estimated seventy biracial children born in the Limburg province of the Netherlands at the end of World War II. Their lives would often be ambiguous and conflicted. Their skin color caused them to be called by many others the "Little Americans," though they most often knew nothing of their biological fathers and their American origins. As they grew, they might have heard something of the fleeting contact of their parents, or they might have heard nothing at all, or something that was not true.

Each was born into a unique situation. Some were immediately given up to other caretakers or placed in Catholic orphanages of varying quality. Some would have a single mother, or eventually a stepfather who could be loving or abusive, and in some cases a man whose wife had been unfaithful while he was away at war. Some would be accepted into large, loving families of half-siblings. Just a few would be known to eventually end up touching the shore of their father's America.

And, as children of World War II, they would become part of a universe of millions of such children of war before and since. Their experiences were often differentiated by the respective differences in the relationships between the countries of origin of their mothers and fathers. The children of parents from countries allied in war might have the least conflicted of outcomes. Where power imbalances existed, the outcome could be more difficult, and sometimes violently so. Racial difference in those relationships could only push outcomes for the resulting children to an even more complicated realm, further aggravated in many cases by the already existing social and stated racial practices of both victors and vanquished.

Each of the principal European nations of the war had different results.

For the most part, the presence of American troops in England had been long sought after and most welcomed. The two countries shared intricate history and had similar cultures and language, albeit with different racial experience before the war. The Americans arrived after 300 years of racial division dating back to the first transport of enslaved Africans by Dutch traders to Jamestown in 1619. Britain, too, had engaged in the slave trade into the mid–19th century, but it had little of the subsequent American experience of racial segregation and animus. The British were at first socially welcoming to the Black Americans in their midst.

A common estimate was that British women and American men had parented 22,000 Black and white babies over the course of the war. At least 130,000 African Americans passed through the United Kingdom in the war with a result of perhaps 1,700 of what came to be called the "Brown Babies" of England.[6] Most would lead lives as outsiders starting in childhood and without the full force of social, religious and government support available to all children and parents in those circumstances. (Chapters Eight and Nine).

In postwar Germany a defeated aggressor that had premised its pursuit of war on the purity of its own race was now occupied by a multi-racial force with its own racial conflict. And it was a society in which dissension against the country's rationale for war could previously have been severely punished to the point of death but was now allowed to go to opposite extremes. Sex with an African American man could even be a statement of rebellion on the part of a now liberated German woman.

By 1953, however, the Reuters news service reported on "a conference to discuss the problem of the 3,000 Negro 'Occupation Children' in West Germany now old enough to enter elementary schools."[7] The nature of the "problem" was not identified and the number of all such children fathered by Allied troops in the nation was estimated at 90,000. With the continuing presence of Americans, the number would rise to 5,000 bi-racial children by the mid–1950s. They would play an intricate role in the coming years of the development of postwar West German society.

Austria had been annexed and subsumed in a malevolent Reich in 1938. Its name was changed—twice—and its self-identity obliterated until its liberation in April 1945. The subsequent Allied force was either occupier or liberator depending on how one had lived through the previous seven years. Of an estimated 8,000–30,000 occupation children of American servicemen perhaps as many as 500 were biracial.[8] For the most part, they were marginalized people, and some were said to have been turned into child laborers to the point of a form of enslavement. (Chapter Ten).

In all cases, however—England, Germany and Austria—the biracial children of the 1940s and 1950s would resurface in public consciousness in the first 20 years of the 21st century. Many of those still alive sought to know the identities and the lives of their fathers. And no less so in the smallest national number of them in the Netherlands.

That number was set at seventy, but it could only be estimated in retrospect and by observation. There were no bureaucratic checkmarks to note at their births and many had been born ambiguously with various surmises about their appearance, if a difference was even noticeable at birth. If the father wasn't known, his name would be recorded only as *Miles Americanus*, American soldier.

It was not easy, at the outset, to determine the exact number of liberation children of any race. Many had been legitimized by the stepfather if the mother was already married, as in many cases, and there was an uncountable number of marriages between actual American fathers and Dutch mothers. Estimates of the number of children born to fathers of all Allied forces in the Netherlands range from 4,000 to 8,000. Because of the early liberation of south Limburg and its position as the marshaling point for the continuing war with Germany, a large number of white and biracial children were born in the province, as well as its neighboring provinces.

As the liberation proceeded, the Dutch Federation of Institutions for the Unwed Mother and Her Child (FIOM), located in the Hague, began to send out alarms that a wave of illegitimate births seemed to be taking place in the province and that many of the babies were being given up to, or coming under the care of, related social agencies. The FIOM had been created in 1930 as an attempt to bring the various independent homes for unwed mothers under a common and consistent direction. Illegitimacy in the Netherlands was met with solutions that could be more judgmental than practical. An attempt in the previous year to mandate government support for unwed mothers had been defeated by a morality lobby supported by Catholic and Protestant interests, which felt that such women were not entitled to the same kinds of benefits that went to those who were incapacitated by illness. The need for private and religious institutions operating on their own resources was re-affirmed and FIOM marked a more enlightened approach to the needs of mothers and their children that was less restrictive and punitive than it had been up to that time.

During the war, occupation and liberation, there was still no government policy in place regarding unwanted pregnancies and unwed mothers, and effective adoption law would not come to the Netherlands until 1956. Nor was there any meaningful responsibility taken by military authorities, although the German government had begun to take some responsibility for the children of its occupying soldiers.

By far, the largest number of war babies in the Netherlands were those of German fathers over five years of occupation. In Adolf Hitler's mind, the people of Germany and the Netherlands were of common Aryan stock and the birth of Dutch children fathered by German soldiers was desirable. The Nazi *Lebensborn* program would seek to promote and support the birth of Aryan children, within or without marriage, throughout Europe during the war years. For many years, it was believed that perhaps 10,000 children had been born of such unions, half of all illegitimate births during that time.[9] Their births were recorded by German officials up until the year 1944, and the mothers involved were eligible for one-time financial support while fathers were not discouraged from adding whatever other support they might. In 2004, German military archives would look back on the time and suggested that the actual number of German-Dutch children of the war might be close to 50,000.[10]

With the alarm about illegitimate births sounded in 1945, FIOM was able put pregnancy prevention and education programs in place that led to a reduction of unintended births in 1946. Still, they would have their own challenges as children of foreign fathers. The white children could more easily blend into Dutch society, but the biracial children could not; nor could they know of each other and form community as they became older.

It would not be until late in life that Rosy Heuts, now Rosy Peters, and Wanda Van der Kleij would meet each other by chance and form a relationship in which they would come to call each other *Zus*, Sis. One day in Maastricht, Wanda and a young woman named Maureen waited together at a bus stop. "I couldn't help but ask her if she too perhaps had an African-American father," said Maureen, "because that was how much she looked like my mother Rosy."

The chance meeting took place during the time of an oral history project to develop the stories of the biracial children of Limburg, the origin of this book. At Maureen's urging, Wanda became involved and relationships between the children, now in their retirement years, were finally formed.

The American liberators had rolled into the village of Nieuwenhagen, not far from Heerlen, in September of 1944. One of them had been Edward Brown, who started a relationship with Wanda's mother, Wanda Dera, the wife of William Van der Kleij. When William returned from service in Indonesia in 1947, he expected to meet a two-year-old daughter, but quickly observed that she was not his own.

Wanda and William would subsequently produce two sons and remain married until 1985, but never happily so. Young Wanda adored the man she thought of as her father, but he could only respond to her dismissively at first. One of Wanda Dera's brothers had emigrated to America and volunteered to adopt the child to her country of half origin, but the mother would not agree. The entire matter was a forbidden topic for all parties, and the daughter was caught in a devastated childhood. She could not understand why until she began to realize that she was different from everyone else.

As with many of the biracial liberation children, Wanda would have to grow into an understanding of her situation on her own and with her own young resources to deal with it. And she would not be the only one of the children, male and female, to eventually become victims of abuse. By Wanda's account, William would accompany physical abuse with name calling. When Wanda entered adolescence, the abuse became sexual; her attempts to gain the help of her mother were met with a turning away.

As she grew older and began to seek a place for herself in society through education, she heard William say, "You do not need to go to school, Blacks are only good for laborers." Her mother would not intervene. Fi-

Wanda van der Kleij, born September 24, 1945, with her mother Wanda Dera (courtesy Wanda van der Kleij).

nally, gaining entrance to a course of home economics, her first job took her to a home where the woman opened the door and, after a flustered pause, exclaimed "A Black?!" and slammed the door in her face.

Eventually, Wanda's life would take a turn for the better. But, in its totality, its circumstances, and those of the small number of biracial liberation children of the Netherlands would offer an intricate reflection of the evolution of American and European racial attitudes and practices as they extended back into the 19th century, and forward to the 21st.

Wanda van der Kleij at age four. At the time, she was the child of an ambivalent mother and a stepfather who would become sexually abusive, and beginning to understand that she was different from other children in some way (courtesy Wanda van der Kleij).

Two

Social Reality,
Military Policy

We do not seem to be able to get the thing quiet.—Pres.
Herbert Hoover, 1931

Jefferson Wiggins' time in Limburg in 1944 would be short, arduous and gruesome. He would not be associated with the births of children, but with the deaths of the thousands of Americans brought to the farm fields that would become the American cemetery at Margraten.

In 2009, Wiggins would be called back to the Netherlands to offer an epilogue to his own experience as an African American soldier in the first months of the liberation and the understanding that had come to him, as he grew into a distinguished educator and writer, of its place in the racial history of the United States. In a book based on that journey, published in 2014, he would be the catalyst for the discovery by the biracial children of Limburg of their commonality and community.

In 1942, he was a 15 or 16-year-old child of rural Dothan, Alabama. He had been born at a time when the birth records of Black babies were an afterthought, which perhaps allowed him to pass as an 18-year-old when he was offered an opportunity to escape his life in a family of sharecroppers. The work on a large cotton plantation had been sunrise to sunset and taken priority over time for schooling. There was not always enough to eat.

And Wiggins had known the fear of confrontation with the Ku Klux Klan (KKK).

"If you met a white man," he told an oral history, "you had to step off the pavement and continue walking on the road, because you could not walk with them on the same sidewalk. We knew that because our parents realized well that it was their duty to us to rub it in how we should behave, as heard in those days. I was always angry about that,

16

but what could we do? We lived between a smile and a tear, between fear and hope."

The KKK had first emerged during Reconstruction after the Civil War as a white supremacist movement that was resistant to the rights and equal status implied in the freeing of the slaves after the war. Its method was violence and murder and it had an effect: the crippling of organization, politics and social safety of people who were trying to establish themselves in the American ideal. It lost power and influence fairly quickly due to its own lack of organization, an inherent tendency toward criminality and vicious racism, and specific laws against it, but was reinvigorated in Georgia in 1915.

One night after midnight, perhaps 40 men in white hoods and robes appeared in front of the Wiggins family's shed intent on a lynching. As was their method, a cross was lit in the yard, but the father was able to escape. He returned in the dark of night a week later and the family moved to another location. The event reinforced the instruction that was given to Black children. Wiggins had grown up knowing that the white man's rules needed to be followed. "If you do not like it, they can come to kill you."

A job as a delivery boy for a drugstore in Dothan brought him to deliver a package to an Army recruiter named Faulkner who seemed at once to treat him as most young Black men were treated in the time and place, but with the cast of an abrupt Army sergeant preparing a young man to fight in war.

"How much is it, boy?" Faulkner demanded of the very nervous Wiggins.

"The price is on the package, Sir," he replied.

In Wiggins' memory, Faulkner bellowed back at him. "But that was not my question. Can't you read, boy?"

In truth, Wiggins' only real experience with reading was with the family bible and at the insistence of his grandmother. He took the sergeant's three quarters and headed toward the door, but Faulkner stopped him with another bellow. "Stop right there," he ordered. "Do you know this country is at war?"

"Yes, I do," he replied faintly.

Faulkner's voice softened. "You look malnourished. You would probably do a lot better in the Army where you'd get better treatment."

The young man did not know the meaning of "malnourished." Faulkner understood and asked, "Do you get enough to eat?" Another truth of Wiggins' life was revealed.[1]

Sharecroppers, or tenant farmers, did the hard labor of planting and harvesting the crops of white landowners. In theory, the two would share in the resulting proceeds, but it was an agreement that seemed always to be abrogated or modified by some circumstance or another. Often, the living costs of the sharecropper family owed to the landowner would exceed the amount of the proceeds, leading to more debt.

In the year that Wiggins met the recruiter, the landowner had decided that the prevailing price of cotton was too low; better to store the harvest until the following year when things might be better. Without the sale, however, there would be no proceeds to share and, with credit exhausted in local stores, the family fell into near starvation. Wiggins' father pleaded with the landowner for just one bale of cotton to sell, but finally had to sell it on his own. He gave the landowner his rightful proceeds from the sale and his family "ate until we could hold no more."[2]

It was later that night that the KKK came looking for his father.

Wiggins had never thought of joining the Army. But Faulkner's promise of a new life took hold.

"For the rest of the day, as I rode around town on my bicycle making my deliveries, I was thinking about some of the things Sergeant Faulkner had said. Medical care, three meals a day and if you get sick they're going to look after you. And on top of all that, the Army was going to pay me $21 a month! That was a fortune to me. My job at the drug store only paid $2 a week."

Though he had been raised to practice strict honesty, he answered a question from the sergeant about his age with "Eighteen." It was probably not believed by his inquisitor, but the nation was at war. Wiggins, however, did not then go off to fight the war, but, at first, to bury its dead, landing in the Normandy Invasion in June 1944 and arriving in Limburg as a member of the 960th Quartermaster Corps. His first job was to dig graves in fields appropriated from local farmers in a community with which he was told not to interact, and whose members had been similarly warned.

"Each morning, when we arrived at the cemetery, there were six, sometimes eight, young females who stood at a distance and waved at us. It seemed as if they were afraid to get too close. Looking back, we later realized that this was probably the first time in their lives that they had seen a Black person. They were cautious, and, in some cases, they seemed afraid. But as the days turned into weeks, instead of waving from a distance, they abandoned caution and began to speak with us."[3]

In 1936, the U.S. War Department, in an attempt to appear to be proactive about the place of Blacks in the American defense force, produced a short film that seemed to show once again that it was actually ambivalent on the matter, and to set the tone for its actions in the war to come.

Its order to the Signal Corps was to produce a film that was 763 feet in length to be titled *Training of Colored Troops in the U.S.*[4]

A story should be worked out showing the negro soldier from the time he is shown in his home, through the processing and training camps and when he received letters from his home folks. The story should stress, of course, the military training phase, scenes of which should be cut long.

All pictures of white troops in this section are to be removed.

The last direction would not be realized in the final film, as white officers were occasionally caught directing the Black troops about, or in a couple of cases noting the camera and trying to get out of the frame. The script was precise in time and content:

Scene 11.	Long shot showing the newly enlisted men learning a Squad drill.	59 ft
Scene 12.	Long shot of men entering the mess hall.	37 ft
Scene 13.	Closeup of 9 men eating watermelon.	15 ft
Scene 14.	Closeup of a man eating watermelon.	14 ft
Scene 15.	Long shot, washing mess kits.	28 ft
Scene 16.	Long shot of the men now in uniforms as they form in line. On the left can be seen their newly given bedding equipment.	4 ft
Scene 17.	Long shot of the men marching away for drill.	18 ft

Excerpt of the working script for "Training of Colored Troops in the U.S.," produced by the U.S. Army Signal Corps in 1936. The stereotyped relationship between African Americans and watermelon dates to the time the U.S. Civil War. The fruit was seen as a source of nutrition and economic freedom by Blacks, who could raise and sell it to support emancipation. As a symbol of that freedom, however, it was derided by Southern white people as indicative of Black childishness and uncleanliness. They continued the use of watermelon as an indicator of irresolute messiness that had gone back to nineteenth century stereotypes of European and Arab peasantry (National Archives).

A scene of nine men eating watermelon may or may not have been intended to cater to a pejorative social stereotype of Black people and watermelon, but the film's non-military scenes of a Black family made proud by a son's enlistment in the Army fulfilled similar stereotypes with costumes, makeup and props down to a corncob pipe held by a gray-bearded grandfather at just the right angle.

The history of African American participation in the defense of the nation is a push and pull of racial attitudes, racial aspiration and the practical manpower needs of war.

The French and Indian Wars of the mid–18th century saw the enslaved used to defend the land holdings of their owners. In the Revolutionary War, it was, ironically, the British who promoted equality leading to

The older members of an African American family listen to a letter from their soldier relative read to them by a younger member, from "Training of Colored Troops in the U.S.," 1936 (National Archives).

potential freedom for African Americans. At first, Gen. George Washington, a slave owner, would not allow Blacks in the Continental Army. The British governor Lord Dunmore responded by offering freedom to those who escaped and joined British forces, which, in turn, led the Revolutionary forces to offer the same. Slavery would continue as a matter of national policy after the war, but a door would be opened in the Northern states to the new thinking and social movement opposed to slavery.[5]

The War of 1812 saw a similar and successful promise by the British to deliver those enslaved who joined their effort, particularly at sea, to places of freedom when their service was completed, a factor in the development of an African Canadian population. And an estimated 200,000[6] of the enslaved or escaped eventually became participants in the Civil War after an initial resistance was worn down by the need for more men. Most naturally, the vast majority fought with the Union Army and Navy. Thousands could be found in the Confederate effort, however, "actuated by a type of loyalty unsurpassed in human annals."[7]

During this course of American history, the country did not maintain much of a standing force but relied on scattered militias and regiments throughout the land. They included two regiments of Black foot soldiers, and two of Black horse cavalries occasionally involved in Indian conflicts on national frontiers.

The Spanish-American war of 1898 required the quick raising of an effective national fighting force which included newly created Black regiments with little training or sufficient equipment. They would supplement a handful of standing Black regiments dating to the Civil War. The end of that and related conflicts, and the turn of the century, saw an increased emphasis on a standing peacetime defense force, but it would eventually be caught short by the sudden demands of the American entrance into World War I in 1917.

African American participation during that time had been undercut by general ambivalence on all sides. As the nation looked at the European war in 1915, a civilian effort was begun to prepare a force of Americans ready to be converted to military enlistment if needed, but it did not even think of Black participation. The effort was led by many distinguished Americans, including former president Theodore Roosevelt. By some accounts, Roosevelt's *Rough Riders* had fought successfully side by side with Black soldiers in the Spanish-American War. Roosevelt, however, would only attribute their success to the work of white leadership.[8]

The 20th century years leading up to World War I were racially toxic in America. The initial shock of the end of slavery after the Civil War had soon evolved into social and economic segregation of the formerly enslaved and their ancestors. Restrictive laws and unspoken norms came to be named after Jim Crow, a blackfaced minstrel show caricature played by white performers across the country and in England, from a time that predated the Civil War.

The ultimate expression of the tone of the time was an epidemic of extrajudicial public lynchings of Blacks by angry mobs as events of public spectacle. All groups who were marginal in American society could be subject to lynching over a period beginning with the first Black lynching in 1835 and lasting well into the 20th century, but African Americans paid the highest price by far. A study by the Tuskegee Institute of the years 1882–1968 catalogued 1,297 white lynchings, often of immigrants, Catholics and non–Christians, but 3,446 of Blacks.[9] As with the attempted lynching of Jefferson Wiggins' father, most were driven by the actions of the Ku Klux Klan.

The advent of World War I was marked by the popularity in 1915 of a cultural icon of the Jim Crow era, the film *The Birth of a Nation*. Its three hours were a telling of history since the Civil War from the same perspective that had created Jim Crow; most of its Black characters were white actors in blackface. Credited with the reinvigoration of the Ku Klux Klan, it would be the first movie to be screened inside the White House under President Woodrow Wilson, who would be judged by history to have been both progressive and bigoted.

As Wilson finally took the nation to war, it would be with the willingness on the part of African Americans to enlist in the effort, met, however, by a reluctance to bring them fully on board. The National Association for the Advancement of Colored People (NAACP) had been founded to promote equality and reduce prejudice by W.E.B. Dubois and others in 1909, but with the declaration of war in 1917 Dubois declared a pause of sorts. "*First* your country, *then* your rights!" he declared in the NAACP's publication *The Crisis*.[10]

Dubois and others believed that Black participation in the war would offer the opportunity for African Americans to gain respect and equality. He continued:

> Certain honest thinkers among us hesitate at that last sentence. They say it is all well to be idealistic, but is it not true that while we have fought our country's battles for one hundred fifty years, we have *not* gained our rights? No, we have gained them rapidly and effectively by our loyalty in time of trial.
>
> Five thousand blacks fought in the Revolution; the result was the emancipation of slaves in the North and abolition of the African slave trade. At least three thousand Negro soldiers and sailors fought in the War of 1812; the result was the enfranchisement of the Negro in many Northern States and the beginning of a strong movement for general emancipation. Two hundred thousand Negroes enlisted in the Civil War, and the result was the emancipation of four million slaves, and the enfranchisement of the black man.[11]

Those may have been results of previous wars, but in this case the War Department was determined not to go into a war as a military agency of social change. The Secretary of War, Newton D. Baker, made that clear. It could not "undertake at this time to settle the so-called race question," although Black soldiers would be "fairly treated."[12]

When Blacks went to enlist, they were often turned away, in large part because there were no Black regiments to take them in. When, however, a race neutral draft law was enacted in May 1917, it yielded 31 percent of the eligible black population as opposed to just 26 percent of eligible whites.[13] In keeping with military resolve not to try to solve society's racial problems and despite DuBois' aspirations, those Blacks were placed on segregated transportation, taken to segregated military bases in segregated communities and placed in segregated regiments that were for the very most part non-combat. They were to become truck drivers, janitors, road builders, grave diggers, dock workers and general laborers. Those given the opportunity to prove themselves in fighting, however, were met with inferior equipment, a paucity of Black commanders because of previous discrimination, and white leadership that could be antagonistic.

Most notably, an exception was the 93rd Regiment, which was sent to blend in with the French army and fought effectively and without incident. Of the 367,000 Blacks first drafted (of a total force of 404,00 over the course of the war), 140,000 would end up in France, but just 40,000 of those in combat and the rest in support and infrastructure roles.[14]

The position of the War Department was that it was not in a position to solve America's problem with racial segregation, but it seemed to take pains to inflict that problem on others. A condition of the American donation of Black soldiers to French forces was that the norms of American segregation be continued in France. By some accounts, liaison officers, worried about the effect that French integration would have on American soldiers after the war, passed along secret memos to French commanders warning against equal treatment of Black and white soldiers. In particular, relationships between Black soldiers and French women were to be discouraged.[15]

> It is requested that the civil authorities concerned take steps to co-operate toward the prevention of these harmful relationships by enlightening the residents in the villages concerned of the gravity of the situation and by warning them of inevitable results.
>
> The question is of great importance to the French people and even more so to the American towns, the population of which will be affected later when troops return to the United States. It therefore becomes necessary for both the colored and white races that undue mixing of these two become circumspectly prevented.[16]

The instructions were largely ignored. Since the late 1800s, France had been a place to escape American racism and an international stage for the abolitionist efforts of Black American leaders and thinkers like Dubois and Frederick Douglass. DuBois, in particular, was a Francophile who had created a 500-picture exhibition about African American life and commerce for the Paris Exposition of 1900, the largest World's fair to that date. His praise of French attitudes and actions about the Black man was a regular feature of *The Crisis*. "It was France—almighty and never-dying France leading the world again,"[17] he wrote of the nation's ceremony in honor of those men of color who had fought valiantly for France.

At the end of World War I, no African Americans would receive the Medal of Honor. In France, however, the first American, Black or white, to receive the Croix de Guerre would be Henry Johnson of the Black 369th Infantry, and 170 members would follow him with that honor after the Armistice. Similar honors would come to the Black American prize fighter Eugene Bullard for his actions in the French Foreign Legion. Henry Johnson would eventually receive a Medal of Honor—eighty-five years after his death in 2015. It would be preceded by the only other postwar award of a Medal of Honor to an African American in 1991, to Freddie Stowers for a heroic attack on a German trench.[18]

The poster depicted the 369th Infantry in successful combat against German soldiers in full American colors as Abraham Lincoln, who had emancipated the slaves, looks on (Wikimedia Commons).

The 369th was derived from the New York Army National Guard and was also called the Harlem Hellfighters. The reluctance of the War Department to send Black troops into combat led to a decision that the unit should fight alongside French forces, where they would be welcomed. France was not in the practice of racial discrimination generally, and they were needed. An attempt by Germany to convince the men through propaganda that they should not fight in the name of a country that had treated them so badly seemed to have the opposite effect and the 369th would become celebrated in France for valiant fighting from Chateau-Thierry to Champagne. It was believed to have spent more continuous days in combat, and to have suffered more casualties, than any other similar combat unit: 191 days and 1,400 dead and injured.

In another light, the 369th brought a previously unseen view of America across the ocean in the form of its marching band. Its combat work done, the band then took the music of Harlem and the introduction to the first stirrings of American Jazz throughout Europe and, finally, returned to the United States with a march up New York's Fifth Avenue.

"How splendidly you have vindicated the confidence of the people of New York," orated former New York Governor Charles Whitman. "You have acquitted yourselves as men. High officials say that no soldiers have behaved better on the battlefield, in town and city, and on shipboard than have the colored boys of the 369th Infantry."[19]

He continued, curiously, but perhaps in a reflection of the ambiguity with which African Americans were considered. "In all your dealings with people of other nations and races you have committed no act which reflected on the character, dignity, and manhood of your regiment." He went

The **369th Infantry parades in New York City on February 23, 1919** (U.S. National Archives).

on to urge them to "show their mettle by fighting for good citizenship and law and order at home."

The speculation by W.E.B. Dubois that service in the war could bring progress and equality for African Americans would not be fulfilled. And the unspoken fear of white military leaders that Blacks who fought in war would be emboldened to fight at home was continued in postwar society. Black leadership saw the need to take pre-emptive action.

In January 1919, the Tuskegee Institute held a conference entitled "Problems Connected with the Demobilization of Negro Soldiers." Its focus was particularly on the return of Blacks to the American South, and plans were already in place to allow them to leave the military community only as employment became available to them in the civilian community, thus lessening the economic disruption of their return. The keynote conference speaker was Special Assistant to the Secretary of War and Secretary of the Tuskegee Institute Dr. Emmett Scott. His words were stark.

> The returning Negro soldier will not be the foul wretch from which to shrink in terror, or a plague from which to flee in fear, as some seem to think. He will return both physically and mentally benefited by reason of his military training and experience during the Great World War and, naturally, he will return to the Southland and other sections with a broader vision and appreciation of American citizenship, as well as with new ideas of what Liberty and Freedom (not license) really mean.
>
> He has clearly shown his eager willingness to discharge the duties and responsibilities of American citizenship, and it is devoutly hoped that fair minded Americans in all parts of the country will calmly and justly recognize the fact that he is, therefore, entitled to all of the rights and privileges which the laws of our country offer to all other classes of our common citizenship.[20]

The resistance to that hoped for sentiment rose quickly in postwar society and it became ugly. One strain insisted that claims of Black bravery in war were lies meant to cover up Black cowardice and incompetence. An opposite voice spoke to the abuse of Black troops by white commanders and the prejudicial actions of white troops. Where Blacks were used in combat it was as cannon fodder for the white troops that followed. When they weren't used in combat they were given the most menial of hard labor.

A more subtle—and predictive of what would occur in World War II—part of the argument was about what had occurred in France. American leadership, according to the complaint, had attempted to convert France to the American norm of second-class citizenship for Blacks. France would not go along with it, and in many cases actively resisted it. American leadership pushed back. And so it went.

A result of the experience of World War I and its aftermath was the reoccurrence of the ambivalence about African American participation in national defense by all sides, but a Second World War was coming into view in the 1930s. The 1936 film about the training of Black troops seemed to be an official reflection of an unenthusiastic response to the situation. If it was intended as a recruitment tool, it was hobbled by racist stereotypes and poor production values. There was nothing compelling about it.

If anything, the intervening years had been more unsettling than any other time. An anti-lynching bill introduced in Congress in 1921 failed to carry. Murders of Blacks took place on a regular basis and without resolution. They were often premised on perceived transgressions of Blacks upon white women. In 1921 in Tulsa, Oklahoma, as an example, an accusation of attempted rape by a Black man upon on a white woman set off riots that ended with an initial count of 36 dead and the destruction of a Black neighborhood of 1,200 homes. It had been known as the Greenwood District, and called by some "The Black Wall Street" because of the relative affluence of its residents.

It was soon realized that the man had only stepped on the woman's foot by accident. The event would reverberate into the 21st century with a new accounting by the 1921 Tulsa Race Riot Centennial Commission of perhaps 300 dead and buried in mass graves that were yet to be fully rediscovered.[21] In 2019, the question of mass graves was rekindled in the framework of a homicide investigation and was met with renewed determination to use modern technologies to confirm the nature and extent of their existence, if indeed they could be found. In 2020, as the nation entered a period of attempted racial reconciliation, the history of the Tulsa riots was introduced to the national discussion.

The KKK had a membership of 4 million in 1924 and staged a march down Pennsylvania Avenue in Washington. Increasing migration of Blacks from the rural South to the economic opportunities of the northern cities was met by the economic rigors of the Depression. In 1935, one third of the Black population—4 million people—received social welfare. The weekly relief payment for Blacks, however, was $9 as opposed to $15 for whites. Anti-lynching bills introduced in 1933 and 1940 were largely opposed by Southern legislators and not enacted into law. President Franklin Roosevelt, who needed the support of the same politicians for New Deal and pre-war legislation, could not be counted upon to support anti-lynching and civil rights initiatives, Alternatively, his wife, Eleanor, would be a powerful voice in their support, a marital contrast that was perhaps by design. As of mid-2020, though "Hate Crime" laws were on the books at the state and federal level, there were no federal laws against lynching. Since 1882, 200 similar attempts had failed in the U.S. Congress and an estimated 4,700 lynchings had taken place between 1882 and 1968.[22]

It was also during the 1930s that Black intellectual life and community, especially among leadership, writers and artists, entered a new stage of effect within the national conversation and culture. Rising labor leaders like A. Philip Randolph of the Brotherhood of Sleeping Car Porters became more assertive. In a nation of thousands of daily newspapers, African American newspapers gained influence based on in-depth reporting and writing.

But there would be no Black progress during this time in the policies of American defense and the War Department. The prejudices and stereotypes, spoken and unspoken, coming out of the now-called Great War remained virulent through the 1930s. Though there would be an eventual national reluctance late in the decade to become involved in yet another European war, active planning for an effective standing defense force had been taking place. But it seemed that every time the subject of Black participation in that force came up, it withered away or was diverted to a dead-end channel.

The definitive post World War II study of the role of African Americans in the military would be a 750-page document produced for the Center of Military History of the U.S. Army and written over the years 1947–1951, *The Employment of Negro Troops* by Ulysses Lee. Lee had risen through the officer ranks in the war, and at the time of writing was a professor of English at Morgan State University. When, in 1944, the Army had finally felt compelled to become smarter about its Black soldiers, he was the author-editor of the manual *Leadership and the Negro Soldier*.

The Employment of Negro Troops was direct and also sometimes relentless.

> Where Negroes and whites worked together in civilian life, Negroes were generally in subordinate positions or in types of jobs traditionally reserved for them. They were the unskilled workers and helpers where whites were the skilled workers and foremen; they were the porters and janitors and watchmen in office buildings where whites were the accountants and salesmen and managers; they were the domestics and heavy laborers for white employers. The skilled and professional workers, the tradesmen and craftsmen among them, though engaged in a broader variety of pursuits than was generally realized, were few in comparison with the vast majority of unskilled workers who held neither responsible nor leadership positions in civilian life. Working relations between Negroes and whites in the same plant were seldom characterized by the upward and downward flow of both authority and confidence so essential to esprit in a military unit. Army planners took note that the United States Navy no longer employed Negroes in peacetime at all, except as mess boys, because of the problem of "mixing the races" aboard ship. Even the Navy's traditional Negro mess boys were giving way to Filipinos, Chamorros, and Japanese. Abandoning the separate Negro units was not seriously considered by the Army at all.[23]

Lee's narration continued through the telling of a military resolve that Blacks would have to be segregated in any coming war just as they were in the last. That the policy of separate facilities and materiel, and the need for white leadership, would create a logistics burden seemed to be blamed on the Black soldier; too bad if that reduced his presence and opportunity. There were troop strength allotments in place, but they were in support of developing divisions of the military effort, like the Army Air Corps, in which Blacks would not be welcomed because of their lack of training and education. There was no space for new enlistments in the Black regiments and cavalries that had been institutionalized in World War I. Although military service was increasingly seen as an opportunity for advancement by Black young men and the Black press, they met with increasing frustration. And the existing units were denied the benefits of youth and fresh thinking. A number of regiments that had fought with distinction in the first war would be diminished or converted into service regiments in the second. The 369th Infantry would dwindle to a division with labor and security responsibilities in the South Pacific.

Ulysses Lee asserted that although white enlistment had continued through the 1920s and 1930s, even during a time of constriction, Black volunteers could only be used to replace retirements from existing units.

> [A] Negro seeking to join the Army had to find out what posts had elements of a Negro unit, discover where vacancies existed, apply to the commanding officer of the post or unit where service was desired and present himself at the post at his own expense once enlistment was authorized. The Army explained that it had no funds for transporting recruits over the great distances outside their own corps areas which many Negroes had to travel to reach posts where vacancies existed. Often a trip from the east coast to Arizona, where the 25th Infantry was stationed, was involved. As a result, few prospective enlistees got beyond the stage of making inquiries at a recruiting station. But the popularity of prospective military service was such that requests for enlistments in the old regiments sometimes came from great distances-even from as far away as the Philippines.[24]

Tuskegee Institute President Robert Moton wrote to President Herbert Hoover in 1931.

> I would respectfully ask you to consider the long and honorable career of Negro troops in the service of the United States. It is the universal testimony that they are excellent soldiers and possessed with eager willingness in the performance of their duties under all conditions of service. It is more than unfortunate, it is an injustice, that regiments that have distinguished themselves in the way the 10th Cavalry and the 25th Infantry have done, should be reduced from combat service to be menials to white regiments, without chance for training or promotion and be excluded from other branches of the services. It is merely a pretense that Negroes are accorded the same treatment in the United States army as are given to white troops. It has never been the case and is not so now. This applies both to

the rank and file, as witness the presence of the highest ranking Negro officer in the United States army at Tuskegee Institute at the present time, who, by reason of his color is denied service according to his rank and with his own regiment.[25]

The president's response was to write to the Secretary of War: "We do not seem to be able to get the thing quiet. I am wondering if there is anything you can do in the matter."[26] But all that seemed to be done was to assert that there was no problem found.

In 1937, the War Department produced a revised plan for the employment of Black troops, at first kept secret so that it would not become the subject of a national argument. In 1940, an exchange between Assistant Secretary of War and "Advisor on Negro Affairs," Judge William Hastie and Army Chief of Staff Gen. George C. Marshall was succinct and comprehensive. Military segregation, wrote Hastie, was not working, and his words seemed, ironically, to support the unspoken argument of white leadership of the past. "In the army the Negro is taught to be a man, a fighting man; in brief, a soldier. It is impossible to create a dual personality which will be on the one hand a fighting man toward the foreign enemy, and on the other a craven who will accept treatment as less than a man at home."

Marshall replied. "Your solution ... would be tantamount to solving a social problem which has perplexed the American people throughout the history of this nation. The army cannot accomplish such a solution, and should not be charged with the undertaking."[27]

The mobilization of troops begun in 1940 included, among other provisions, the requirement that the percentage of Blacks used be in proportion with their percentage in the male military age population of their geographic origin. The effect would be to limit Black participation in the war to 10 percent of forces. They were, with few exceptions, to be placed in all-Black regiments and corps with Black officers. The plan required the creation of Black infantry, cavalry and artillery regiments, but heavier emphasis was placed on secondary defense, ordinance and quartermaster services.

The results could be demonstrated in a Protective Mobilization Plan of 1940 which projected the status of 44,537 Black troops. Those in fighting and reactive artillery battalions would total 18,115 and the remaining 26,422 would create engineering and quartermaster corps.[28]

Of those 44,537, and the eventual one million African Americans who would participate in World War II, students of the Army War College who would soon enter combat leadership positions in the war offered an official estimation of their fellow Black soldiers.

As an individual the negro is docile, tractable, lighthearted, care free and good natured. If unjustly treated he is likely to become surly and stubborn, though this is usually a temporary phase. He is careless, shiftless, irresponsible and secretive. He resents censure and is best handled with praise and by ridicule. He is unmoral, untruthful and his sense of right doing is relatively inferior. Crimes and convictions involving moral turpitude are nearly five to one as compared to convictions of whites on similar charges.

On the other hand the negro is cheerful, loyal and usually uncomplaining if reasonably well fed. He has a musical nature and a marked sense of rhythm. His art is primitive. He is religious. With proper direction in mass, negroes are industrious. They are emotional and can be stirred to a high state of enthusiasm. Their emotions are unstable and their reactions uncertain. Bad leadership in particular is easily communicated to them.[29]

It was probably the case that most of the African Americans who arrived in Limburg in 1944 had little knowledge of the full burden of the history of their own people in the American military. But they had a job to do on behalf of others who had been liberated from years of the oppression of German occupation.

And it was certainly the case that the people of Limburg had virtually no knowledge of who these Black men were, nor of the social rules that accompanied them, and how they were to respond to it all.

Three

Liberation and Slavery

Can you imagine how we wept...—The mayor of
Maastricht, 1945

Henry Van Landingham had been born in 1920 in the Black neighborhoods of Buffalo, New York. Well into his time in the war, he would
tell his own diary, he had begun to forget the streets of home, and even
his wife.

> I can't even get Mary's face in my mind like I used to. All I see are all these
> scrubbed Dutch faces in her place. Home is so far away it's unreal. We pretty
> much stopped talking about home. I know it's no good getting used to being here
> in one place. As soon as you get used to something, the army moves you on to
> something else and you have to try not to let it bother you.[1]

Henry would move on from Limburg in not a very long time, but his
passing through would cause him to return a half century later. Now, in
1944, however, he would be a mystery to the people of Limburg, but one
which they did not have the luxury of taking too much time to figure out
after years of Nazi domination.

"You know, at first, they were looking at us kind of suspiciously. We
heard that [from Germans] the rumor was that Blacks had tails, like mon-
keys. But after we were here for a few weeks, all that Dutch friendliness
came pouring out to us." At one point, Henry's presence in Limburg, and
the way he carried himself, would become so noticeable, that some gave
him the nickname Napoleon, meant as a compliment.

Much of the activity of the war near Valkenburg took place in and
around the old sandstone caves of the village of Geulhem, the Geulhemmergroeve (the Geulhem Quarry). The caves, or approximately fifteen
miles of underground corridors, dated back to Roman times, created as
a particular kind of sandstone that was useful to construction was quar-
ried out of the hills of the region. They would play various roles over the
course of the war: a nearly impenetrable hiding place for Jews, escaped

A relatively modern view of the exterior of the Geulhem sandstone caves, which date to Roman times, approximately 50 BC–400 AD. The caves would be used by various parties in World War II and play a role in the postwar stories of one of the children of a Black American liberator (Romaine/Wikimedia Commons).

Allied troops, and members of the resistance, and for the food and materiel needed to support them, as well as shelter against bombing for the people, and for artifacts that needed to be kept from theft by the Nazis.

The Black American soldiers were restricted in what they could do in their leisure time, and they were subject to separate facilities for everything from food to health care. But the caves were a frequent setting for their work and socializing. Henry's work as a truck driver for the Red Ball Express put him there often and their entrance was just down the hill from the home of the Nols family. With the quick acceptance of the Dutch people of their Black liberators, he formed a relationship with the family that would be a source of respite for both of them. He was naturally outgoing, curious and social; they were inclined to be friendly and, like much of the Netherlands at this time, living on the edge of desperation and in need of any help they could receive. Trinette Nols had six children, and her husband, Harrie, a miner had followed the first American units into Germany as a medic.

It was not an unusual relationship and similar to a number that had been formed between Black soldiers who worked in the delivery of supplies and Dutch families that had nothing after years of war. Each of the men in Henry's unit had adopted a village family and it was not uncommon for food to accidentally fall from a Black-driven truck as it passed the family home.

The German conquest of the Netherlands had required five days of attack, culminating in the destruction of Rotterdam on May 14, 1940. Overwhelmed in almost every respect by the German force, the strength of Dutch resistance, however, had been surprising to German Chancellor Adolf Hitler and he ordered the Luftwaffe to bring it to an immediate end. A prolonged negotiation, starting with just the threat to bomb the city, eventually failed. An estimated 2,000 aerial bombs were dropped over central Rotterdam and its residential areas.

Over the following days, the smoke and haze of resulting fires seemed to create constant nights of falling buildings. When the firestorm subsided, at least 1,000 had died, 25,000 homes and 2,300 stores had been destroyed.[2] The docks, factories and warehouses at the heart of the Netherlands' economy were gone and one of the world's historically largest and most active ports was stilled. The Germans threatened the same fate for Utrecht, and the Dutch surrendered. By that time, the Netherlands royal family, led by Queen Wilhelmina, had moved to London along with military leaders and the nation's treasury with the assistance of parts of the Dutch navy and merchant marine force.

The queen's time in London during the war would turn out to be a powerful and saving grace to her country and to the Allied effort, but she had been doggedly insistent that it was a trip she did not want to take. In the 20th century, Dutch royalty did not have the authority and effect that had marked the years in which the Netherlands was a predominant world power in trade and governance. She had become queen at the age of eighteen, eight years after the death of her father, King William III, in 1890, and she had determined at that time to be a leader of consequence. But, as World War II approached, she found that, among her countrymen, hers was perhaps the most strident voice warning of what was to come, and it was pretty much ignored. She saw in Adolf Hitler and the German people what others in the Netherlands and some of the rest of Europe seemed not take seriously, thus she was not taken seriously herself until Dutch mobilization was begun in August 1939, too late to be effective.

As the German destruction of Rotterdam approached, the queen's handlers and security forces began to process of removing the royal family from the country. It was against her stated wish that she, herself, stay behind. And she thought that would be the case, but as she boarded a British ship that she had expected to take her to the Zeeland province and her fighting troops, she was told by the captain that his instructions were to take her to England and he would do as he was told. She then determined that when she got to England, she would use the opportunity to implore

King George VI for more help for her country and demand that she be returned. That plan, too, was frustrated as she was put on a train at Harwich and met by the king an hour later at Liverpool Station. He kissed her on both cheeks and took her to Buckingham Palace.

In London, she was joined by Dutch citizens from other points in Europe and from the Dutch possessions to begin to form a military and intelligence force in exile. Eventually, Wilhelmina would find a powerful voice in the outcome of the war.

Despite the Rotterdam Blitz, there was an initial feeling among the people that their occupation by the Nazis might be difficult but relatively benign. Hitler's view of the common Aryan heritage of the two countries caused him to assume that the Netherlands would easily be blended into a larger Germany and Aryan hegemony. That idea was shared by some Dutch who would become collaborators with the enemy, or enthusiastic workers in the Nazi administration. And the physical space and infrastructure of the country would be key to the continuing plan to take over all of Europe, but the participation of the people would be required.

At first, the newly occupied Dutch seemed ready to go along with the rules of what most thought at the time would be a shorter period than the eventual five years until liberation. In addition, the Germans put in place a civil government, rather than German military, regime. Intent on Nazification of Dutch Society, it was harshly managed, but with the necessary participation of Dutch citizens. They were inclined to be law-abiding and driven by strong social ethics, and the occupiers at first seemed to blend in with their fellow Aryans with benevolence. The laws and restrictions that the occupation began to post on public bulletin boards, however, became increasingly untenable. The occupation required a strong Dutch labor force, but if one refused to take an assigned job for professional or patriotic reasons, his or her family could be exiled to another location at the very least. Any German soldier could commandeer any of the ubiquitous Dutch bicycles on a whim and the protesting bicycle owner could be shot dead. The radios and movie theaters offered only German propaganda, and one million of those radios able to receive signals from outside of the German sphere would be confiscated, though many were hidden under severe and sometimes arbitrary penalty of law.

The human results of the occupation as it progressed became profound. The assigned work requirements often led to a crisis of conscience complicated by dissension within families. As a worker, a man would become an employee of an enemy that had taken his country and increasingly engaged in atrocity. If he could not do that, others in his family could find their lives disrupted and antagonistic to his decision. When he was most often forced to decide for his family's welfare, he could become broken.

Interviews of the children of the time would describe fathers who lived in resignation and tears.[3] As the industry of the removal of the nation's Jews, Roma and Sinti to Nazi death camps developed, it encompassed Dutch workers who maintained infrastructure and ran the streetcars and trains.[4]

The persecution of Jews in the Netherlands was among the most aggressive in conquered European nations. Seventy-five percent of the Jewish population would be lost to the Holocaust, the largest percentage of a national population of all countries, save Poland.[5] At first, they were segregated in commerce, transportation and education. When the rounding up and transportation of the Jews commenced, many of their fellow citizens met it with resistance, culminating in a short-lived regional strike in February 1941. Instigated by the Communist Party of the Netherlands, it was a response to the rounding up for transportation of more than 400 Amsterdam Jews. The strike was viciously suppressed by the Germans in two days' time, but it would become the first European protest against Nazi Jewish policy and the only of those to be organized by non–Jews.[6] Jews were required to identify themselves with the wearing of Stars of David beginning in spring 1942, and, when the Catholic church protested increased transportations in the summer of 1942, the Nazis responded by enforcing the deportation of Jews who had converted to Catholicism. It was then that an estimated 25,000 Jews over the course of the war were taken into hiding. Only two-thirds of those would survive, however.[7] In the Netherlands, more so than in France or Belgium, the penalties for assisting Jews could be fatal.

In the 1960s, an assessment by Yad Vashem, the Holocaust Remembrance Center, would hold that the persecution of Jews in the Netherlands would be the most fatal of all the German occupied countries aside from Germany itself, due in large part to a vicious Nazi-based civilian regime with a large portion of civilian support. It would note, however, that Dutch names formed one of the largest portions of its Names of the Righteous who had assisted the Jews in World War II.[8] Other postwar considerations of this particular history, however, would assert that the number of Dutch that assisted the Jews was small, and that the numbers of those in the Dutch resistance was smaller than the number of those who had willingly joined the Waffen-SS, Hitler's most brutal force in civilian repression, control and murder.[9]

The last year of the German occupation of all the country but Limburg and some regions to the north would come to be known historically in occupied areas as the *Hongerwinter*, the Hunger Winter, a national famine during a brutal winter that would kill 18,000[10] as a minimum estimate (21st century studies would suggest that those gestated and born during this time would live shorter lives than those born before or after).[11]

The Hongerwinter had been accurately predicted by the Dutch Prime Minister, P.S. Gerbrandy, in a letter to American Gen. Eisenhower in December 1944 and it would be informed by what he saw in Limburg. "[I]f the now occupied part of the Netherlands has to go through the same process as the liberated part, we shall witness a calamity as has not been seen in Europe in centuries, if at all."[12]

> In the liberated Netherlands the means of transport have been taken away by the Germans, in many regions few livestock are left, communications have been destroyed, power stations have been demolished, many little towns are nothing but ruins, larger towns ... are severely damaged, tens of thousands of houses have disappeared, the fuel situation is nearly everywhere heartrendingly bad, clothing is lacking.

It was certain, he said, that as the rest of the nation was liberated the Germans would take or destroy everything. "There, all the disasters mentioned above will be ten times as horrible as in the southern liberated part of the country."

Gerbrandy could not predict that, on top of all of that, his country was about to face one of the most brutal winters in its modern history. The *Hongerwinter* followed years of war that had seen a reduction in agricultural production matched with increasing export of that production to the German homeland. Ration coupons for food had

Children in the Friesland province dig up wooden ties from tram rails to burn for heat in the *Hongerwinter* (National Archief of the Netherlands).

been instigated, along with similar restrictions on clothing and basic goods.

The demoralization that came with conquest and occupation by Germany grated against the very certain, strong and complex sense of Dutch identity, but with mixed results. There was no avenue for the common citizen to escape a country that was surrounded either by the enemy or the North Sea. Many became collaborators out of whatever motivation, and a relatively dormant fascist movement of the 1930s, the *Nationaal-Socialistische Beweging in Nederland* (NSB), became the only political movement allowed by the Nazis, with an eventual membership reaching 100,000. Most Dutch could only go along with what had been presented to them, but a resistance developed, albeit slowly and in a particularly Dutch way. In a paper presentation to the United States Holocaust Memorial Museum, psychologist and Holocaust historian Linda Woolf would describe it as "passive resistance or non-violent active resistance."[13]

At the time, according to Woolf, Dutch society, confronted with new and difficult circumstances, did not think of its response as actual resistance, but more simply as behavior that was now illegal within the strictures of the occupation. When German films replaced American and British films in the theaters, the people walked out and newsreels were met with derision. It was illegal to listen to the Radio Oranje service of the BBC in London, but daily fifteen minute programs each day were heard on the hidden radios and included more than thirty speeches by Queen Wilhelmina over the course of the occupation. Her audience did not hear a formerly distant and lofty queen, but a passionate and very human voice that was not restrained from anger and the use of colorful language to express her fervor for the well-being of her people and her resolve that they would survive the years of harsh occupation. Her regular admonishment of her subjects about the ways in which they should conduct their lives in this time reminded them of who they were as the Dutch people and who they would remain.

Tough though her words may sometimes have been, they were gratefully received. When subtle opportunities arose to protest the occupation through fealty to royalty they were taken: the wearing of orange (the national color)[14] carnations on the birthdays of the queen's stepson Prince Bernhard, and the placement of a stamp on an envelope in a way that would reflect the primacy of the Queen as their leader, as examples. A vast majority of University students went into hiding when oaths of loyalty to the occupying force were to be presented for signing, and NSB membership of 100,000 amounted to one percent of the national population.[15]

The hiding of oneself or of others was especially prevalent. The protection of the hidden *onderduikers* (under divers) and those who helped them, was a special interest of the Resistance, as was the smuggling out of

Queen Wilhelmina saw her country through both world wars. Though her removal to England at the outset of World War II was at first resented by the Dutch people, her regular broadcasts back to the country through the BBC became essential to their morale and motivation during the Nazi occupation (Wikimedia Commons).

the country of Jews and young men who would otherwise be conscripted by the Germans. Fallen Allied airmen and escaped prisoners of war were secreted to safe borders so that they could fight again. Dutch women, in particular, developed networks and alliances that made them particularly effective protectors of the hidden.[16] Among those who escaped the country were 1,700 Engelandvaarders (England sailors), named after others who had successfully crossed the North Sea to England and had made it to London to assist the government in exile.

Speaking and publishing against the regime could lead to banishment to the Mauthausen complex of labor and starvation camps in Austria, but the voice of resistance persisted. It was often expressed from the pulpit and in underground newspapers, among the most important of them those that could offer translations of broadcasts from Allied countries, especially from the BBC in London which served as the media connection between the exiled Queen and her people. Strikes of laborers and municipal workers, some promoted by the illegal Dutch Communist Party, took place throughout the occupation years and in response to forced labor of Dutch citizens in Germany. Some Dutch would assume the role of collaborators so that they could spy on genuine collaborators. These kinds of passive acts were called *illegaliteit*.

Proactive resistance expanded dramatically in 1943, driven in part by the requirements that Dutch men be sent to labor in Germany and university students be required to pledge loyalty. It ranged from hiding away from the occupying force, to the bombing of bridges, railroads and other infrastructure, and the murder of German soldiers and Dutch collaborators in the streets. The forces of organized resistance grew out of expanding family and social groups, Protestant Christians, Catholic youth leagues and Social Democrats. This despite almost certain transport to concentration camps, and the possibility of execution if caught.

The occupied nation would be powerfully influenced by its two main churches. In the 16th century, the Dutch Reformed Church had evolved out of the Protestant Reformation in reaction to the perceived corruption and authoritarianism of the Catholic Church. The spread of Protestantism moved throughout Europe, entered the Netherlands at a time of Spanish Catholic rule of the country and was effectively repulsed into what would become modern Germany. There, it was allowed to evolve into a force that would eventually be able to return to the Netherlands on footing solid enough to see the nation through the Eighty Years War that ended in 1648 with Dutch independence.

Eventually, the Dutch Reformed Church took on the core beliefs of Calvinism, which held that man lived and died by God's will and not his own: original sin determined that all were sinners and had no choice in the matter, and predestination determined the individual's ultimate journey to heaven or hell as a matter of God's decision. Those non-negotiable beliefs aside, the spirit of revolt from Catholicism also allowed tolerance for other, non–Catholic, spiritual beliefs in the Netherlands, including Jewish and other Christian religions. That led, in turn, to a diverse in-migration to the Netherlands in the 17th century.

During the 19th century, developing beliefs began to split the Reformed Church into differing factions as the evolution of Catholicism brought it more acceptably into the nation's spiritual life, and all beliefs seemed able to live separately in faith and society, under common governance. The Catholic Church would then be able to renew social and spiritual mechanisms of the past as they modernized into new tools like newspapers and broadcast, especially in various parts of the country, particularly in Limburg in the south. With that modernization, however, came enhanced mechanisms to exert influence on thought, belief and practice.

Though they had operated in different worlds at the outset of World War II, the Reformed and Catholic churches seemed quickly able to work together against the cruel excesses of the Nazi occupation and the persecution of Dutch Jews. In September 1942, the combined Catholic and Protestant churches of the Netherlands sent a letter to the Reich Commissar protesting increased transportation of Jews.

> The sufferings which the execution of this measure will inflict on thousands of men, women and children and entire families and the realization that it contravenes the profound moral and ethical feelings of the people of Holland compel us urgently to request that this measure shall not become effective.[17]

The letter noted that whole cities were being made "Jew proof" within the time of a few days, but it was to no avail. As the churches continued to become public and hidden collaborators with the resistance, many of their clergy would pay the ultimate price for their choices of conscience.

The most aggressive Nazi persecution and deportation of Dutch Jews had taken place in the urban and industrial northwest. In August 1942, the Nazis moved to be more effective at the task in the south of Limburg province. A number of Catholics in the region, as an example, were converted Jews and the Catholic bishops were ordered to make those people known.

New research in the early 21st century suggested that, despite the effort, the province may have been an island of relative safety for Dutch Jews and those who had crossed the borders of nearby Germany and Belgium. Unlike the search and roundup Nazi tactics of the cities, identified Limburg Jews were generally told to report for arrest within a short time period, which allowed them to go into hiding, and many Limburgers were willing to help them. In the view of historian Herman van Rens it was a community in which everyone seemed to know everyone else and everyone else's business.

"When you betrayed someone to death in Limburg, everybody knew and it carried different social implications than in Amsterdam," he told the Jewish Telegraphic Agency in relation to his 2014 book *Persecuted in Limburg*.[18] In addition, Limburg's low population and varied geography offered more places to hide. It was also in the business of supporting those passing through from Germany and points east to refuge in Spain and Switzerland, approximately 3,000 over the course of the war.

During the 1930s, many Jews would move to Maastricht from the northwest of the country. In population studies for the book, Rens determined that the 1933 Jewish population of 800 in Limburg had reached 2,200 by the time of the liberation of the province, while 75 percent of Dutch Jews had been lost nationwide. While one third of those in hiding in Amsterdam would eventually be found, the figure was just ten percent in Limburg. Those who could not escape were walked to Maastricht station, from which they were deported into the Nazi camp system.

It would not be until 2020 and upon the observation of the 75th anniversary of the liberation of the Auschwitz concentration camp in Poland that the Netherlands would officially apologize for its compliance in the Nazi destruction of the Jews. It was given in Amsterdam by then Prime Minister Mark Rutte. In the previous year, the Dutch national railroad had begun a program to pay restitution to families that had been damaged by the company's complicity in transportations to the Nazi camps.

Except in small pockets of the largest port cities, the Netherlands of the 20th century had virtually no experience with Black people. The country did, however, have a significant history with the enslavement of Africans. Its victims would never enter or be used in the Netherlands proper, but they would be part of the economic life of New Netherland of the early 17th century. The Reformed Church, the officially designated religion of the colony, would play an influential role in how that would work in society. New Netherland comprised much of what would become New York, New Jersey, Pennsylvania and Delaware with New York City at its center. As important to Dutch commerce at the time was New Holland in the northern portions of Brazil, where slavery was an important part of a sugar plantation economy and would become integral to other pursuits of what was then the Dutch West India Company (WIC).

WIC was preceded by the Dutch East India Company formed in 1602 to engage in trade with India and the region of the Indian Ocean. The West India Company was formed in 1621, partly as a result of the East India Company's effort to find a shorter route to India through an imagined Northwest Passage through North America. In 1609, the British explorer Henry Hudson set out to find the passage, giving his name to the Hudson River. The river did not ultimately lead to a shortcut to India. But it helped to establish Dutch trade in North America.

Both companies became involved in slavery. The East India Company used captured Africans mostly for its own labor needs, but the West India Company used them primarily as commodities of trade. Its businesses ranged from West Africa to the Americas and its initial products of trade were sugar, agriculture and gold. But it soon fell into the slave trade in a triangle defined by the Netherlands, the African slave coast and South America, with the Dutch island of Curaçao as its most active point of transfer and distribution onward. As presented, WIC regulations were designed to allow humane treatment of its human cargo, but they were mostly ignored in support of increased profitability. Some assessments of history would call the Dutch slave traders the most brutal of the European nations.

The first of the enslaved arrived in New Netherland in 1626. They were needed to do the hard labor of settlement that was not of interest to those Dutch who came to the territory to make their fortunes in trade. By mid-century, they would be credited with helping to establish the agricultural infrastructure of the lower Hudson River Valley. With that accomplished, New Netherland was able to convert the most important product of its economy from fur trading to agriculture.

This was slavery in all of the terror and dehumanization of the capture and transportation of one group of humans to be subservient to other humans, but, once in New Netherland, the lives of the enslaved could be more benign. In the practices of the Reformed Church, slave family relationships were respected; they were allowed to marry, and their children could be given the grace of baptism. They were given the legal protection of the courts, could challenge those who held power over them and were allowed to work for their own economic benefit.

In Dutch sensibilities, slavery was an economic expedient. It was not *ostensibly* a racial or power subjugation of humans deemed to be inferior or subhuman. Without an apparent basis of racial animus, it would be easier for Blacks and whites to live and work together. The Dutch values of family were proactively transferred to Blacks with this kind of inclusion. A result for some was an integration into a society of Dutch mores and a taking on of Dutch identity and language.

The legal system did not put up unreasonable barriers to the earning of freedom and integration into a society in which Jews were subject to more social discrimination than freed slaves. That status could come at the end of a process which rewarded good work with a conditional "half freedom" that required an annual payment, usually of agricultural produce and the agreement to perform occasional labor as needed by the Dutch West India Company. A benefit to the Company was the occasional free use of labor without the expense of maintaining enslaved people.

The half-freed were given documents identifying them as "free and at liberty on the same footing as other free people."[19] They could obtain the benefits of membership in the militia, own real estate, intermarry with whites and could themselves own white indentured servants. By mid-century they had created their own residential communities, often out of land that had been given to them with their grants of half freedom, which allowed the development of commonality and commerce within the larger community. Called the "negroes houses" or the "negroes plantation," the largest in New Amsterdam was settled in what would eventually become Washington Square Park.[20]

By 1664, the number of enslaved and freed Blacks in New Netherland reached 6 to 8 percent of the population, perhaps as much as 17 percent in New Amsterdam.[21] On August 27 of that year, however, a flotilla of English warships appeared in New Amsterdam harbor to fulfill the wish of

King Charles II that New Amsterdam cease to exist in the midst of the British colonies. The Dutch could only succumb. They had not fortified their holdings with sufficient committed Dutch population and the mechanisms of physical defense. An attempt to win New Netherland back in 1673 would succeed only briefly and lead to unchallenged British rule in 1674.

As a result of the environment of quasi-freedom and opportunity for betterment for the New Netherland enslaved, many were able to move into the expanding geography of the new nation and become founding members of its historic African American community.

By the mid–19th century, the trade and use of African slaves was coming to an end in fits, starts and war. In most cases, determinations to end their involvement in slavery were declared years before the traders would actually bring it to an end. In the United Kingdom, the difference between those two steps was abolition in 1807 and actual cessation in 1838. In France, the years were 1794 and 1848; in Denmark, 1803 and 1848; in the Netherlands 1814 and 1863. The United States legislated the end of the importation of the enslaved in 1807 but allowed slavery to continue until the Civil War settled the matter with the Emancipation Proclamation in 1863.

During these years, both the United States and the Netherlands were pushed by abolitionist movements to end their involvement in slavery. The American movement was active and aggressive, and the Dutch effort was quiet and persistent, while paying attention to the course of abolition in the United States. American literature was popular with the Dutch. The most translated and republished of American authors was the abolitionist Harriett Beecher Stow, especially her book *Uncle Tom's Cabin*.[22] The book, about the human results of enslavement for all who participated in the practice, influenced the conversation about slavery in both nations.

The interest in literature was accompanied by books and writing about America written by Dutch travelers to the country. They experienced the United States from their positions as the wealthy and educated who would be able to afford the trip, and most criticized the treatment of Blacks as slaves, or as freed slaves in the years after Emancipation. Two of them were businessman C.A. Crommelin in 1866, and Amsterdam newspaper editor Charles Boissevain twenty years later. Both saw slavery, its postwar result for the formerly enslaved and the continued separation of the races as impediments to American civic and economic progress.[23]

After World War I, relations between the two countries were mixed by the aftermath of that conflict in both countries, the boom and bust of economies and positioning for the coming of the next war. A post–World War I Dutch ambivalence about America increasingly gave way to interest in American culture, complimented by American interests in Dutch culture loosely associated with the Dutch heritage of Pres. Franklin Delano Roosevelt. Intellectual exchange between the two countries increased in the 1930s, and as both were drawn into the next war, economic and political relations became more important.

Three weeks after the liberation of Limburg's largest city of Maastricht, a long and heartfelt letter signed by mayor Michiels van Kessenich in the name of "All Inhabitants of the City" appeared in the *New York Times*. Addressing all Americans, the inhabitants of the first liberated city of the Netherlands wanted "an opportunity to thank you for the arrival of your boys who have brought us the liberty for which we have longed so fervently."

> We need not describe to you our suffering and our want. The tyrant robbed us of everything that has been dear to us. He tried to destroy our culture; our unions were dissolved, our religion was hindered, our men and boys were carried off, our food was stolen, our horses and our cattle were stolen, our bicycles were transported to Germany and even our hens had to lay their eggs for Huns. Only German music was heard, and with great danger we had to listen secretly to our friends who brought us news…. Each day brought new pain and new care. Our young people have had no youth. They were chased and hidden in cellars and woods.
>
> Such was our situation and then your boys came. Can you, readers, realize with what joy we welcomed them.

The U.S. Army 30th Division, known as Old Hickory, arrives in the Sint Lambertuslaan neighborhood of Maastricht, Netherlands, on September 14, 1944 (Regional Historisch Centrum Limburg—RHCL).

Can you imagine how we wept when we could shake hands with the first American boys.[24]

The letter, which continued at length, reflected a feeling about America's role in the war that would influence events in Limburg—and in many other parts of Europe—well into the next century.

The liberation of Limburg and Maastricht had not been the primary goal of Allied forces, as they continued the march they had begun in Normandy a few months earlier. It was, instead, the opening to industrial Germany through Aachen, 40 kilometers to the east of Maastricht, which would require breaking through the Siegfried Line that stretched from Basel, Switzerland in the south to the Netherlands north. As the Al-

The U.S. Army assists the people of the Limburg city of Roermond in returning to their homes in March 1945 (National Archief of the Netherlands).

lies moved northeast across France and Belgium, the Germans sought to fortify the line with the use of slave labor, but it would not be enough. The 21st Army Group under British Field Marshal Sir Bernard Montgomery and the 12th Army Group under American Gen. Omar Bradley had moved toward Germany at an unexpected and relatively breakneck speed. On the morning of September 12, the 117th Regiment of the 30th American Division, known as Old Hickory, crossed from Belgium into the Netherlands village of Mesch.

Most striking in old newsreels of the American entrance into Maastricht on September 14 were the ravages of bombing on the Dutch Revival architecture that had fallen into the streets, or lay demolished in place, and the bridges fallen into the Maas River. Whole formations of captured German troops were assembled in open spaces, their hands held above their heads, and members of the higher command were marched down the steps of official buildings, their hands held higher. Where breaks in the rubble allowed, the people lined the streets to welcome their liberators.

The arriving soldiers were unmistakably American, in uniforms that seemed to have marched for hundreds of miles and helmets that may not have been removed since the beginning of the war. Many walked hand-in-hand with small children who had joined the parade along the way. The young women of the city were well dressed and joined the walking Americans as if with easy familiarity. Everyone was happy, and all faces were broadly smiling, all of them white.

The liberation of Limburg would continue with Operation Market Garden, commencing on September 17. "Market" would be an attempt to seize bridges across strategic canals and the Rhine and Meuse rivers with air forces dispatched from England, and the ground forces of "Garden" would cross the bridges north of the Siegfried Line to reach into the important industrial Ruhr Valley of Germany. Key to its hoped for success would be the capture and holding of the bridge over the Rhine at Arnhem. The goal was met, but ground forces were not able to meet the schedule as they came from the Belgian border. Among other impediments on the path to Arnhem were the citizens of Dutch towns and villages that were liberated along the way, including Nijmegen and Eindhoven. The troops and tanks needed to move quickly; the people wanted to celebrate with them, and the convoys bogged down in the crowds.

Market Garden would fail. It would be remembered in the history of the war as too complicated and ambitious in its strategy and supported by inadequate intelligence, a mistake that may have had the effect of extending the war. Nevertheless, no one would call the effort anything but heroic.

And, while it liberated Dutch cities in the provinces of Limburg, North Brabant and Gelderland, German reprisals against Dutch citizens where it had not succeeded led to the starvation of many and the destruction of their homes. Market Garden would become the subject of a book and film in the 1970s, *A Bridge Too Far*.

FOUR

Aftermath

While the Army accepts no doctrine of racial superiority or inferiority...—Classified Army pamphlet *Leadership and the Negro Soldier*, 1944

In Limburg, the change from a German occupying force to an American liberating force seemed to come abruptly and by surprise. One day one would see German soldiers outside of her window, and the next morning they would be Americans. As the citizenry came to understand and trust the change, celebration overtook the streets and public places. Though able to talk to each other on only the most basic level, the Dutch and their American liberators almost erupted into days of partying and dancing in the streets that spread into the countryside and the smallest of villages.

The African American soldiers who had come into the mix as they provided the materiel, structure and pure labor that would address the desperate needs of a formerly oppressed people were at first drawn into the celebration without reservation by the Dutch. Officially, the attempt was made to hold parties and events that hewed to American racial policy, but it seemed natural to the people that the Black Americans would unofficially join the crowds in the streets and in the newly opened dance halls.

It was, and would further become, a time of social loosening and change for Limburg. But, among the Americans, it would serve to harden the social and racial rules which defined the society in which they had grown up, and which—as a matter of military policy—they had not been able to leave behind. Dutch citizens saw that African American soldiers were actively excluded from the movie houses, dance halls and pubs used by their white counterparts.

In February 1944, the War Department had published and immediately classified a pamphlet entitled *The Command of Negro Troops*. Its stated purpose was "to help officers to command their troops more effectively by giving them information which will increase their understanding of their men."[1] It offered the premise that "the Negro in the Army has spe-cial problems," due to inferior education and social opportunity, a limited role in national life and lack of experience with skilled labor. Those char-acterizations were supported by statistics yielded from the Army General Classification Test (AGCT) given to all inductees over a six-month period in 1943. The test was intended to predict who would be capable of leader-ship, who could be specialists and technicians, and who would be physical laborers. They showed large differences between Blacks and whites in the basic results of an overall grade.

Grade I, the highest possible, for example, was attained by 6.4 per-cent of white inductees and just .2 percent of Blacks. Grade V, the lowest possible, was attained by 4.1 percent of whites and 35.1 percent of Blacks.

> Assignment to class IV or V based on a soldier's AGCT score is not to be accepted as evidence that a man is unteachable, but it does indicate that his train-ing requires extra patience, skill, and understanding on the part of the instruc-tor.*[2]

The asterisk referred to a notation which reminded that illiteracy was a measure not of learning ability but of learning opportunity, nor was the grade to be taken as a final word on the matter. Further tests could "sort out those men with a high degree of native intelligence but inadequate schooling from those in a lower range of native ability." Officers would be further aided by *Form 20*, which would indicate the man who would be able to "surmount the disadvantages of inadequate formal education, [and] may prove to be a real asset to his unit and to the Army."[3]

Taken in the whole of its twenty pages, *The Command of Negro Troops* was a nuanced study of the situation presented to the Army, with remind-ers throughout that the problem was not with the quality of the inductees themselves, but one which could be corrected with proper leadership that took into account where these men had come from and the good potential for where they could go. In addition, the Army had created special train-ing units in most commands to address deficiencies, with varying degrees of success.

One result of the Army's study of the difference between Black and white soldiers, however, could not and would not be changed as a mat-ter of policy, as noted in a 1944, classified pamphlet *Leadership and the Negro Soldier*. An assessment of the relative social needs and attitudes of Blacks and whites, it was frank and candid: Blacks disliked racial segre-gation, whites accepted it as a matter of course, and the two groups had no common understanding of what it really was, let alone the ability to deal with it together. The pamphlet allowed that, in relation to social and other facilities available to Blacks, "The protesting Negro ... knows from experience that separate facilities are rarely equal, and that too often racial segregation rests on a belief in racial inferiority."[4]

That said, however, the pamphlet went on to reinstate policy that while "the Army accepts no doctrine of racial superiority or inferiority.... It is important to understand that separate organization is a matter of practical military expediency, and not an endorsement of beliefs in racial discrimination."

To be effective, an army needed to run on as little friction as possible, thus the practice of combat and social segregation was necessary. The results of a 1943 survey conducted by the Research Branch of the Morale Services Divisions of the Army were offered as an explanation. It involved 13,000 men across 92 Army organizations derived from a full geographic spectrum of the United States. They were assembled in segregated groups, promised anonymity, and led through a series of questions that were facilitated by trained supervisors. In describing the survey protocols, the War Department took pains to emphasize the care that had been taken to account for the educational and cultural backgrounds of those surveyed. Whites were interviewed by whites and Blacks by Blacks.[5]

"Do you think white and Negro soldiers should be in separate outfits or should they be together in the same outfits?" Just 38 percent of Black soldiers, but 88 percent of white soldiers thought separation was preferable.

"Do you think it is a good idea or a poor idea for white and Negro soldiers to have separate P.X.'s in Army camps?" Forty percent of Black soldiers, but 81 percent of white soldiers thought this was a good idea.

"Do you think it is a good idea or a poor idea to have separate service clubs in Army camps?" Forty-eight percent of Black soldiers thought it was a good idea, but 85 percent of white soldiers agreed with them.[6]

Indeed, the results reflected the reality that had existed before and which would continue through the war. Recreation and social facilities in and around military bases in the United States were heavily segregated and inferior for Blacks. Where Black training bases were hastily created almost anywhere, recreational facilities for Blacks often had to be improvised, and, outside of a spirit of care by the military, they could be sometimes unsavory.

The survey gave the direction. The reinforced, 1944 version of War Department policy, therefore, was that these sentiments could not be ignored, and continued segregation of military units was required. As to segregation through the management of social facilities, however, "The burden of deciding whether or not there shall be some separation in the use of camp facilities is placed on the local command, with the assumption that local conditions will be taken into account."[7]

In the case of the Netherlands, however, local conditions would suggest one response to the appearance of African Americans in the forces of their liberation, but the Army command would continue to maintain an opposite response brought with them from the United States.

Additionally, the response of the people of Limburg would be the opposite of what the War Department believed to be the case with the other nations and societies of the world. Upon America's entrance into the war it was the considered opinion that its Black troops should not be sent overseas. The question had first shown up in the documents of the Department in March 1942, under the signature of then Brigadier Gen. Dwight D. Eisenhower. Eisenhower's beliefs about race would show up in his presidency of the United States during the 1950s. The press for racial integration would begin to gain traction during that time, but he believed that it would be a slow process that derived from the hearts and minds of the citizenry. During his presidency, he would meet with civil rights leaders just once from 1953 to 1961 and would be seen by history as having failed to exert the moral authority of a president in the matter.[8] Earlier, his time as a successful leader of U.S. forces in the war would seem to be constantly challenged by the contradictions of military racial policies, and his own attempts at leadership in racial matters to be somewhat dithering.

In 1942, Eisenhower reported to the War Department that he had found no other allied country where America's Black troops would be welcomed, and the decision had been made that, where necessary, Blacks and whites would be sent abroad just as "American" troops without notice of their racial composition.[9] Some reluctant countries and territories objected to this policy, giving specific reasons:

Alaska: fear of the mixing of Blacks and native Indians and Eskimos.

Australia: in contravention of its "White Australia" immigration policy.

Bermuda, Trinidad, St. Lucia, Chile, Venezuela: various reasons or not given.

British West Indies: well-paid and well-clothed Blacks might upset colonial authority.

Iceland, Greenland, Labrador: by request of the U.S. Air Force.

Panama: requested withdrawal of Black troops in the Canal Zone.

Liberia: rate of pay inequality between Black Americans and Black Liberians.

British Isles: the request came from the American command rather than the British government. (See Chapter Eight.)

Not all requests were realized or were variously realized based on the developing factors of the war. And, by 1944, too much had occurred to worry about what color of person was where, though the structures of segregation still applied.

As the forward white American troops commenced their move into Limburg, their Black counterparts began to appear quietly, and at a seeming distance in the background.

On September 13, twelve-year-old Matthieu Marres and his father set about to pick apples from the family fruit yard in Eckelrade, between Maastricht and Margraten. Suddenly, the quiet pursuit was broken by the sound of shots fired. They knew that both Americans and Germans were nearby and took off in the opposite direction, but into the range of American fire which they avoided by moving from tree to tree until they arrived in the center of town and an air-raid shelter beneath a neighbor's home. They could see the German soldiers walking back and forth from a small basement window.

Realizing that in their haste they had left a gate opened on their property, they eventually gained the confidence to see if their cows had wandered out and saw them milling about at a nearby farm among a few remaining German troops. Upon returning to the village they came across soldiers who now wore American uniforms and moved cautiously. They seemed not sure that they could trust the villagers, but the elder Marres, who spoke some English, told them that they were now in Dutch territory and were most welcome. The Americans gave the young Marres a rare piece of chocolate.

Later in the year, Matthieu and his friends in school heard that something was happening near Margraten that they should see. During a lunch break, they ran to the place they had been told about and saw "a big mess with a lot of dead people." It was there on subsequent days that they saw Black people for the first times in their lives. "They emptied the trucks that arrived, filled with corpses that were dumped out on the muddy ground. The weather was bad, and it was very cold."

In late September or early October, the Marres family was asked to accommodate the soldiers, which they, as with most Limburgers, did happily.

"In the barn there was a concrete floor where we normally stored hay and such. Some twenty black soldiers were sleeping there," while white soldiers were assigned to sleep in the house. "We noticed the lesser jobs, such as kitchen work and standing guard, were done by Blacks, and we also noted that now and then there was some tension between the black and white soldiers."

One day, the children were told not to go to their school because it had been commandeered by the Americans. "We did go there, because the Americans had made it into some kind of club house, and we were allowed to watch the movies they were playing. Now that I think back, no Black soldiers ever joined us there. We did not know anything about racial segregation."

Soon, the soldiers were gone, probably sent to fight in the Belgian Ardennes and never to be seen again.

Matthieu Marres was not alone in his first observations of American racial practices. The Limburgers saw that most whites acted superior to the African Americans, and that the military command stringently controlled their interactions. Upon arrival in Limburg, the Army, with the assistance of local authorities, started setting up centers for rest and recreation in Maastricht, Heerlen, Valkenburg, Kerkrade and other locations. The cream of American celebrity of the time, including Fred Astaire, Marlene Dietrich and Mickey Rooney, came through the Netherlands to entertain the troops away from home. The Blacks who had done much of the physical labor in setting up the R&Rs were excluded from the centers in many cases, or excluded from integrated use of them, once completed.

If a Black soldier wanted to enter a Dutch bar, he had first to be sure that there were no white soldiers already within. The Blacks had to take care of their own entertainment and the Limburgers were invited to join them. Harrie Rouvroye of Elsloo, north of Maastricht, remembered one of the evenings when the program included a band and a striptease in the streets. "Of course, I had never seen anything like it! As the lady continued to strip, and took off her wig, it became clear the lady was a gentleman, albeit a very feminine one. The crowd started yelling wildly and tried to storm the band, but the Military Police who were present quickly restored order."

As housing for the Americans became more necessary and fell into routine administration, the people of Limburg were asked to conform with an American practice that they had not been previously aware of, did not expect and could not always abide.

At first, many of the Americans, Black or white, would be housed with local families as space permitted. The Dutch had long since been inured to this kind of imposition as a sometimes unpleasant and dangerous feature of the German occupation. It could be a manageable situation for all, and stories would emerge of relationships formed that would transcend the war, but for those family members unable to accept the occupation it could be perilous.

The American liberators presented the Dutch with a different kind of problem. Whatever their own social norms, the liberating force had brought overriding requirements about how society was to work, although they would not be enforced with the threat of harm that was characteristic of the Germans. White soldiers were entitled to housing in homes with families, but Black soldiers were relegated to other structures where necessary. One way or another, however, some Limburg households could and did follow their own social inclinations.

It was the proactive openness of the Wetzels family on Nieuwstraat in Heer that had led to the eventually interrupted romance of Lenie Wetzel and Edward Moody, and the birth of their son, Ed. Jr. The attic was given over to the four African Americans who showed up at their door. They had been moving from place to place for a long time and would be moving on again. Lenie's mother, three older sisters and their husbands would offer them a respite away from the war. They taught the Americans the popular Dutch card game *Klaverjassen*, a sixteen-hand tournament of point accumulation played through constantly changing partnerships around a table. *Toepen*, usually a drinking game, arrived at a winner through the one-by-one elimination of the other players around a table. In exchange, the Americans would sing the songs of their country and upbringing.

The skin color of the young men was only a matter of interest. The Wetzels family's only real experience with dark skinned people had been through pictures in the mission magazines of the Catholic church. Only one of Lenie's sisters had seen a colored person up close: a child brought to her school by a missionary who was seeking charity to address African poverty.

Edward Moody was a further curiosity. He was himself the child of a Black mother and white father, unusual in the America of the time. He was the favorite of Lenie's mother, known to the men as Ma Wetzels. When out with his truck he would take it on an extra spin to drive down Nieuwstraat and wave at the woman as he drove by, and he would sing to her when he arrived home after his shift (during his time there, it was believed that he had made some recordings with a record company in Maastricht, but they could never be found).

Then he and Lenie had conceived a child and committed themselves to each other, and then he was gone. It was understood—though the policy cannot be documented—that when the military command became aware of a pregnancy of a local woman and a Black soldier, the soldier would be ordered on to a distant point of the war. There would be no responsibility felt to take steps to keep the new family intact, and there would be no interest in helping the mother to track down the father if he had moved on.

Many of those interrupted families would attempt to put themselves back together decades later, sometimes in the most tenuous of ways and with technologies of communication that had not been thought of in the mid–20th century.

One of those pathways had begun in the end of slavery after the Civil War, run a course that would include the lifetime of America's greatest racehorse and come to a resolution in a computer connection between the Netherlands and suburban Washington, D.C., in the following century.

Maddoxtown, Kentucky, had been created as a "free town" after the Civil War, a settlement of freed slaves designed to support the development of families and their farms. Its first church/schoolhouse was erected in 1875, and it was in that year that the Kentucky Derby was inaugurated in Louisville. Before the war, the tending of horses was a common job of the slave economy, and it followed that in the new Kentucky the men of Maddoxtown would supplement their incomes with work in the state's iconic agricultural industry. Nearly all of the jockeys of the first Derby were African American, as were those who tended the horses, with skills passed down through generations.

Will Harbut had moved to Maddoxtown in 1885 and built one of its first homesteads. As his family grew to 12 children, Harbut began to develop a reputation as a "horse whisperer," one of those who seemed able to cross the barriers of communication between human and animal with extraordinary results. Eventually, he was introduced to the thoroughbred *Man o' War*, and the two would not be separated, perhaps sharing a confidence with each other that could not be breached by others, until Harbut was stopped by a stroke in 1946.[10]

The eleventh child of Will and Mary Elizabeth Payne Harbut was born in Lexington in 1922. At age 21, James Harbut was married in a shotgun wedding, but enlisted in the Army before the expected child was born. By the time he had worked through France toward Germany he had been divorced and arrived in Limburg in a second wave of American liberators. The Black soldiers were housed in a pub in Nieuwenhagerheide. All of the Americans were welcomed, and their spirited behavior brought life to a place that had been oppressed for years. As elsewhere, the Black soldiers were a curiosity, but well received.

The arrival of the Americans in the Netherlands brought significant support to the beginning of the postwar recovery of village economies. It fell to the soldiers to take responsibility for the repair of their own uniforms, and Toos (a fictive name requested to be used for this book) was a skilled seamstress. She had set up shop on a parlor table in sight of the street, and the Americans learned that they could receive her services with a tap on the parlor window. Her work was a boon to her family. Payment could take the form of food: cheese, canned fruits and chocolate and other goods that were difficult to find in an economy that was strictly controlled by ration coupons.

Jimmy Harbut began to tap on the window for nothing more than an invitation to take a walk. He was a compact and handsome young man and, as the two walked arm in arm about the village, they were well received by others. Toos' parents saw him only as an American without regard to his color and welcomed his attention to their daughter. Eventually he would sometimes stay in their home overnight.

When Toos became pregnant, other family members helped her to receive the extra rations available to pregnant women, and her father's initial anger over the pregnancy melted away with the arrival of the baby girl, Petra (a fictive name requested to be used for this book). Subsequently and very soon, James Harbut disappeared. During the time of Toos' pregnancy he had been sent back and forth to various jobs in the region, and now he was gone. The military command would or could not tell her where they had sent him. Though Toos would never see him again, he appeared to attempt to stay connected. One day, a friend of his still in the village brought baby clothes that James had sent to him through the Red Cross from an unknown location. And they were able to exchange letters, which Toos kept in a shoe box found decades later.

As Petra grew up, her mother remained elusive on the subject of her father. Bedridden a week before her death in 2008, Toos surprised her daughter after she had asked for perhaps the last time for more information. She reached into the

Petra's father, James Harbut, was likely removed from Limburg by the Army as a result of her birth. He would attempt to take some responsibility for her in subsequent years, and she would have a brief telephone conversation with him before his death in his nineties (courtesy Petra).

nightstand beside her bed and handed Petra a sealed envelope. It contained three photographs. "You're entitled to these," she said. One of them showed a cheerful young Black man with a bicycle, probably taken in France in 1944, with the name Jimmy written at the bottom.

Gerritt Linssen of Buggenum, on the Meuse River and north of Roermond, was a good man and the child he would come to accept as his own would eventually have a very good life. But, for his troubles in 1944, Gerritt was a forced laborer in Germany, sent there by the

James Harbut, probably in France, 1944 (courtesy Petra).

Nazis, probably because he had stolen food and given it to some Russian prisoners of war. At some point, he escaped from Germany, but could not return to Roermond until it was liberated in March 1945. Toward the end, its residents had been forced to evacuate the city by German edict. Gerritt's wife, Mia, and their two children had moved away to live with friends in Noord-Brabant, and they, too, returned.

Through the municipality, Linssen got a job at the U.S. Army barracks as the Americans were assisting in the repatriation of Roermond. He made friends with the African American soldiers there and often brought them home for dinner, an invitation commonly offered to the American liberators. One in particular became a good friend. His identity would never be known. Decades later, a neighbor of the time could only describe him as "a gorgeous, dark, tall man," who was a regular visitor to the family home.

The Americans pulled out of Roermond on June 17, 1945, and on March 4 of the following year Mia gave birth to a son, Cor. The attending midwife thought that the baby looked odd and called for the family doctor, who found a perfectly healthy newborn. They quickly realized the truth of the matter of the "yellowish" child but kept it to themselves. It was a truth that would be only tacitly be acknowledged for years. When the family moved back to the smaller town of Buggenum, Mia would grow uncomfortable with the attention she received when out with her new child. They went back to the larger Roermond, still in ruins, but the attention was easier to live with. Mia had developed the response to the quizzical looks she received: "He looks like one of our cousins in Swalmen who is also really dark." By the end of the 1940s, and the birth of two more sons, Mia's presentation of her children to the rest

Cor Linssen and his brother Herman at the Maasniel fair in Roermond, undated (courtesy Cor Linssen).

of the world had grown more nuanced. "This is our Huub, our Jo, my Cor, our Herman, and our Ben."

Months after Henry Van Landingham and his truck had moved on, Trinette gave birth to a daughter, Els, at the School for Midwives in Heerlen. It was September 9, 1945, and the next day the traditional registering of the birth done by the absent father was instead completed by the student midwife. Els was formally a member of the Nols family of Berg en Terblijt.

It was a family based in gracious warmth and openness. When Henry first appeared in its midst, a driver in the difficult and endless transports of the materiel of war and liberation, he was, as described years later, physically and mentally exhausted. And he was a man with a lively mind—he would write about his experience with a unique voice. When he got sick while working in and around the sandstone caves across the street from the family home, Trinette took care of him, and brought him back to the health he would need for the miles of driving that were to follow. They had known each other for just two months.

Els' birth date indicated that she had probably been conceived in one of the last moments of that relationship. She was unmistakably different from Trinette's other children, but, in the eyes of others in the village and other relatives, the family's sense of itself made her just one of its seven children—albeit darker than the others. But that acceptance was confounding to her. She knew that she was different, and vaguely that she had a father somewhere in the United States. She was accepted, but she knew that she was still an outsider of sorts in the village. She would later remember that the village hairdresser could never figure out what to do with her hair. The woman never asked questions, however. Nor did Els. It was not a topic of discussion.

Decades later, the story of Els and the others like her would be little known. Then, in 2014, as Jefferson Wiggins told a nationally published biography, *Van Alabama naar Margraten (From Alabama to Margraten)*, his story of the caution overcome of children who had never before seen a Black person, Huub Schepers was able to finally understand himself. Wiggins had laid out the whole history of racial segregation in America from a personal perspective, and not given a quarter in his description of the life he had then lived in the U.S. Army and during his brief time in the Netherlands. The narration was not angry, but matter of fact. It recounted the difficult work that the African Americans had done, particularly in the service of the dead. And it described the discrimination they had had to face in its performance. It was respectful, though, of the country for which he labored at first and later fought, and of the people of the countries like the Netherlands in which that took place.

It was revelatory information for Huub Schepers. His had been a life in which most every early foundation had been first attained, then crumbled or disappeared, or even worse. Not much could be known about his mother, and less about his African American father. She was the wife of Lei Schepers, a member of the fascist *Nationaal-Socialistische Beweging* (NSB) that was allowed to operate by the Nazis. He and his brothers had also served with German *SS* forces and would be arrested during the liberation.

After his birth, Huub's mother put him in the basement of the family home in Geleen, to keep him separated from her other two children. An aunt, however, would bring him upstairs when she could and place him in a carriage with her own child so that he could get fresh air, which his mother would never do. She was ashamed to be seen with him.

The birth occurred when Lei Schepers was imprisoned in Valkenburg for his activities and he knew that the child could not be his. He demanded of his wife that the boy be gone before he returned home. "And if you don't do that, then I'll drown him in a bucket of water."

It turned out, however, that Lei could be released if he recognized the child as his own, but when he returned home Huub had been moved on, as he would be a number of times in his first years. This time it was perhaps at the instigation of his mother's family to the care of an elderly widow in Sittard. Years later he would learn that when she first saw the child, she scrubbed him repeatedly because he seemed so dark. In the first vestiges of his memory, however, he would remember seeing her often sitting in the dark and praying, though he felt warm and safe. Then he was taken from her by social services to a foster family with four daughters, which he remembered as a happy time, until he was taken away again. This time it was in a car to Maastricht, where he was placed in a children's home under the care of Catholic nuns. "That was when the lights went out," he would later say.

After a lifetime that will be considered in a larger context, Huub, to whom this book is dedicated, would become the key that would help to solve the mysteries faced by many of the children of African Americans of World War II.

When the American civil rights leader Martin Luther King, Jr., died in April 1968, Huub Schepers had flown an American flag in his yard at half-mast. When Huub died suddenly in January 2016, his memorial service was held on January 18, Martin Luther King, Jr., Day in the United States. Huub's American flag was draped across his casket.

FIVE

Margraten

Fear was in the air. Or perhaps it was sadness. Every
day was the same.—Jefferson Wiggins, 2009

Toward the end of his life, Jefferson Wiggins would remember well
what he had wanted to say to the woman who had given him a celebratory
bottle of Calvados outside of St. Lo, France.

His impulse to lie about his age and take advantage of the offer of
the Army recruiter in Dothan had been vindicated. Among other things,
it had led to a dramatic acceleration in his literacy and his ability to make
use of his basic strengths. Remarkably, he was now a 19-year-old first sergeant in the 960th Quartermaster Service Company. His captain counted
on him to lead men who were much older, and, with that leadership, the
whole corps had managed to pass through the gauntlet of D-Day in good
condition.

Now, they were marching toward an unknown destination that
would turn out to be the Dutch province of Limburg. Outside of St. Lo,
the woman appeared along their way with several bottles of the French
apple brandy to give to the passing men.

"Soldier," she said to Wiggins, "you don't understand how it is to have
your freedom, to lose it and then to regain it."

That was powerful to me and I realized how much I had missed.
    I wanted to answer her, but I didn't because I couldn't speak French, but I
wanted to say to her, "Madam, you don't understand how it is never to have had
your freedom and here you are in the middle of a country that you have never
been to before, marching through a town which you know nothing about, risking
your life to free someone that you will probably never meet again and knowing
that the freedom that you deserve at home, you won't have."[1]

The nature of the racism he would experience in the Army would be
different, and not as hard edged as it had been in Alabama. At one point,
when he felt compelled to correct the lie he had told about his age, he had

had to confront a very real fear that he would be sent back to his previous life. His desire to leave that life had been so strong that he had signed up without his family's knowledge. He was ashamed that he had lied, and just disappeared—run away—to his first posting in Kansas, not knowing that his parents feared that he had been taken by the KKK. But the measure of the opportunity the Army had given him was found in his mother's eyes when she arrived at his posting in Fort Wadsworth on Staten Island, New York. His conscience had directed him to tell his commanders about his deception, and his mother was called to New York to either sign a parental release or to take him home. She had been determined to do the latter, but when she saw him, she was surprised at how healthy he looked. She told him that she would not have recognized him if she walked past him in the street.

And it was on Staten Island that a kindness occurred that would become the pivot upon which his whole life would turn.

He had asked one of his officers where he could go to improve his education. He had never been to a library, but that was the officer's suggestion, and there was one nearby. The Stapleton branch of the New York Public Library was located several blocks south of the ferry stop at St. George. In Alabama, the libraries were labeled "Whites Only," but at Stapleton Wiggins was greeted by Mrs. Anne Marie Merrill and a relationship was formed. He spent much of his free time at Stapleton, and it was Mrs. Merrill's tutoring that drove the dramatic change in his literacy.[2]

It was in long discussions with her that he gained a world view that could be articulated, particularly in the strength of his self-concept of a Black man still in his teenage years. The effect, combined with the honorable way he had dealt with the lie about his age, did not go unnoticed in the Army command. He was given space to continue his education on his own, and occasional staff car transportation to the Stapleton library.

That demonstrated esteem on the part of the Army would be one of the factors in Wiggins' later promotion to first sergeant, but, after Staten Island, he and his fellows would be subject to the same War Department drill in relation to the segregation of its white and Black troops.

The 960th Quartermaster Service Company set sail from New York to Glasgow on February 27, 1944. The *Frederick Lykes* was a freighter that had been converted into a troopship. The outer decks were accessible to all, but Black troops were quartered in the lowest decks of the ship. Fresh air was difficult to find, the water on the other side of the hull was frigid and movement that produced seasickness was more pronounced. On the third day of the crossing, the rudder became inoperable and the ship simply drifted for several days in an ocean that was menaced by German U boats.

As per military policy, and in Wiggins' view of it, the ship carried two armies, one white and one Black. Black soldiers were not allowed on the deck with recreational facilities, but they were able to find places in their own quarters for games of cards and dice, religious services and gospel singing. The latter attracted white sailors from the upper decks who were welcomed by the Black soldiers below.

"It was a time," said Wiggins, "when people who were non-religious, who were non-believers, all became believers, because I don't think any of us thought we would survive this.

"At the same time, they knew and we knew, that they were not supposed to be there, but that once we got to Europe ... you know, war is a great equalizer."[3]

But the strength of the power of inequality persisted. Upon arrival in Scotland, the white soldiers were disembarked first, and the Black soldiers had to spend another night in their shipboard quarters. At first, they were led to a large yard and told to create their own camp. From there they traveled by train to Wiltshire in South England, where all were housed in traditional barracks, but without recreational facilities for the Black soldiers.

It was Wiggins' understanding that the British had been told that the Black Americans that would soon be in their midst "were like wild animals, couldn't be trusted, don't get close to them."[4] As the men marched, people came out of their homes to stare at them. And in a trip on his own to Birmingham he would find that even Black immigrants from the Caribbean considered him carefully, perhaps probably more because he was American than because of his color.

In England, segregation of recreational opportunities was not as highly enforced but was highly policed. In one case, a fight between a white and Black American was resolved when MPs shot the Black man dead. In the following days, both groups were restricted to quarters though less so for the white group.

On June 6, 1944, the men found themselves off the coast of Normandy at the outset of Operation Overlord, the code name for the Normandy Invasion that would set the course toward the end of the war. Their recent training had taken a turn into landing craft and their use, and they had been issued extra clothing and equipment without explanation. Now they were told that they would be arriving on the beaches after the heaviest of fighting, but that what they would see would be gruesome. They could still be hit by fire, but if their fellows fell, they were to keep moving forward. By now, Wiggins, though promoted to first sergeant, was still 19 years old, and he was not confident in his ability to lead and survive. He was frightened without reservation.

A landing craft arrived to take them within two or three hundred feet of the beach. The men jumped into water that was dark red. They had to step over visible bodies of the dead but stumbled over those that were submerged and hidden as they went forward. The beaches extended for another hundreds of feet beneath the machine guns of German pillboxes atop the dunes, and mortars fired from a point further inland.

> So if anyone ever talks about hell on earth I think that is what they mean.
>
> Once on that beach I was really upset. I had no idea where the men of our company were. It took a while before I discovered some of them in the chaos, because that was what it was. A complete chaos and ear-splitting noise. A nightmare. In that enormous racket we started looking for our comrades and the group became gradually larger.[5]

The march toward the front passed first through St. Lo. It had been totally destroyed and its remaining residents had been evacuated, but, as they walked, more people emerged from the surrounding hills to welcome them, to celebrate, and to pass out bottles of Calvados. The war was going faster than expected and their next stop was Liege, Belgium, 600 km to the northeast. There, the Black soldiers were better received than they had been in England and France, but Wiggins detected a frame of mind that would perhaps never see the non-combat Black Americans as liberators as much as they were laborers; albeit laborers who would work to restore their lives, and appreciated as such. Even that, in Wiggins' view, was an improvement, and perhaps a portent of what was to follow.

In Liege, Wiggins was told quietly by his captain to prepare the men for a new assignment, which he would not further describe. They traveled by truck to Gronsveld, across the river Maas in Limburg, to housing in a school building, where he was told that they would be heading out again at 4:30 the next morning. He could still not learn where they were headed. "You'll see," he was told.

In the dark before dawn, they were taken to a field outside of the village of Margraten. "We're here, first sergeant," the captain told him. "get your men together. You'll be given picks and shovels and this will be your job in the near future."

> I was completely confused. I didn't understand what we were to do in this field. I also noticed there was a heck of a smell, but I didn't realize that this smell came from what would become a cemetery. Going through France and Belgium, there was always a peculiar smell, but not like this. I saw large fields in front of me, full of dead bodies. Only dead bodies. I couldn't grasp the reality in front of me.
>
> I asked the captain why we needed picks and shovels. His answer was clear and took me completely by surprise. "This will be the newest American military cemetery. It will be your duty to make sure that each grave you dig meets all specifications—six feet deep, six feet long and two and a half feet wide—and that each soldier you and the men place in a grave is buried with the utmost respect."
>
> I was 19 years old! All I could think was, "where are the caskets?" I was totally

lost. I guess the captain must have seen the confusion and dismay in my face. I asked him, what else, other than picks and shovels would be brought to us because I didn't see anything else. He said there would be nothing else. I was stunned.

I couldn't grasp the reality before me. I was still waiting for the big trucks to bring the caskets in. I still thought we couldn't start burying and told a white sergeant that we couldn't bury these guys because the coffins had not arrived yet. He reaffirmed the captain's words, "There are no caskets."

The sergeant showed us a stack of mattress covers that we would use to bury the bodies, tying the bags with a cord at the top and the bottom.

"You'll get used to it," he said. "You place the body in a mattress cover. You tie each end and lower it in the grave."

And that was my introduction to Margraten.[6]

The dead bodies of war, and, in this case, the mattress covers in which to place them, were the responsibility of the Quartermaster Graves Registration Company, which had been derived from the devastation of the American Civil War. Before that time, there had been no comprehensive and organized way to deal with the dead of war, but the 620,000 dead on both sides of the War Between the States now demanded that they be registered, located and buried, and reburied as necessary, in defined spaces that met uniform specifications.

Graves Registration then went on to respond effectively to the conditions of subsequent American wars, but, by 1944, it seemed to be floundering. In a 1955 retrospective review of its own work, the Quartermaster Corps pointed to a problem begun in 1942 when a reorganization of the corps lessened the strength and profile of the (then called) Memorial Division just as the size of America's armed forces began to rise from 1.5 to 8 million.[7]

As the war progressed, the lack of personnel and training led to Graves Registration services that "were characterized by improvisations," and "inadequate and ineffective service in the field." In one theater of war, as an example, the prescribed ratio of Graves Registration personnel was one man per 650 troops, but the actual ratio was one to 1,200.[8]

That was the reason that Jefferson Wiggins had been shown a field of dead bodies, given a pick, shovel and supply of mattress covers and been told to put his men to work. At the time, no one could predict the heroic work that he, his fellows, those who would follow them over three years, and the people of Limburg themselves would have to accomplish against tremendous odds to establish the American Cemetery at Margraten.

And the reason that Jefferson Wiggins, by now a very literate and self-educated leader of men at age nineteen, found himself faced with the hard, gruesome labor of grave digging was another feature of the

Jefferson Wiggins, third from right, training with his unit before deployment to Europe (U.S. Army).

Quartermaster corps, one that would also apply to many of the African American men who would participate in the liberation of Limburg.

The problem was circular. Official War Department policy was that the number of Blacks in the services should approximate their portion of the population, approximately 10 percent. A semi-tacit feature of that policy was that Blacks generally should not be sent to combat units, therefore they were sent to non-combat units. A result in 1943 was, "the Quartermaster Corps is required to operate its highly specialized and technical units with 33.39% of its personnel Negro enlisted men."[9] Emphasis on "specialized and technical units" offered an unspoken contrast to the continuing language of the Department's assessment of many of its Black recruits as not sufficiently experienced and educated—albeit due to life experience that was no fault of their own—to take on technical work, let alone assume positions of leadership.

In other words, the Quartermaster Corps suffered from a surplus of Black soldiers. When the Quartermaster Gen., Maj. Gen. Clifford L. Corbin, asked for relief from the burden in January 1943, the response he received from the General Staff was that a decrease in Black personnel "cannot be favorably considered at this time due to the fact that personnel so rendered surplus would have to be absorbed by combat units."[10]

Eventually, Jefferson Wiggins would find himself broken out of that circle at the personal instigation of Gen. George Patton, but, in the next few months he would ultimately be working under the command of the 611th Quartermaster Graves Registration Company. Captain of the 611th was James J. Shomon, a good, albeit casually racist, man who would lead his men to an extraordinary accomplishment under dreadful and relentlessly brutal circumstances.

In the time frame of the Normandy Invasion to the crossing of the German border at the Rhine River the 611th would start its work with the collection in Southampton, Weymouth and Plymouth, England of Allied bodies sent back across the English Channel from the D-Day landing. That had been a relatively easy task; they could be registered and buried either permanently or temporarily in the calm of English soil. These were the dead found in the water at Normandy, or still on ships of the Allied fleet.

Those who had died on French soil, however, would be dealt with in France as conditions allowed, and with the same seemingly endless supply of mattress covers. They were buried in temporary cemeteries, or already established American cemeteries as possible. On the way to Paris, the 611th split into two branches. One traveled into the Loire Valley with the 5th Infantry Division, and James Shomon took the other in the direction of the Belgian border. By that time, the unofficial count for Operation Overlord stood at 37,000 American dead and 10,000 missing, and Shomon traveled on to Brest, France.

The port city had been a German stronghold, submarine base and supply depot since the fall of France in 1940. The battle to reclaim it would last from August 7 to September 19, 1944. A convention of war was that enemies had responsibility for tending to each other's dead as possible. The enemy dead were found in the submarine pens at low tide, weighted to the harbor bottom by rocks. The civilian dead were found in seemingly endless corridors of the city's underground, described by Shomon as "the abysmal pits beneath the shattered city."

> Here we found a nightmare of hell. Our lanterns hardly gave us good light, but we saw that the walls of the inner tunnels were charred black from a terrible fire. We descended a winding stairway littered with hundreds of dead French people. They were in crawling positions, headed for the main exit. The dead on the stairs were so that we had to slide on top of them in order to descend. Some of the charred and burned women had reached the very exit before they were caught in flames. Their faces were horrifying.[11]

From Brest, Shomon and his men moved on to Dutch Limburg. There, it would be his job to convert the daily arrival of the dead and multiple acres of farmland into a cemetery that would be filled first with 28,000 bodies, then be taken apart and reconfigured for the 8,000 dead who would forever give their identities to one of the great American war cemeteries of Europe. It was October 1944, and the demands upon the land that would become a cemetery were only going to increase and accelerate.

Shomon had appeared in the town hall at Margraten to tell officials what would occur. The United States Ninth Army was headquartered in Maastricht, and its quarter million troops would be involved in the coming attacks on the Ruhr and Rhine Valleys on their way to Berlin. In preparation for the expected large loss of life, Graves Registration had requisitioned what would finally total 65 acres, most of it productive farmland along a former Roman highway that had been used in wars from the time of Charlemagne in the 9th century to Hitler in the current day.

As it would turn out, there would always be an undercurrent of unhappiness on the part of the farmers involved, but it would not detract that much from the general good feeling about the American presence in the province. "Nothing can be done about that, it's war," the mayor reportedly told one of the farmers, advising him that he would eventually be compensated and that he should just look for new land to farm. Hearing the protest that this was otherwise good and productive farmland, Shomon was reported to have said, simply "The best soil is not good enough for our boys."[12] Eventually, the cemetery would reconfigure much of the surrounding agricultural land and change the very nature of the region. The farmers would wait until 1952 to receive their compensation.

For the next seven weeks, Jefferson Wiggins and the men under his command were brought to Margraten by truck each morning. On the first day they saw a scene that had never before been in their experience.

> We didn't know there was such a place, anyplace in the war such as Margraten and we were totally unprepared for the establishment of the graveyard. We knew Americans and Germans were being killed, but we had never given any thought at all to what happened to all these people who were killed.[13]

The work would begin as soon as surveyors laid out the initial burial plots. Wiggins was not yet told that at the other end of the land before him were the bodies of four or five thousand soldiers who had not yet been identified. The next day, his force of 260 Black gravediggers was confronted with a long line of bodies beneath tarpaulins. He was told just to start with grave number one and continue through the first collection of 200.

> Captain Shomon came over and he said that—and I kind of liked him—"I know that this is the most gruesome task, that any of us has ever had to do, but it is a necessary task. I don't envy you, but at the same time I don't feel sorry for you because someone has to do it..."
>
> "Sometimes a chaplain will be here," he said "but you have to bury the soldiers respectful. It will be hundreds a day and just remember that each young soldier

that you bury, could have been you, your brother or your cousin and is a fellow American."

"First Sergeant," asked one of Wiggins' soldiers, "what happens if we do all we can and we find that we just can't do this job, what happens?"

"I'm not sure what happens," he replied, "but I am certain that each of you will do the best that you can."

The work took place from 7 a.m. until dark, at which time there would always be a religious service, the blowing of "Taps," and a rifle salute. Large trucks arrived at regular intervals with bodies "stacked like cordwood," and often with attached trailers of assorted body parts. Some bodies were freshly dead and easier to manage; others had to be handled with chemicals that dissolved rubber gloves. Standard procedure was to place a dog tag in the body's mouth, for one soldier to place the body in a sitting position, another to slip a mattress cover over its head, both to bring it to a standing position and bring the cover to its feet. As the days progressed into an historically brutal European winter, the work got harder. In the first weeks it was the constant cold rain. A body needed to dry before being processed, but the tents could not always provide full shelter. A grave once dug would only fill up with mud and water before it could accept its occupant and be closed. The ruts worn into the ground by the trucks became deeper and impassable. When the logs that were dropped into the mud to allow traction sank too low, they were topped by whole tree trunks. The war continued nearby, and buzz bombs filled the sky.

When the hard winter set in, the water-saturated land became frozen and impermeable, but the bodies kept coming, many of them also frozen. In December, a last gasp of the enemy would evolve into the Battle of the Bulge in the nearby Belgian Ardennes. Though most American dead were interred at the American Ardennes cemetery, German soldiers entered the mix of the dead at Margraten. Some of the gravediggers did not have sufficiently warm clothing and were allowed to take boots and coats from the corpses that came before them. Each was required to dig three graves each day, but that was not always possible. The ground needed to be attacked with blowtorches and axes. Many of the bodies once successfully interred had to then be disinterred for bureaucratic reasons.

If the men were lucky, a shower truck would show up outside the cemetery once a week. Sometimes the school in which the grave diggers were quartered would provide hot water, other times it could be heated in their helmets. Drinking was a problem wherever alcohol could be found or created, and Wiggins would later remember that in their drunkenness many of his men would be driven to bouts of crying.

"In all those eight, nine and sometimes ten hours a day that we were digging there, fear was in the air. Or perhaps it was sadness. Every day was the same. Nevertheless, you didn't get used to it."[14]

Despite the wish of military policy that the American soldiers and the people of the community avoid interaction, the horror of the first months of the cemetery that would eventually help to define their small region could only lead to a coming together of the Dutch citizens and the American liberators. But, with few exceptions, the Black gravediggers would always be seen almost as distant ghosts. They were billeted by themselves and moved about as a group in marching formations or in trucks.

Like others, schoolboy Huub Bessems, then of Termaar, had been shown pictures of Black people but had never seen one in person. Suddenly, with the arrival of the dead, the area of the fruit market was now the home of hundreds of the gravediggers and the truck drivers that delivered those they would bury. He would watch them march off to the cemetery each morning and would sometimes encounter them at night. "If you were out on the street in the evening—there was no street lighting or anything—you were just walking along, and they were wearing rubber shoes ... you couldn't hear them and you didn't see them, and suddenly, 'swish' there was somebody next to you and you were scared silly. That was a very weird experience."[15]

Sjeuf Felder, then of Vijlen, was the fifth child of a Dutch mother and a German man who had fled to the Netherlands. Like a large portion of the Dutch, Sjeuf had invested in an effort to learn and be able to speak English. One day, he and a friend heard that something was going on in Margraten that they should see. As they got closer to the village, they came upon "a whole queue of trucks that were fully loaded with ... corpses, just call it that. 2000 American soldiers were killed in the liberation.... It cost the lives of 2000 boys."[16] The true and uncounted number, however, was probably something less than that.

Years later, it would be difficult for Felder to withdraw full memories of the moment from the emotions that had accompanied it. But he could remember the common smell of the Black soldiers and the cadavers that they tended. His understanding of English, however, was not enough to allow him to understand what they were saying.

> They were almost all Black soldiers, coming from poor backgrounds ... who spoke dialect, let's say, and I didn't understand a word of it. I thought to myself: You didn't learn it properly because you don't understand a word they're saying. I thought: You spent so much money on it and studied so hard, yet you don't understand it at all.

Although the young women who had stood at a distance while they observed Jefferson Wiggins outside the cemetery gate eventually talked with him, when one of them ventured to respond to his proffered handshake, she could only briefly touch his hand, then look at it closely to see if anything had happened to it.

And what the Dutch citizenry could observe about the relationships between white and Black Americans might have become a model for their own behavior. Frans Douven's family, as an example, owned a dance hall next to the fruit auction in Margraten. As the number of Black soldiers in the region increased, a number would be quartered in the two locations. Frans noticed that the two groups did not get along. When white soldiers entered the dance hall, the Black soldiers who may have been present would usually withdraw.

In time, the proscription on interaction between soldiers and civilians had to give way to unavoidable reality. The building of the cemetery soon came to dominate the life of the village. The trucks brought with them trails of blood and the smell of death. When one of them had to wait in line, one of the driver's duties was to spread gasoline on the ground over which it had idled and set it afire to burn away the blood. The chaos of it all became overwhelming as the winter deepened. Perhaps the first acknowledgment of the shared burden of the Americans and the people of Limburg came in the Christmas Eve mass at the Catholic church in Margraten.

As the Battle of the Bulge raged just to the south, the night sky was filled with an air war and the reach of anti-aircraft artillery from below. The church was full to the rafters with the people and children of the town, clergy and nuns, and American soldiers. The choir was led by an accordion player, and the priest gave his sermon in English.

> Pray hard, my friends, for only through prayer will come good weather for battle. Only through prayer will come airplanes, tanks, courage to hurl the invader back into his scheming, turbulent world of evil and lawlessness....
>
> Be stout of heart, be courageous, be prayerful, my beloved, for the Almighty is with us. The free people of the world will march to victory and trample down the heathens.[17]

The Battle of the Bulge would lead to a symbolic endpoint for the war with the crossing of the Rhine River by Allied troops on March 22, 1945. It would be deemed the bloodiest battle of the war, with more than 19,000 American dead. German deaths were estimated upwards of 12,500, and the conventions of war dictated that the Americans would have responsibility for the temporary burial of some of those. With the coming spring, the construction of the Margraten cemetery would become easier, but now it would be overwhelmed.

The artificial wall between the American soldiers and the citizens of Limburg would finally come fully down. James Shomon went to the mayor of Margraten to plead for help.

Quartermaster soldiers remove a body from the vicinity of Malmedy, Belgium, on or about December 17, 1944, the date of the Malmedy Massacre in which German troops executed 84 Americans by machine gun or point-blank range (U.S. National Archives).

> Can you help us? We need men. We need men with shovels. Can you issue a call to all able-bodied men of Margraten to report to the cemetery at once? We have more than a thousand bodies that must be buried.
>
> The Burgomaster took off like a shot for the town hall. "Just leave it to me, Captain," he called, "just leave it to me. The men will be there."[18]

The thousand were buried over the course of two days. The people of Margraten were now fully engaged with the cemetery and would remain so in their attention and adoption of every grave and name on the memorial walls by regional families into the 21st century.

Jefferson Wiggins had left Margraten a few months earlier and gone further into the war. He would eventually, and for most of his life, put the experience out of his mind, but the conundrum of it would never be forgotten: in all of that horror, he had never buried the body of a Black man killed in combat (172 African American burials would be discovered in the cemetery in 2014). "I thought, as did others, if only they would give us a gun, then we'd finish the job together. The sooner the war is over, the sooner we can go home."[19]

> Our job was to dig the graves, place the body in a mattress cover and lower them into the grave and cover them. The worst part of it for me was watching all these

young Americans who weren't even old enough to vote, seeing them … in many cases their bodies mutilated and mangled, and had to be put in the mattress cover. That was the hardest part for me.

I recall a conversation with the others that once you're dead, you're dead, and color doesn't mean anything. Our job was to be as respectful and bury these soldiers with as much dignity as they deserved. Someone said to me "How the hell do you bury a guy with dignity when you're burying him in the uniform he was killed in, you're placing him in a mattress cover, and many times the grave is filling with water while you're trying to bury him.

"Forget about race. That's what we were trying to do. We weren't burying a white soldier, but we were burying an American soldier."

Six

Limited Service

What the hell is there to think about?—Gen. George
Patton to 1st Sgt. Jefferson Wiggins, 1945

On June 6, 1944, and in the days that followed, the Normandy
beaches would take on another burden, without which the deaths of Allied
soldiers would have been futile. It was one thing to begin the recapture of
a continent with a massive invasion from the sea, and then to reclaim lost
territory more quickly than expected, but it could not happen without an
intense chain of the supplies needed to do so.

The port of Cherbourg would not be recaptured from the Germans
until June 29, but it was barely functional. The recovery of the port of
Brest would wait until September 19, but it would be in even worse condition. The port of Antwerp would not be fully usable until November. So,
after the troops and graves registration had come ashore at Normandy,
the soft beaches had to become the hard port of entry for food, fuel, materiel, and the infrastructure and consumer goods that would be needed
for the advance to Germany and the recovery of liberated territory. There
were, however, few intact railroad lines to move them inland. The roads
were not in much better condition, but they could be made passable with
hard work and determination, which fell in large part to the heavy trucks,
drivers and mechanics of the Red Ball Express.

At some point during or after his time as a driver who wore the patch
of the Red Ball Express, Henry Van Landingham began to write about his
experience:

> This old truck groans like a woman in labor. It never runs smooth, even on a
> good paved road. I know I am out running [sic] the convoy now, but I can't help
> it. Every time I get close to the Berg [Berg en Terblijt], the truck seems to pick up
> speed by itself and fly all the way home like a runaway horse heading for the barn.
>
> Twenty miles back Charlie woke up and asked me where we were. I told him
> to go back to sleep. He always seems to have a good sense of when I am getting
> tired. But I really like to do these last few miles myself. I saw the steeple of the

75

Berg church from way up in the hills around Maastrict [sic]. But the trees hide
the steeple on the way up the hill to the Berg. When I can see the steeple again I
know I will be only five minutes away from my bunk.

Charlie is my favorite copilot on the road. That boy is really black, with only
big eyes shining out at you. He grew up in Cleveland pretty much the same way I
did in Buffalo, poor, but scheming how to do something different than go into the
plant like all the other colored boys. But the war messed up both our plans. Now
we are both here in Holland with no idea of when or if we will get home.[1]

The Red Ball Express would become perhaps the most visible
non-combat contribution of African Americans to the gathering last year
of the war. It derived out of the first efforts of supply for the advance to
Germany that had been part of the planning of the Normandy Invasion.
The components, floating dockage and ramping necessary to create artificial cargo harbors were first brought together in England. All arriving
vehicles would have full gas tanks, and a supply of filled 5-gallon gas cans.
Despite the destructive winds and tides of a subsequent three-day storm
on the English Channel, and because it had been difficult at first to move
inland against the enemy, the improvised port became a parking lot of
170,000 vehicles, with reserves of 7.5 million gallons of fuel, and 500,000
tons of supplies by the end of June.[2]

The supply chain was finally able to move inland with a break in the
German lines at the end of July, and the path forward became easier than
anticipated. Unexpected opportunities created the replacement of old
strategies with new, but the provision of supplies could not always keep
up. The movement into France of Gen. George Patton's Third Army consumed 380,000 gallons of gasoline each day, and reserves were exhausted
by August 7. Each day thereafter required supply from rear positions.
Consumption and the need for fuel only increased as the month went on
and culminated on August 24 with 782,000 gallons consumed by the First
Army. On August 25, the Allies entered Paris, and the Red Ball Express
shifted into first gear.

In the absence of usable railroad lines, the Express took on the imagery of railroading. In America, the Santa Fe Railroad had been running
Red Balls since the turn of the century. With the placard of a red ball
on their locomotives, the trains sped through switches that were made
straight, through rights of way that were made clear and past stations and
yards that would only know their passing wind.

In this version and following a similar model that had been used in
pre-invasion England, 132 trucking companies were combined into a force
of 6,000 trucks over 36 hours of planning. Each was manned by two drivers who shared 22 hours of daily driving, with two hours down-time for
maintenance. The trucks were predominantly 2.5-ton GMC "Jimmy's,"

along with 1.5-ton Dodges and Macks. In the retrieved geography of Europe, the trucks of the Red Ball Express were set in convoys 60 yards apart from each other mapped out to travel nonstop for hundreds of miles, and which followed the heels of the advance of Allied troops. By the time of its replacement by restored rail lines on November 16, it would transport more than 400,000 tons.

The concept and basic design of the Express had been the work of Gen. Dwight D. Eisenhower and derived from his study and use of the French highway system. The routes were one way in each direction east and west, or on divided highways, and allowed no other traffic. Although the roads were marginal, pockmarked, broken or more imaginary than real, the system was designed with pull-outs and rest areas, and could only function with makeshift bridges or the repairs of hundreds of others. As the American president in the 1950s, Eisenhower would initiate the American Interstate Highway system on the same model. Not all drivers who wore the patch of the Red Ball Express were Red Ball drivers, but part of alternate and extended routes that took on similar names, like the Green Diamond in the region of Cherbourg, the White Ball Express between Le Havre, Rouen and Paris and the Lions Express between Bayeux and Brussels. The ABC Express out of Antwerp and eastward moved more than 51,000 tons, not including oil, over the course of one month in 1944. When the need for these circuits was alleviated by rebuilt railroads, the trucks moved on to other transport tasks that would eventually take them deep into Germany.

The trucks would frequently break down and have to be pushed off the road or destroyed (the Dodge trucks were reputed to have the most stamina, but the GMC Jimmys were easier to repair). They could be randomly attacked by one of the few remaining Luftwaffe planes, and one estimate claimed that those that had made regular runs toward Aachen could accumulate as much as 1000 pieces of flak over the three months they were driven. Most rode on the same large 11-inch tires that were used by American city buses. In December 1944, the Office of Defense Transportation announced that 1945's planned allocation of 2.5 million of the tires for domestic use would have to be cut in half, the other half sent to the war.[3]

The large wheels could not protect the trucks from their most menacing enemy: mud. The larger wheels could bog down more deeply. The transmissions could be worn out with the attempt to escape. The brakes could be immobilized by hardened clay. Bulldozers could help, but not always.

The drivers fared not much better than the trucks. The long hours over difficult roads and highways in trucks that always needed mainte-

Despite breakdowns, attack by German airplanes, the exhaustion of its drivers and barely usable roads, the Red Ball Express would move 400,000 tons of supplies through Europe between August 25 and November 16, 1944 (Archives Normandie 1939–45).

nance led to exhaustion and illness. When it seemed necessary, they overrode the speed governors on the truck engines, which often led to crashes and injury. The pace was relentless.

Seventy-five percent of the drivers were African American, but they would emerge in the postwar popular culture as just minor players. The chief protagonists of a 1952 theatrical American movie, "The Red Ball Express" were a Black driver, played by Sidney Poitier, and his white captain, as portrayed by Jeff Chandler. While a casual line in the movie asserted that half the drivers were Black, the actual number of Black actors in the cast of drivers was less than that (in one scene, 18 white drivers and 6 Black drivers honored the death by landmine of another Black driver). Any racial tension that may have existed in the actual Red Ball Express was expressed in just one scenario in the movie, when Poitier asked politely if someone else would hand him a doughnut.

A white driver says, angrily, "Black boy, you give orders to no one. You take them."[4]

A brawl ensues, and in the subsequent scene Poitier tells Chandler that he's going to apply for a transfer because he can put up with any danger, but he will not put up with that kind of behavior.

"Look Robinson," says Chandler, "I'm not educated at all in the subtleties of race relationships, but it was never my intention to treat you any different from anyone else in this company."

Later, Poitier grouses to a friend, "He outranks us the way we've been outranked all our lives," to which his friend replies, "I've been all over the world, seen all kinds of people, and this is the greatest bunch of fellas I've ever worked with, even if half of them are all white."

The American Third Army forged the path from Normandy to the Rhine and into Germany under the leadership of Gen. George Patton. In many respects, Patton was emblematic of all of the contradictions and dysfunction of racial policy of the War Department, and then some. He was both a conventional and a conditional racist, and, in his particular lack of human empathy for the Jewish victims of the Holocaust, he was probably more harmful than the rescuer he was intended to be. Added to the mix, and making it difficult to fully consider his racism, was his self-admitted theatricality. He blustered, cussed in extreme and proclaimed whatever he felt was needed to move his troops, keep the support of his audience, and get the job done.

Some thought that he was mentally ill, or perhaps brain damaged as the result of a propensity for accident and bodily damage. He had fallen off horses and been kicked in the head by them. A lamp had blown up in his face. He would die in 1945 after being projected through the windshield of a car.

Conventionally, he was a white man of the times and of the insistent, practically applied prejudice of the army of which he was a general: those who were not white were inferior in some way that may not have been in their own control. As he worked through the Pancho Villa expedition, which preceded the American entrance into World War I in 1917, he expressed the opinion that the Mexican peasants, who lived in dire poverty, should be exterminated because "they are so far behind that they will never catch up they are much lower than the Indians. They have absolutely no morals."[5]

Of the Japanese in the 1930s, he admired the Samurai and the Warrior, but upon a visit to Hawaii in 1936 he saw the Japanese residents as potential traitors and called them "Oranges." He compiled a list of 128 Japanese whom he believed should be arrested and held under a suspension of the writ of habeas corpus in the event of war. They could never be loyal and their immigration should be restricted, under imposition of martial law if it came to that.[6] In his private life, he was a property owner in San Marino and South Pasadena, California, and was a signatory through the proxy of his sister to covenants limiting real estate sales in the regions to Caucasians.[7]

"Nigger" was a common word of his vocabulary, but it was also not uncommon in the language of many of his contemporaries. "Niggers" and "Coons," after all, had shown up in the written correspondence of World War II President Harry Truman as late as 1939.[8] Truman would eventually become an advocate for equality in the military, and, as the war progressed, some of Patton's contemporaries in command began to change their behavior. Patton's evolved into a conditional approach to those who were inherently inferior in his view but could appear more or less so on the basis of their behavior.

The Jews, the most tragic victims of the European war, were clearly victimized again by a defect in Patton's humanity. With the war's end, Patton had been put in charge of the Displaced Person camps of Southern Germany. These were, for the most part, the surviving Jews of the concentration and death camps of the Third Reich. They had been caught up in the will of the German people, and of many nationals of the occupied countries, to strip them of their humanity, sever human and family connections, and to work and starve them to death, if not to murder them outright in gas chambers, disease-ridden barracks and forced marches.

Upon an inspection with Gen. Eisenhower of one of the camps of the displaced, Patton complained, "these Jewish DPs, or at least a majority of them, have no sense of human relationships."[9] Eisenhower spoke to the inmates gently and with compassion, but Patton described them to his diary of September 17, 1945, as "the greatest stinking bunch of humanity I have ever seen."[10] With that kind of belief, Patton had set up camps in which some of the former Nazi guards were put in charge once again of their former prisoners. It did not seem to matter to him if the Jews were forced in some cases to wear Nazi uniforms in the absence of other clothing. The camps were to be closed off. If they were not, he warned, the inmates would "spread over the country like locusts and would eventually have to be rounded up after quite a few of them had been shot and quite a few Germans murdered and pillaged."[11]

President Truman could not help but learn of Patton's behavior. After an investigation by others, he wrote to Eisenhower, "we appear to be treating the Jews as the Nazis treated them except that we do not exterminate them. They are in concentration camps in large numbers under our military guard instead of SS troops. One is led to wonder whether the German people, seeing this, are not supposing that we are following or at least condoning Nazi policy."[12]

Patton's response to his diary of September 15 was that the criticism had apparently come out of the belief "that the Displaced Person is a human being, which he is not, and this applies particularly to the Jews, who are lower than animals."[13]

The reconciliation that many would try make between the American general who was credited with magnificent effort in the war and the sometimes breathtakingly non-empathetic racist would come in the often-quoted exclamation of the conditionality of his prejudices. It was seen as a positive indicator of the man:

> I don't give a damn who the man is. He can be a nigger or a Jew, but if he has the stuff and does his duty, he can have anything I've got. By God! I love him. You've got to be proud of them. You've got to give them loyalty when they give you loyalty.[14]

And, as a supplement to the assertion that a racist utterance could be read positively, the quote was often followed by the true reminder that in regard to African Americans Patton was an advocate for their inclusion against the grain of War Department policy when he saw their merit. He played a role in being sure that African American judges would be involved in military justice for Black soldiers, and his closest, long-time aide, and a pallbearer in his funeral, was the African American Master Sergeant William George Meeks.

Whatever the confusion of George Patton's racism and its effect on his work, it became most evident at the crucial time in which the war was finally turning and required the maximum effort. And it seemed to be mirrored by the War Department itself as it began to accede in a limited way to the need to become more flexible in its racial policy.

In December 1944, Germany opened its last offensive action of the war in the Ardennes region of Belgium. Its purpose was to break supply lines from Antwerp, and to defeat the Allies on the battlefield soundly enough to bring them to a negotiation for the end of the war. The Battle of the Bulge would become one of the most deadly, vicious and storied battles in American military history.

In early December, Jefferson Wiggins and the men of the 960 QMSC, left Margraten and moved closer to the Belgian village of Bastogne. The gathering winter had already shown itself to be potentially brutal, and the coming German offensive was in the wind. Wiggins' status in the unit had only been increasing since the promotion to First Sergeant. Since then, he and the Captain who had promoted him had become full confidantes. One evening the unit was ordered to put together a reconnaissance group to check out the feeling of the Bastogne villagers that the Germans were afoot. Wiggins was asked to join the group, but was not able to because of a previous commitment and deadline. The men never returned, and the unit had lost its commanding officers. They seemed to have been replaced by the increasing roar of the approaching offensive.

When a colonel came looking for an officer of the unit the following day, Wiggins had to tell him he held the highest rank. It was not a responsibility that he wanted, and he asked when a new officer would be assigned. "You're it, First Sergeant," said the colonel, "You know what has to be done and you know how to get it done."[15]

Wiggins' first response was a kind of anger. "The colonel made very clear that he was absolutely frustrated, just like I was. Here I was, a farmer boy of 19, responsible for 259 men. I was unexperienced and had no idea at all where I was. Something was terribly wrong, because normally no superior would have brought us in such a position."[16]

His job was to command his men in preparing and maintaining the roads that would carry the American advance and the returning dead and wounded, and which were beneath a constant snowfall. He was to inform the command on routes and conditions on an hourly basis. On the sixth day he was visited in the old barn that was the company's headquarters by a retinue of officers with Gen. George Patton at its center. Wiggins would later remember him as surprisingly smaller than expected, but with two pearl-handled pistols on his gun belt. He knew that he would have to follow very strict protocols in the encounter that was to follow.

"Are you a real First Sergeant?" the general demanded.

"Yes, sir. I am a real First Sergeant."

"You look damn young to me. How old are you, First Sergeant?"

Wiggins was frozen and could barely remember how to form words. "Get your company commander in here," Patton ordered.

Wiggins recovered. "We have no company commander, Sir, nor do we have officers."

"Are you telling me you're the ranking man in this outfit, First Sergeant?"

"I am, Sir."

The colonel who had put him in that position explained the situation.

"Colonel," said Patton, "this is a perfect example of the caliber of soldier this country can produce. This soldier and millions like him enable me to kick kraut asses all over Europe—and I'm not finished yet." He looked Wiggins directly in the eye.

"First Sergeant, I believe you would make an outstanding officer. I think I may give you a direct field commission. What is your reaction to my thoughts?"

Wiggins was nervous. "Can I think about it, Sir?"

"What the hell is there to think about?" Patton uttered, perhaps in theatrical anger. "Too much thought leads to hesitation. But since you need to think, I'll give you thirty seconds."[17]

Five days later, Wiggins was given the bars of a lieutenant. He had never before even seen another Black officer, nor, he supposed, had any of his men. The promotion was celebrated by the colonel and the other white officers with champagne.

Patton was racist at his core. Whatever his true thoughts and motivations as he promoted Jefferson Wiggins to Second Lieutenant, it came at the time of a delicate crossroads for the War Department. In its struggle to maintain a segregated force in the face of increasing need for fighting troops, it had come to the verge of a duplicitous adjustment in policy that might have been even more damaging than it already was.

At the time, the demand for infantry riflemen was beginning to exceed the supply. Training programs had been converting those in other services to the infantry, but the numbers of them coming from training in the United States were declining. By one projection, the Ardennes fighting would be short 29,000 men by the end of December.[18] The other service units from which the new infantry would have to be converted included the Quartermaster Corps and other branches of the Army with large numbers of Black members—those who had been previously determinedly excluded from combat. The need for more fighting men was dire, but, by the formula of segregation, Black soldiers would have to fight in Black units that for the most part did not exist.

The challenge fell to Lt. Gen. John C.H. Lee, a controversial figure in the last years of the war. Lee was an engineer with added administrative skills that brought him from his first experiences in the Panama Canal Zone in 1909, to a Croix de Guerre for his command of the U.S. Army 89th Division in World War I, overseer of the recovery from the Mississippi River Flood of 1927, command of the Pacific port operations in the first years of World War II, now to the creation of the Services of Supply organization to supply the European theater of the war in 1942.

He was a deeply religious man and wore his beliefs as he did the stars on his uniform. His initials, JCH were often said to stand for Jesus Christ Himself or John Church House. Sometimes, the name would be John Court House, the issuer of judgmental proclamations, and commands beyond the pale. There seemed to be enough stories of the times he would reach into garbage cans and eat the thrown away food as a demonstration against waste that they had the ring of truth.

Depending on one's point of view, Lee was seen as a petty tyrant or a quiet and humble man. He had once reportedly enraged Eisenhower by requisitioning for his staff the best of the Paris hotels that had been quickly vacated by the fleeing German command. His reputation for pomposity and ostentation extended to his own private railroad cars to move him through his work, but he could point to their usefulness in the quality of that work, for which he would be highly regarded by history, although some would fault his inability to match the speed of the advance from Normandy to Germany with the speed of the supply lines to support it.

Perhaps most controversial about Gen. John C.H. Lee was his proactive advocacy for the aspirations of Black soldiers to be treated as equals, at least in the actual fighting of the war. The plan he offered for the conversion of many of his own quartermaster troops to combat positions was one that might be interpreted differently in the sensibilities of the 1940s than it would be in more enlightened times. It would start with the recruitment of infantry volunteers from the Black units of the Communications Zone forces (rear units supporting the communications needs of forward fighting units). On December 26, he distributed a letter that could be read either cynically or with great welcome depending on one's attitude about how he had been treated as a Black soldier, excerpted:

> The Commanding General makes a special appeal to you. It is planned to assign you without regard to color or race to the units where assistance is most needed, and give you the opportunity of fighting shoulder to shoulder to bring about victory. Your comrades at the front are anxious to share the glory of victory with you. Your relatives and friends everywhere have been urging that you be granted this privilege. The Supreme Commander, your Commanding General, and other veteran officers who have served with you are confident that many of you will take advantage of this opportunity and carry on in keeping with the glorious record of our colored troops in our former wars.[19]

Leaving aside its assertions of a past glory that had never genuinely been voiced in the annals of Army history, and the supposed urging of everyone else that they be given this opportunity, Lee intended the plan to finally integrate the fighting units that would be needed to carry through the end of the war.

Gen. Dwight Eisenhower's chief of staff, Gen. Walter B. Smith, saw the promise, however, as "a clear invitation to embarrassment to the War Department."[20] Writing to Eisenhower, Smith asserted that, although he agreed that the two races should be mixed, this was not Army policy, and if the letter got out to the general public, it would put the Department in "grave difficulties."

> It is inevitable that this statement will get out, and equally inevitable that the result will be that every negro [sic] organization, pressure group and newspaper will take the attitude that, while the War Department segregates colored troops into organizations of their own against the desires and pleas of all the negro race, the Army is perfectly willing to put them in the front lines mixed in units with white soldiers, and have them do battle when an emergency arises. Two years ago I would have considered the marked statement ["without regard to color or race"] the most dangerous thing that I had ever seen in regard to negro relations.[21]

The pressure groups and newspapers were worthy of Smith's concern. In 1942, the same NAACP publication, *The Crisis*, that had urged Blacks to see World War I from the perspective of "First your country. Then your rights!" took on a very different view. Civil rights leader Roy Wilkins editorialized that this was not the time to be silent about inequality in America.

> It must be that we declare the life blood of our fighters and the sweat of our workers to be a sacrifice for a new world which not only shall not contain a Hitler, but Hitlerism. And to thirteen millions of American Negroes that means a fight for a world in which lynching, brutality, terror, humiliation, and degradation through segregation and discrimination, shall have no place—*either here or there....*
>
> A lily-white navy cannot fight for a free world. A jim crow [sic] army cannot fight for a free world. Jim crow strategy, no matter on how grand a scale, cannot build a free world.[22]

The Crisis was just one voice, and perhaps belated, in what was coming from a list of strong African American newspapers of the day. A letter to the editor of the *Pittsburgh Courier* of January 31, 1941, started what would come to be called the Double V campaign. "Should I sacrifice to live 'half American'?" asked the writer, urging that "colored Americans adopt the double VV for a double victory. The first V for a victory over our enemies from without, the second V for a victory over our enemies from within."[23]

A writer to the Chicago Defender on March 7, 1942, asked, "With America trying to spread the gospel of the Four Freedoms worldwide, why should we cease our fight for them right here at home."

The Double V campaign would continue throughout the war and extend into the demand for equal opportunity in the factories and services that supported the war effort. As the demands of the war became more dire in terms of lives lost and sacrifices in the national treasury, demands for equality evolved into the assertion and belief that the part that Black Americans would play could lead to that second victory.

But, by the time of Gen. John Lee's stated plan to recruit non-fighting Blacks into white fighting units, Blacks had been involved in fighting in only limited ways. Gen. Smith's stated caution to Gen. Eisenhower was premised on a truth: Blacks had been excluded based on a policy of racial segregation, but now that the need was dire (and the potential of death in combat was increased) they were perfectly welcome to join the fight with comrades who were "anxious to share the glory of victory with you."

Smith succeeded in getting Eisenhower to retrieve and rewrite Lee's invitation, but it had already been posted and seen. Eisenhower's version did not rescind the notion that Blacks and whites could now fight together—with a proviso—but it seemed only to devalue further the humanity of one of those groups.

The Supreme Commander desires to destroy the enemy forces and end hostil-
ities in this theater without delay. Every available weapon at our disposal must
be brought to bear upon the enemy. To this end the Theater Commander has
directed the Communications Zone Commander to make the greatest possible
use of limited service men within service units and to survey our entire organization in an effort to produce able bodied men for the front lines.[24]

Further into the letter, the concept of "limited service men" was
evolved into "suitable negro [sic] volunteers," but it came with a proviso
that seemed to hark back to an aspect of the segregated army that could
be seen as one of the causes of everything that had excluded most African
Americans from the fight.

In the event that the number of suitable negro volunteers exceeds the replacement
needs of negro combat units, these men will be suitably incorporated in other
organizations so that their service and their fighting spirit may be efficiently uti-
lized.

The Black volunteers would go to Black units before they would be
integrated with white units. But as Eisenhower's policy evolved, it could
not even go that far. There were already a number of all Black fighting
units in the form of long-standing artillery units with the supplements of
tank and tank destroyer units. The conversion of "limited service men"
into those battalions was needed and welcomed. But there were no existing Black infantry units in the immediate West European theater to accept
volunteer riflemen. When it came down to it, the determination was made
that it was not Eisenhower's desire to place individual Black trainees in
white units, but to create all Black units which could supplement white
units.

Whatever was actually promised by the new policy, or the new version of the old policy, 4,562 Blacks had volunteered for combat by the
end of February 1945. They had been truck drivers, longshoremen, cargo
checkers and construction foremen. But once again, as in the initial draft
complications of the war in 1942, supply exceeded places to put them and
the effort was stopped. In an assessment from the perspective of history,
they would present fewer disciplinary and absentee problems than their
white counterparts.[25] Eventually, an official number of 2,221 Blacks would
serve in 37 platoons beside white platoons and, in some assessments,
helped to reduce racial friction in the common pursuit. Some of them
had had to take a reduction in rank so that they would not outrank the
white soldiers with whom they fought. That sacrifice made, and their valor
proved, all of their platoons were decommissioned at war's end.[26] Their
records would not reflect the ranks they had given up until the 1950s.

Gen. George Patton would play a constructive role in the development of Black infantrymen as he moved toward the capture of Berlin, and

he was particularly associated with what came to be considered the very successful all Black tank battalions. The most storied of them would be the 761st, which called itself the "Black Panther Battalion," but it would be in relation to the battalion that Patton's hypocrisy would be most evident to himself, if not to anyone else.

The 761st had come together early in 1942 with six white officers, thirty Black officers and 676 enlisted men. In November, the battalion became part of Patton's Third Army and came before him for inspection on November 30. His proclamation to the men would become often quoted in the history of race relations in the U.S. military.

> Men, you're the first Negro tankers to ever fight in the American Army. I would never have asked for you if you weren't good. I have nothing but the best in my Army. I don't care what color you are as long as you go up there and kill those Kraut sons of bitches. Everyone has their eyes on you and is expecting great things from you. Most of your race is looking forward to your success. Don't let them down and damn you, don't let me down![27]

After that oration, however, he told his autobiography, that his firm belief that Black soldiers were not capable of combat remained paramount. "Individually they were good soldiers, but I expressed my belief at the time, and have never found the necessity of changing it, that a colored soldier can not think fast enough to fight in armor."[28]

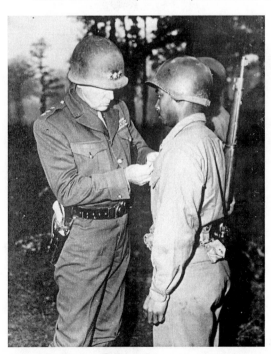

Lt. General George S. Patton pins a silver star on Pvt. Ernest A. Jenkins of the 761st Tank Battalion, a.k.a. the Black Panthers, France, October 1944 (U.S. National Archives).

But the 761st would serve for 183 consecutive days under George Patton, and, like the 769th of World War I, a longer time without respite that any other tank battalion. It had started its epic journey at the front of the push through France, supported airborne forces at Bastogne in the Battle of the Bulge, helped to clear the way for the breakthrough of the Siegfried Line by the 4th Armored Division, and was one of the first American units to connect with the Red Army's march from the east. It would lose 34 members during that time, and more than 200 would be wounded. It would receive a presidential citation for its work—in 1998.[29]

For the most part, the war would enter its final months still fully supported by the soldiers of the Quartermaster Corps, as well as those of the Ordinance Corps, Signal Corps and Engineer Corps. In a speech to the Third Army in advance of the Normandy Invasion, Patton, had not given them short shrift. Whether or not he had the race of these soldiers in mind, what he told them was accurate.

> All the real heroes are not storybook combat fighters. Every single man in the army plays a vital role. So don't ever let up. Don't ever think that your job is unimportant. What if every truck driver decided that he didn't like the whine of the shells and turned yellow and jumped headlong into a ditch? That cowardly bastard could say to himself, "Hell, they won't miss me, just one man in thousands." What if every man said that? Where in the hell would we be then? No, thank God, Americans don't say that. Every man does his job. Every man is important. The ordnance men are needed to supply the guns, the quartermaster is needed to bring up the food and clothes for us because where we are going there isn't a hell of a lot to steal. Every last damn man in the mess hall, even the one who boils the water to keep us from getting the GI shits, has a job to do.[30]

SEVEN

Liberation Children

All of those children, all of those soldiers, Black and white. Just forgotten children.—Arzeymah Van Landingham Raqib, 2019

In 2019, the American daughter of the truck driver Henry Van Landingham would sit at her kitchen table in Ocala, Florida, and begin a consideration of the story of her father and his Dutch daughter Els with a pause for tears.

"These children ... that they were just left and forgotten." Her brother, Henry's son, Philip, had served four years in the Vietnam war of the 1970s and he had told her of what he had seen in yet another war.

"Those children were forgotten also," said Arzeymah Raqib. "All of those children, all of those soldiers, Black and white. Just forgotten children."

Henry had died in 2006 after a very successful life in postwar Buffalo, New York, and retirement in Florida. He had been preceded in death by his Dutch daughter Els in 2004. Arzeymah and Els had become very close and their families had been able to visit each other in their respective countries. This was a truly, though not completely, blended family of African American, white Dutch, and Els with her children and grandchildren in between.

In Arzeymah's knowledge of it, the full family had been founded when Trinette Nols had saved her father's life across the street from the sandstone caves of Geulhem.

The wear and tear on the trucks of the Red Ball Express was something that could be observed and quantified. They could be repaired if possible, or abandoned at the side of the road if necessary. But the toll on their mostly Black drivers was hidden beneath the relentless pace of the Express and their stoicism in performing the task they had been given to do. The endless convoys over long, circular tracks were absolutely essential to the race from Normandy to the Rhine. The rules and restrictions by which they operated—governed speed on the trucks (that could be overridden), the number of hours they could drive—were often necessarily forgotten. The speed could get up to 60 mph over roads that barely existed, through artillery fire and the debris of war, wandering cattle and the destitute along the way who begged them for food. At night, the drive was without head-lights or minimal lighting of the road ahead. One man slept while another man drove. When they could not stop to change positions, they had to do so while the truck was still moving.

Henry had been exhausted in the Red Ball Express and couldn't eat. He could not keep anything down, and at one point he thought he had contracted dysentery (and would receive a disability payment from the Army for the rest of his life). Henry would rarely say much about his time in the war, but he would say that Trinette had "nursed him back to life."

And of the biracial children of the war in Limburg that Els had known she had once told Arzeymah that, by the definition of a fully completed life, hers, though also problematic, "was probably the only positive story in there. Because everyone else was either neglected, abandoned, abused or adopted. There have been a couple that have found their parents, but their families here have rejected them."

In the first years of the 21st century, the existence of 8,000 Liberation Children of World War II in the Netherlands was well known, at least from the perspective of the white children of the soldiers of America, Po-land, the United Kingdom and Canada. They had formed the Liberation Children's Association in 1984 to assist each other in looking for their fathers. The effort was largely unsuccessful and ended in 2006, with oc-casional meetings thereafter. In 2012, national awareness of the reality of their lives was expanded with the publication of the book *Trees krijgt een Canadees* (*Trees Gets a Canadian*) by Dutch journalist Bonnie Okkema. Trees was a common name for a Dutch girl, and the title meant loosely that a Dutch girl was having the baby of a Canadian soldier.

The book was titled after a popular Dutch song of 1945, "Trees Heeft een Canadees" (loosely, A Dutch Girl is in a Relationship with a Canadian Soldier). In the song, Trees spurns the attention of a Dutch boy, and, in-stead, is learning English, but she is uncertain what will happen when her boy from Canada "Will return, sooner or later, To his home in Ottawa."[1]

It had been the Canadian army that did the hardest work and paid the heaviest toll of 18,000 casualties, including nearly 8,000 dead, in the rec-lamation of Antwerp and the opening up of the Scheldt estuary to Allied Forces in 1944 and 1945. It had constituted the left flank of the Allied push from Normandy to the Rhine river, and, while the Americans fought in the

Belgian Ardennes, the Canadians held portions of the line in France and the Netherlands, then helped to push it forward. In the Netherlands, they fought a patchwork of German units still in place, and during the *Hongerwinter* they brought food and fuel to the starving towns and villages.

The relationship between Canada and the Netherlands was based in human relations, as well. After the departure of the Dutch royal family to England, its crown princess Juliana and her children moved further west to Ottawa, where her third child, the daughter Margriet, was born. The Canadians were beloved by the Dutch, and the largest number of Liberation Children in the Netherlands, perhaps more than 6,000, had been fathered by Canadian soldiers, who were not able to immediately return home because of the lack of troopships. In all of Europe, an estimated 30,000 children would be born of Canadian fathers from 1940 to 1947. The largest number, 22,000, would be found in the fellow Commonwealth nations of the United Kingdom. The 6,000 in the Netherlands was the largest number on the Continent, 4,500 of them to single women.[2]

The perception of these children, Okkema wrote, had always been that they were the products of the happy times and fathers who served with the benign forces of the liberation of their nation from Nazi oppression and atrocity, and happy times meant to overcome the deprivations of the *Hongerwinter*. But the happy times had been times of excess, most notably of unwanted pregnancies and venereal disease. The response had ranged from the warnings of the Federation of Institutions for Unwed Mothers to an edict from the mayor of Eindhoven that dancing would not be allowed without his permission.

In Okkema's reporting, the result was a Dutch motherhood indifferent to the lives of its children. They were to be lied about, given away or ignored. The mothers suffered a high rate of suicide. If identified as out of wedlock and caused by foreign soldiers their pregnancies had been met with little family, government and social support. The Catholic church seemed more willing to be of assistance, but that came with moral judgment and condemnation. And the condemnation in most cases came from the same sources that had not allowed young women to know about contraception and the intricacies of sexuality.

A result for the children was the constant sense of illegitimacy, and frustration as they followed the natural human instinct and desire to know who one's parents were, and to find them. For the most part, they would receive no help in those pursuits from their mothers, nor from any governmental institutions.

An exception for the child of an American would be Donna Bastiaans, whose mother Mia was certain of the where and who of her daughter's conception. As to the "when" of the event, it had been during one of the best times of her young life: riding around with the other girls of the neighborhood in the big trucks of the U.S. Army driven by the African American soldiers. And Donna's father was without a doubt Adolphus Graves of the small town of Stony Creek, Virginia. The relationship between Mia and Adolphus was not frivolous and they would try to keep it alive into the 1950s. But Mia may also have been rebelling against the admonishments to young women of the time and place.

In November 1944, the Catholic churches, schools, newspapers and government joined in a campaign to discourage the women of Limburg from engaging in romantic relations with liberating soldiers. A *New York Times* story on the effort used the word "vamping" in its headline and noted the fear that this kind of activity "might break up the married life or engagements of their liberators in America."[3]

> In the churches, priests and ministers have been pointing out that soldiers fighting on foreign soil are bound to be homesick and they abjure the girls not to take advantage of this understandable lack of resistance to feminine wiles. It is stressed that the Americans should be greeted warmly, but that the greeting should not be carried too far.

The word from the pulpit had derived in part from a September letter from the archbishop of the Netherlands that was to be read in each church. The war's end, it said, had not brought the end of original sin, but, contrarily, had made the need to fight against it more necessary than ever. "The suction force of paganism hauls in a lot of things, and frighteningly so, and the convictions and morals of many believers are being contaminated by unchristian elements."[4] The way that people were dressing, it said, mocked "any sense of Christian modesty, and is reaching not only dangerous, but provocative heights.... The conduct of many girls, and married women even, is exasperating and seductive ... relationships are being entered into that defy all standards of a sensible and Christian engagement."

The vigilance of the Catholic church against "the suction force of paganism" had been preceded in official Netherlands with an unspoken but much deliberated concern over the expected sexual demands of the liberation. In April 1944, the arrival of victorious American troops was still on the horizon, but a meeting was held among military and health authorities to anticipate and plan for what was expected to be a dangerous rise in prostitution.

A summary of the meeting was premised on the necessity to be practical rather than "hypocritical" and "hyper-moral."[5] The incidence of prostitution and venereal disease had increased during the German occupation due to "poor material conditions ... as well as the collapse of all kinds of moral norms." That was only likely to increase in the liberation, and among both liberators and the liberated.

This keeps new dangers in sight:

A. Enlargement of venereal diseases

B. More undermining of moral and human responsibility

C. New hostility of the male population towards the new occupiers, especially if they can lure the girls with more and better material means

The following general guidelines are already considered relevant:

I. Intensive, business-like, medical-hygienic propaganda against the problem of venereal diseases. Treatment obligation.

II. Moral action with the help of the Clergy and youth organizations to strengthen the sense of responsibility.

III. Increased possibility of normal entertainment. Lifting dance ban.

IV. Official brothels are not permitted under any circumstances. Existing prohibitions continue to apply. Control of registered prostitutes remains.

It was noted that the American military was "already looking into these issues. They will probably want to furnish their own 'hotels' with their own girls. This falls under their competence." They would be informed by the Dutch of "the psychological danger to provoke Dutch girls," and the memo ended, "We reject a color bar." The last was not further explained, but probably reflected what would be a Dutch resistance to American segregation.

However it was to be accomplished, the goal was to create a wall between American men and Dutch women. When the liberation came, the young women of Maastricht were prohibited from being found on the streets after dark. But that, according to posters and pamphlets that appeared in public places, still left "some two more hours for them to commit their abject antics which cannot bear the light of day. But also during the day, the attitude of a certain category of girls is such that they exhibit signs of having lost even a semblance of modesty." The complaint was believed to have been the work of a group of men under the name of Militant Minds and promised that the girls who persisted in their behavior would meet the same public shaming that had come to women who had consorted with the just departed German occupiers.

In December, the newspaper *Stars and Stripes*, published for the American soldier, described the problem under the heading "Wooden-shooed Away."[6] The posters, it reported, were to be found all over, and when an American officer had tried to take one down, he only found it replaced ten minutes later. The campaign seemed to be found in the parts of the country most dominated by the Catholic church and was "having an effect on the attitude of many girls toward Allied soldiers and is creating fierce resentment among Yanks." Exhortations from the pulpit were daily and loud, and supported by a local newspaper. It was not just that the girls were engaging in behavior that would leave them disappointed when the soldiers inevitably moved on, but the rise in illegitimate births and venereal disease would be certain if they yielded to "temptations of American chocolates and cigarettes."

In Weert, a very small advertisement could be found in the local newspaper addressed to the *Meisjes van Weert* (Girls of Weert). "Weerter Boys Have Chocolate Too," it said, signed by "Some Friends."

The situation was also a concern of the U.S. military, at least in the view of a Lt. Col. Burner, who wrote to a local newspaper after a Rest and Recreation facility for American soldiers had been closed to prevent the meeting of American men and Dutch women.

> With our arrival as American liberators, the level of morality among the Dutch youth has decreased significantly which is very regrettable. Our boys are to blame: they thought they would find the same here as they found earlier in France and Belgium.
>
> On behalf of all American military personnel, I apologize and we are hoping the young people in the region will soon rectify the things they did wrong. I was very sorry to learn that the girls for whom the meeting was organized specifically, probably did not even attend. For them especially, I am hoping they will be getting back on the right track. Provide a sociable time for our boys but please do so in a respectable manner, as many of you have indeed done, and we are grateful to you. Our boys, and all boys in the army, are inclined to do these things, and it is not easy to educate them about this. Therefore, girls of the Netherlands, you will have to be stronger![7]

It may have been the case that Mia Vliegen had enhanced whatever motivated the girls of Limburg with an added rebellion against the racism that had been imposed on the province with the arrival of the Americans.

Mia's family had lived in Maastricht since the 1930s in a house near the eventual placement of tents to accommodate African Americans who would not be put up in traditional housing. In her mother's telling of it, the people of the neighborhood were angry about the treatment they saw given to the men by their white fellow soldiers and commanders. They had just been through years of Nazi propaganda about those who weren't purely Aryan, and the warnings of the previous year that the Black Americans who might arrive with the defeat of the Fatherland might even be cannibals.

"This Hitler had a screw loose," Donna would say. "The population quickly found out that the Black soldiers did not eat people, on the contrary, they brought people food." And the young women of the town saw a continuation of the German obsession with race in the barriers to how they wanted to live their own lives. One night when she and her friends wanted to go dancing with the Black Americans, they all set out for the popular Royal Maastricht dancehall, but the young soldiers were not allowed entrance by their American officers. The message was clear to the girls of Limburg that the privilege of dancing with them was for white soldiers only.

When it became apparent that Mia was pregnant, Adolphus was immediately transferred away. Mother and daughter continued to live with Mia's parents without discord, and, when Mia married Harrie Bastiaans in 1950 he gave Donna his name without hesitation. Adolphus had gone on to fight in the Korean War of 1950–1953 and, upon its conclusion, had written to Mia asking her to bring Donna with her to America. But it was too late.

As she got older, Donna wanted to know her father and had been angry at her mother for not waiting for him. The two had kept up a correspondence in the intervening years, with perhaps an expectation by some that they would come back together somehow. Mia, however, could give Donna no explanation except to say "that was just the way it was in those days."

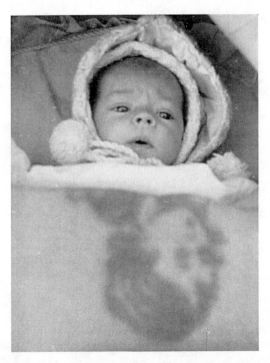

As her father receded in the years of her childhood, Donna became less certain of herself. In Maastricht, like the others of her circumstances, she became socially hesitant. Eventually she gravitated toward Liege, Belgium where there were more people who looked like her and she would not be stared at when she walked down the street. But, as she grew into adulthood, she became occasionally unsettled in her day to day life.

Donna Bastiaans' father, Adolphus Graves, was removed from Limburg after she was born, but would try to stay in touch with her mother, Mia, for a number of years after the war (courtesy Donna Bastiaans).

It would not be until 2015 that the biracial liberation children of the Netherlands would find

Huub Schepers stands to the left side of one of the brothers of St. Joseph House, Cadier en Keer, in 1952. The orphanage would be deeply criticized in a 2011 report to the Catholic church for the prevalence of violence and sexual abuse against its residents while Schepers was a resident (courtesy Netty Schepers Wanders).

their first national recognition in the story of Huub Schepers as told in the newspaper *de Volkskrant* of April 24. The paper had been founded as an organ of the left of center Catholic labor movement after World War I. It had not been published during the Second World War, but started up again postwar, unmoored from the church. By 2015 it was an influential liberal national morning daily with a circulation of 250,000. Schepers' story would, among other things, bring condemnation to the very same Catholic church. His description of arrival at an orphanage run by Catholic nuns as the "time when the lights went out," was replaced in the article's subhead with a damaged rekindling of that light.

"There is a veil over my life," he said.

It was not until 2002 that the Roman Catholic Church began, with a declaration from Pope John Paul II, to deal publicly with the problem of the sexual abuse of children within its dioceses and institutions. In the Netherlands, as elsewhere, it had been a problem for the ages. Up until World War II, the church held a powerful sway over the more than one-third of the Dutch population that adhered to the faith. Inevitably, the end of the war brought the beginnings of social change in the country that would work against its influence. In the eyes of the church, social and moral decline had begun in pre-war years, especially in the actions of young people. In the immediate postwar years, however, it seemed to be the young people who were most victimized by what would come to be understood as the profound sexual failings of the church.

Eight years after the Pope's declaration, the stories of sexual abuse of minors by Catholic clergy and institutions began to show up in the news media of the country. The Conference of Bishops and The Dutch Religious Conference acted to undertake an independent inquiry into the problem. The revelations of the Deetman Report, named after its chief investigator Dr. W.J. Deetman and issued in 2011, were stunning. The report opened with a definition of terms:

> Sexual abuse is defined as: any sexual contact by representatives of the Roman Catholic Archdiocese—priests, religious, pastoral workers employed by the church, lay persons and volunteers working for the church—with a child or youth under the age of 18, entrusted to the responsibility of those representatives, where those persons feel (felt) unable to refuse the sexual contact as a result of physical dominance, abuse of a position of authority, emotional pressure, compulsion or force.[8]

The investigation covered the years 1945–2010 in the Netherlands and the Dutch Antilles islands of Aruba and Curaçao. A context was offered in the narration of the declining influence of the church in Dutch life during that time. Catholics had increasingly "emancipated themselves from the authority of the church,"[9] and blended into the varieties of origin and belief of the larger population. The change was accompanied by more liberal beliefs about heterosexuality and homosexuality. But the line was drawn at pedophilia, which was mostly not talked about and largely understood at the time as a crime of men against young girls.

The Report determined that ten percent of Dutch children had been abused during that time, and that the rate of abuse in both Catholic and non–Catholic institutions for children had been twice that number. The most abuse had occurred in boarding institutions where children were cut off from the protective attention of parents and other caretakers. The actual number of those who had suffered mild, severe or very severe sexual abuse by an estimated 800 Catholic priests or lay workers between 1945 and 1981 could only be estimated at between 10,000 and 20,000.

The Huize St. Josef in Cadier en Keer was specially noted in the Deetman Report for the "use of excessive forms of violence, combined with sexual abuse,"[10] and it was here that Huub Schepers had been placed in 1952.

The home was run by the Fathers of the Sacred Heart and held children of both American and German fathers, and of members of the National Socialist Workers Party, which had collaborated with the Nazis.

Huub was one of only a few with dark skin. He learned to try to stay out of view, to disappear.

The prevalence of violence against the boys of Huize St. Josef was most sensationally told in the 2010 book *Nr. 21* by Dutch artist Frans Houben. "21" had been Houben's number in the home. He described an immediate beating upon entering St. Josef, followed by years of mental, physical and sexual harassment. He had been locked in small closets for hours at a time, given cold showers for bedwetting, regularly kicked and beaten. His personal pictures were torn up, and a duck he had taken as a pet had been killed. His caretakers found frequent reasons to fondle his genitals.[11]

Houben was white, but, as a small, biracial child, Huub Schepers had had to contend with other abuses.

> You felt a lot of things were not right. The Fathers and Brothers were completely unpredictable. Some got hysterical when they were beating you. But nobody ever talked about anything. Every now and then one of the Brothers would hit me and call me names like, son of a bitch, and nigger or jigaboo. Once, I was locked up in one of the cells in the basement, as a punishment. Those were small rooms with a bed, a concrete table and a chair. And a catechism.
>
> In the morning, they would take away the mattress, and then you would just sit there. With this catechism! If you wetted your bed, you got locked in the metal wardrobe, standing up, with nothing but a piece of bread sprinkled with salt. Another punishment was sitting on the balance beam on your knees, hands up in the air, and you were not allowed to move.
>
> Once a week, the boys could take a shower. Before you went in, the Brothers checked the crotch of your underpants. If they found it was stained, you had to take a cold shower.[12]

In all of Huub's time at St. Josef he received no visitors from the first years of his childhood. When other children went to their families on vacations, he stayed in the home. Then one day at age sixteen he was abruptly removed and driven more than 250 km away to a psychiatric clinic in Oegstgeest, north of The Hague. In retrospect, he supposed it was to cover up an expected investigation of abuse, but this was also a time of the setting in of mental issues that would remain with him throughout his life and determine his profession as an adult. It started with a job in a Catholic nursing home after he graduated from high school with the support of a foster family in Maastricht.

For Trudy (Truusje) Habets, it would be the Catholic Institute for Girls in Simpelveld that would vex her childhood. The problem was not sexual abuse, but the oppressive darkness of the place after years of stability in her life on her grandparents' farm in Retersbeek, east of Maastricht.

As the Americans had settled into the region after the liberation, white troops were put up in one of the ancient castles of Klimmen and were feted by the Dutch people. The Black soldiers had to create their own entertainment, and their parties drew the younger population of the region. Trudy's mother, Maria, had already had four children with two men, the last three with her husband, who had recently fathered a son with his girlfriend. All lived together on the farm in Retersbeek, and one evening Maria and her sister in law attended one of the African American parties, during which Trudy was probably conceived.

Maria's husband gave Trudy his name, but the infant was soon sent to a home for children, then retrieved by her step-grandmother. Eventually, the family, burdened with dysfunction, fell apart, and Trudy stayed with her grandparents in what she remembered as a loving situation.

One day, as Trudy and her grandmother were sweeping the porch, they heard a car drive up the road. "As if it happened yesterday," Trudy remembered as an older woman, "I can just see that car driving up to the property again. Two men in dark suits got out, one of them grabbed me and dragged me into the car."

She remembered her grandmother running after the car, her broom still in hand, and her own fear and anger. "I want to get out! I want to go to Oma!" she yelled, to no avail. She would later understand that there were reasons that her grandparents had sometimes suggested abrupt games of hide and seek. Finding her grandparents to be unfit to raise her,

Trudy Habets had found normalcy while living with her grandparents at their farm, but was abruptly removed from her family by social services and placed in an institution that would damage her childhood, and the adulthood that would follow (courtesy Trudy Habets).

Child Protective Services had been trying to take Trudy away for some time and now they had succeeded.

She was given to the care of the Sisters of the Poor Child Jesus, a congregation that had been founded in Aachen, Germany in 1844, then moved across the border to Simpelveld in 1878. Its homes for girls and young women in Germany, Belgium, Luxembourg, Austria and the Netherlands were to fulfill the goal of "promoting a simplicity of character and joyful spirit in imitation of the Child Jesus born in poverty."

Though one of 500 uniformed girls in the home, the nuns treated Trudy separately from the others as a particular kind of charity case, and with special attention to her color and curly hair. That was picked up by the other girls and expressed in names uttered behind her back. But it was the loss of her farm life that set her back the most. She missed the trees, the quiet, the small farm animals with which she had played; now she had only a small brick playground. At one point a soccer ball she had kicked broke a window in the school with the result of banishment to a locked attic for three days without food.

Her questions about why she had been removed from her happy life on the farm would not be answered, and when she stopped asking, she stopped talking. It was the lay people who came to work in the home that were nicest to her, but she thought that she noticed that by the time she came to trust them, they would be gone. One summer vacation she was sent to stay with a childless couple in Geleen, and came to think of them as an aunt and uncle, but when the wife came upon what to Trudy was an innocent physical encounter with the husband, she was taken immediately and permanently back to the home.

The nuns had told her about sex. For the other girls whatever they knew was restricted to a careful biology class, but Trudy was given the further instruction that Black girls had to be very careful because they got into trouble more easily than white girls. The information set her off balance as she entered the years in her life in which she had to begin to understand her own sexuality.

Trudy had finally left her past fully behind at age twelve after a visit with her mother. Either mother or daughter could have used the meeting to come back together again, but neither raised the subject. For Trudy's part, she had no interest. When she was sixteen, she attended a home economics school across the street from the home at Simpelveld. There, a psychologist told her that she was not smart enough to be helped by continuing education and that she should find a job.

In the first years, Ed Moody had not been forgotten by his American father, who had written to his mother Lenie in 1951.

Hello little girl,

Well it has been a long time since I heard from you or any of the family so I thought I would drop you a line to find out how you and Eddy are and all the family. Leny, I know I have no right to ask you this, but I hope you will and do this for me what I would like you to do is have a photo made of you and Eddy. Send it to me please.

Well Leny, I don't know what to say so I will ask you a few questions if you don't mind.

1. Have you a boyfriend now?
2. Can I have Eddy for 2 or 3 months here in America?
3. If I send you the money will you come to America for 2 or 3 months?
4. When you answer my letter tell all about your family. Tell me all about all mother Bettie, Annie, [illegible] Louise and every one.

Well this is all until I hear from you so please answer soon.

So by by give all my love, kiss Eddy for me and I still love you.

P.s. don't forget the photo.

As ever yours,
Ed Moody

Eventually, the long-distance relationship faded away, but the romance that had brought him forth seemed to support a good life for the child. Pictures of his father and mother during the very short time they had known each other showed a young couple who seemed very firmly attuned to each other and set comfortably into a group of Black and white friends and relatives. The picture of his father that Ed would carry with him all of his life was of a confident young man with an easy smile and a thin mustache beneath a truck driver's cap set just so on his head. A picture of a very young Ed and his mother caught a tall young woman with a moth-

Ed Moody with his mother Lenie Wetzel, undated (courtesy Ed Moody).

er's warm smile, her face surrounded by cascading hair, holding firmly to the hand of a loved child who barely came up to the level of her knees. As he gained the age of reading and writing, a picture of him saw him sitting at a desk before a painting of Dutch naval history, pencil above paper with a smile as confident as his father's. His skin was light, but his face was unmistakably African American, beneath a healthy head of curly hair.

At that age, he was not fully aware of the circumstances of his birth, though the subject of the war of recent years was always in the air, as was the family's experience with the Black soldiers who had shared their home. He knew that he was different somehow from his friends, but thought it was because of his hair, which was more notably red than curly. His friends would call him the "red Negro." While still too young to understand the full story of his birth, his uncles were regular visitors in the house and they seemed to replace the father he had not really known to be missing. The truth of the matter became known to him at about the same time similar stories of foreign fathers came to some of his friends, one of them German.

Ed took to music and at age fourteen he and a friend formed a boy band that soon became popular and busy in Limburg, then began to travel with the singer Anneke Gronloh who had been born in Japanese

Ed Moody would form a boy band in 1950s Limburg, and travel Europe as a young musician backing up a popular singer of the time (courtesy Ed Moody).

occupied Indonesia and gone on to write and perform one of the most popular songs in modern Dutch history, "Brandend Zand" (Burning Sand). It was only then that Ed's foreign paternity began to limit him, as it kept him from obtaining the passport needed to travel outside the country. He would instead require special permission of the Dutch military for each trip.

In 2015, Ed Moody and Huub Schepers formed a friendship that would become the subject of a newspaper article in *Dagblad* (Newspaper) *de Limburger*. It caught the attention of a woman whose husband would never talk easily about who he was, but she knew that it loomed large in the background of his life.

Evelyn had been urging Huub Habets to search for his father for years. His mother, Gertruda Hermans, known as Tru, had been one of the young women given a fresh start on life at the end of the war. It was, again, the marl caves of Geulhem that held the story, and in this case the many dance parties of the liberation. Not welcomed in the social settings of their white counterparts, the African American soldiers in the region drifted to events in the caves easily. They fit right in with the spirit of the times.

Tru was the youngest of eight children. Her father had the responsibility of working the signals of the only railroad crossing in Geulhem. The family was accepting and unassuming, as was Tru's steady boyfriend Louis Habets, who would become the hero of Huub's young life.

When Tru was four months pregnant, she and Louis married. Though he was not his child, Louis named Huub after his own father, Pieter Hubertus, and against tradition that he should be named after the paternal grandfather. The child was born on October 10, 1945. The next day Louis registered him as his own in the municipality of Valkenburg. With the exception of her grandmother, who was said to have spent the rest of her life with her hair in a bun and dressed in black, the full extended family accepted and encircled the child.

Everyone knew that Huub was the child of a Black American soldier, but Huub could not give voice to the questions that swirled in his head. He could not talk about it. And as a child, he said, "I never wanted to be out in the sun, because I did not want to get even darker."

His stepfather gave him the full childhood of a loved boy, and when he turned sixteen, Louis, who supported his family on a miner's salary, gave him a brand new moped, an impossible gift for most families of Geulhem. Out in the community, Louis regularly heard questions about his different child. Huub remembered going to the county fair with his family. He and his brother were five or six years of age and wearing identical clothes that Tru had sewn for them. "Is that one your's too?" he remembered someone asking his father, "That one can't be yours now, can he!"

someone else exclaimed. Louis was regularly taunted about his illegitimate child by his fellow miners. It took a friend of Louis to finally tell them to stop the harassment.

When Huub got the courage to ask his parents about these things they would only say "But you have a good life with us, don't you?" It was that, but it was a life with which he could not fully engage as a child. For one thing, in his kindness to his stepson Louis seemed to be a more indulgent father with Huub than with the other children, which had the effect of making him feel further apart from his brother. With the family's support he became a member of both the Boy Scouts and the Valkenburg Boys Soccer Club, but he would always stay in the background. At dances, he was sure that the girls wouldn't notice him, thus stayed out of their sight. In those years, the popular hair style for young men was the pompadour made popular by the American singer Elvis Presley, but it would not be possible for him to join the trend.

Huub Habets had known Els Geijselaers from school in Geulhem, but they had never really met.

Like Huub, Els had grown up as a loved child who could never fully understand the truth about herself. At home, and with the support and protection of her brother and sister, she was no different than anyone else. To the family's immediate neighbors, as well, there was nothing extraordinary about her. She would be teased at school, however, and called a Negro, even if she did not know quite what that meant. Her mother's response was to take Els on her lap and give her candy as if that would solve the problem, but it did not. When she heard her parents being asked who the child was and where she had come from, she did not hear the answers. In her imagination, the answer was perhaps that she had been taken away from somewhere and that at some point someone would come to take her back to something she didn't know. Like the others, she learned to stay out of sight for fear of what might happen if she were too obvious

Els married when she was eighteen and had a son when she was twenty. The child was as dark as she was, and she thought that her parents would finally tell her about herself, but they only offered the same love to the grandchild, and without explanation.

Rosy Heuts/Peters would grow up with an unrelentingly opposite experience. Though her mother had never "given her away to the circus," the life that she provided her daughter was no less chaotic. She had contracted asthma at age six. A small saving grace was that she was sent to a Fresh Air Fund home on the North Sea and north of Amsterdam, twice, but she was not able to keep up in school and was ignored by her teachers. In the mining town of Brunssum she had always tried to present herself well, often with a big white bow in her hair, but often heard herself called names like

"Blackie" and "Negro," and referred to as the Little American. She felt herself to be an accident and inferior. She wished "not to be Black anymore," but that could not change.

Her mother took on a boyfriend who moved in with them. "You're as stupid as they come," she remembered him telling her when she had to repeat a grade. Or, "I can have you placed in a home just like that, because you are not mine." When her mother became engaged, mother and daughter went to meet with the man's family. Rosy's mother had attempted to dress her up for the occasion, and heard "She's a pretty child, too bad she is Black."

Her new stepfather moved the family to Maastricht and times were better until she arrived at puberty and the following years of abuse. The man would physically restrain then sexually molest her. Resistance was met with more violence. If her mother was aware of the abuse, she did not acknowledge it, and Rosy kept it to herself. As she got older, she realized that he had probably been a Nazi collaborator in the war.

She had managed to overcome her asthma at age ten, and a talent for athletics carried her through teenage years. At age eighteen, she escaped home by enrolling in a school for family care workers in Sittard. The school required instruction of religion, and she would make the observation that the bishop who instructed them would remind them that contraceptives were forbidden in their lives. Abortion had been illegal in the Netherlands since 1887 and would not be fully legalized until 1984. She would have four children by age twenty-seven.

It would be Huub Schepers' obituary in 2016 that would help Robert Joosten to open up his past. It had not been as bad for himself as it had for others, and not as difficult as it had been for his mother.

Twenty kilometers north of Aachen and just south of Brunssum, the German occupation of the mining village of Nieuwenhagerheide had been very oppressive for years, and the liberation seemed perhaps out of control. The white American liberators had set up a large tent just outside of the village, and, in an observation that was perhaps more exuberant in memory than it was real, at least one modern adult remembered seeing condoms thrown out its windows in quantities that made them playthings for the village children. Nieuwenhagerheide was dominated by a massive Catholic church that would become a national monument in the 21st century. Condoms were not to be used.

Annie had come to the village with her parents from the city of Eindhoven and she lived as a bit of an outsider with a corresponding wildness, according to the memories of her son. By appearances, she had been happily married to Jack Joosten since 1940 and he was madly in love with her.

Perhaps as a precursor or a cause of what was to come, Annie became pregnant by an unknown African American soldier in 1945. And she contracted a sexually transmitted disease, which would leave her newborn son with a permanently damaged eye. Jack would beat her throughout their marriage, though he would never lay a hand on Robert. A sister to Robert was born ten years later, despite Annie's repeated attempts to divorce her husband throughout that time. The most difficult problem that Robert had to deal with in his childhood had not been his skin color and curly hair, albeit the cause of occasional bullying, but the abuse suffered by his mother. It had led him on one occasion at age twelve to escape his home in his pajamas and run to the police to seek help. As an adult, working in the musical theater world of Amsterdam, he would remember his childhood as a time that he would have to make his own rules and figure things out on his own resources.

Petra, the daughter of Toos and Jimmy Harbut, had gone to kindergarten with Robert Joosten, and Annie had once been heard to say that because they were the only two biracial children in the school, it seemed certain that they would get married one day, but their paths diverged early in life. And, like others, Petra's own life was a divergence between how she saw it and how she was seen.

A favorite candy of the time was "a button of licorice," and that was the complimentary description given to her by most people in the village. She grew up, however, withdrawn and with few friends. Toos married in 1950, and her husband gave Petra his name and support. One time when she was very ill the family doctor refused to treat her. "Just leave the Black kid alone, it will pass," he said. One of Toos' brothers, however, ran to the doctor's house. "If you are not at our house within five minutes," he warned, "I'll start gutting your home."

He admonished the doctor. "If I put a bell on everybody who has had something going on with a soldier, the bell would be tolling throughout the whole village."

As much as Petra tried to learn about her mother's experience with a soldier as she grew up, Toos would only tell her that her father knew about her and had sent her clothes. Occasionally she would read from one of the letters that she would eventually give to Petra while on her deathbed, but that was all she would say.

As adults, all but a few of these children would seek to know their fathers in whatever way they could, and often with frustrating or imperfect results. But it would be in Florida where the two most successful resolutions to the question of "who am I?" and "who have I come from?" would come to pass. One of those fully realized answers would be found in the tears of Arzeymah Raqib as she sat at her kitchen table in Ocala and remembered her beloved Dutch sister, Els, and "all of those forgotten children."

The other would take place the following day in 2019 at another kitchen table, this one in Clearwater, just outside of Tampa. Maria Andres had come to postwar Netherlands as a five-year-old and into a childhood that would be as troubled as that of some of the others. She, too, now sat at the table in tears, but, in this case, they were an expression of the contentment that she felt. She had finally come to the end of her search. She had been born in Germany, one of the perhaps thousands of children of African American occupation soldiers left behind in all of postwar Europe.

Germany had been the last stop in the march of American troops through World War II. Their first landing, and their base of operations for the duration of the war, would be the United Kingdom, where the interaction between white citizens and Black Americans on a very large scale, starting in 1942, can offer context and understanding for what would occur in a much smaller scale in the Netherlands beginning in 1944.

EIGHT

In England

You mean that we have to get over our prejudices? You don't get over a prejudice that easily. There's no use pretending we're different from what we are.—Interaction between actor Burgess Meredith and Gen. John C.H. Lee, 1943

Lt. Gen. John C.H. Lee had arrived in the United Kingdom in 1942 to begin the logistical work that would support the Normandy Invasion of 1944, while supplying the needs of the intervening months as well. Eventually, one quarter of all U.S. troops in Europe would fall under his command. One day in 1943, Lee, with his retinue, seemed to depart briefly from the real world all around him and walk into the fictive depiction of a busy railroad station in Britain where he was observed by an awestruck movie star of the day, Burgess Meredith.

The Americans and the British, of course, had a long and mostly positive history with each other. They were allies in and out of war, derived from a common people, and shared the same language and culture, but there were problems. Three million Americans would move through the UK during the course of the war, and the movement had begun with large and small conflicts in the way American men and the British people lived their daily lives. The social differences were aggravated by economic disparity between necessarily thrifty British and free-spending GIs, which, among other results, changed the sexual dynamics between men and women.

But the conflicts between the two cultures were nuanced and, for the most part, friendly; perhaps easily addressed in an educational film of sorts for the American arrivals. Burgess Meredith was the guide in a dual role of American actor and real-life Captain of the Army Air Corps (and co-director of the film). "A Welcome to Britain, 1943" was co-produced by the U.S. War Department and the British Ministry of Information. Its premise was that Meredith had planned to interview American and British military commanders about their alliance in war, but that they saw the goal of the film differently.

> AMERICAN GENERAL: Wait a minute. This is war. There will be plenty of time for speeches. That's your job, isn't it?
>
> MEREDITH: Yes, Sir.
>
> AMERICAN GENERAL: Let the soldier make the speeches.
>
> MEREDITH: What'll I say?
>
> BRITISH GENERAL: I suggest you tell your men something about our people, and the factories and the pubs, on the farm. The people they'll meet and be with. Tell them about their problems; big problems, little problems.
>
> AMERICAN GENERAL: Put all you've got into it. That's the way you win victories on the battlefield. Put yourself in it.

Meredith then faces the camera and suggests that he's just the person to explain England because he has "been here all of three weeks."[1] First stop on the tour is an English pub, outside of which he exchanges suggestive smiles with a pretty girl, and tells his audience "We'll get to that later." Indeed, the pretty girl rides her bike in and out of the following scenes, with a reaction from Meredith that seems sometimes frankly lascivious, or bad acting on the part of a good actor.

The pubs, he explains, are like clubs where people who don't have a lot of money can spend a few hours a day socializing over *warm* beer, and with elaborate and unspoken rituals. On cue, an American soldier comes crashing into the scene with a loud mouth and American ebullience until he is painstakingly socialized. Special attention is paid to instructing the audience in the meaning of Scotsmen in kilts.

During dinner with a typical British family, Meredith reminds that these are proud people who don't have much, but will not say so. A visitor is likely to find a full dinner laid out on the table, though it will include food and drink that will have to last the family a full week. "Don't grab a handful of tomatoes. They're rare luxuries. Go easy with the meat. They each get just 25 cents worth a week. You can eat it all in one gulp, but don't." As the actor then slathers jam on a piece of bread, the father looks on with disguised alarm.

And so it goes. In a classroom with young children, Meredith learns about the geographic and political divisions of the British Isles in the context of the scale of Europe. It is pointed out that the distance from London to Berlin is less than the width of Texas.

The weather, British tea, American cigarettes, pronunciation of place names are all up for example and discussion as Meredith eventually pulls into a train station and has trouble figuring out that he has to open his compartment door by turning a handle on the outside of the train. He is helped in that realization by a Black American soldier, and when the two have stepped on to the platform they are addressed by an elderly woman with whom they've just ridden. She seems oblivious to the difference in their races and tells them that they must come to her home sometime to have a cup of tea. "Both of you," she emphasizes.[2]

As the Black soldier goes to get cigarettes for both of them, Meredith's direct conversation with the viewer becomes vaguely conspiratorial. He looks about quickly to be sure that no one else in the film hears him, and speaks directly to the camera:

> Now look, men. You heard that conversation. That's not unusual here [looks around again for inadvertent listeners]. That sort of thing happens quite a lot. Now let's be frank about it. There are colored soldiers as well as white here, and there are less social restrictions in this country. That's what you heard: an English woman asking a colored boy to tea, and she was polite about it, and he was polite about it. That might not happen at home, but [looks around carefully again] the point is we're not at home. And the point is too if we bring a lot of prejudices here what are we going to do about them?

The script seems to be both an affirmation of official American military policy on segregation of the races, and an admission of its futility. Then Meredith's attention is abruptly changed to a scene in front of the railroad station's tobacco stand: the chance arrival of Lt. Gen. John C.H. Lee and his retinue.

Respectfully awestruck, Meredith shares with the viewer that "He's got a lot of colored troops under him, and they're doing a big job over here. And I happen to know that Gen. Lee comes from Kansas, and that his family fought for the Confederacy."[3]

Soon, Lee, Meredith and the Black soldier are standing together. In a hesitant voice that almost apologizes for the impertinence of the question, Meredith indicates the soldier with a nod of the head and asks, "I was wondering what the general thought about ... him and me, Sir."

What Lee has brought to this chance encounter in a British railway station is a carefully scripted statement of the belief that would inform his attempts to move African American soldiers into combat positions in the following year. The film seems to stop, then start all over again with a general in full military bearing and a firm voice, reading from cue cards.

> LEE: America has promised the Negro real citizenship. And a fair chance to make the best of himself.
>   When the Army needs Americans to fight for the country, it takes Negroes along with whites. Everyone's treated the same when it comes to dying. And so, the Army wouldn't be true to America if it didn't try to live up to the promises about an equal chance.
> MEREDITH: You mean that we have to get over our prejudices?

Actor Burgess Meredith (center), a member of the U.S. Army Air Force and the Office of War Information, with an uncredited African American actor (right) and Gen. John C.H. Lee (left) discuss the way white American soldiers should interact with African American soldiers in "A Welcome to Britain" (U.S. National Archives).

> LEE: You don't get over a prejudice that easily. There's no use pretending we're different from what we are. But we can try to live up to our American promises. I'd go further and say we can't do less and still feel ourselves patriots. We have promised to respect each other. All of us. That's one of the reasons that makes our world worth fighting for. But you're all together in this small country with the same surroundings. The same amount of pay to spend, the same sort of places to spend it. And we're all here as soldiers. Everything we do we do as American soldiers. Not Negroes and white men, rich or poor, but as American soldiers. It's not a bad time, is it, to learn to respect each other both ways.

Gen. Lee then walks off to the strain of quiet patriotic music, and Meredith lights the Black soldier's cigarette. "Thanks," says the soldier. With an earlier exchange about getting some cigarettes, it is one of just twelve words uttered by the unnamed Black soldier in the full four-minute segment.

In the end, the film does not allow Burgess Meredith to get the pretty girl on the bicycle. She turns up again as the wife of an officer, and a frantic Meredith has to be pulled away from the scene by a friend, though not before he makes a fool of himself.

In many respects, however, his experience was not typical. A common estimate without documentation is that 22,000 children were born of American soldiers and British women in the years of war and its aftermath. Another undocumented estimate is that approximately 1,700 of them were biracial. From 1941 to 1950, the U.S. Immigration and Naturalization Office counted 37,789 British "War Brides" and 472 British children as coming to American shores.[4]

The meeting of British women and American men in World War II England brought together two strains of socio-sexual culture that might have seemed, at first glance, to have been ships that should have passed in the night. The situation also brought the observations of the anthropologist Margaret Mead. They were published in pamphlets of both the British and American armies, and in the *New York Times* in March 1944.

The American practice of "dating," she said, was not instinctive to the British. The boys and girls of England were mostly brought up separated from each other, and the men seemed more likely to continue that practice into adulthood, leaving the women still with their gender cohort, but essentially adrift as they entered childbearing years. In that environment an assertive move by a male focused on a given woman, like asking for a date, was full of portent and meaning, good or bad. In the American scheme of things, however, it was perfectly natural. "The idea of a social pattern in which a boy looks for a girl who is smart, attractive, has a line, dances well and gives him a wholly satisfactory evening because he has been able to take her out and let other people see that he could take her out is—just missing [in Britain]."[5] Thus, the seeking of a date by an American man could be misunderstood, and if a kiss occurred it could have a different meaning to each of the participants. For the American it was traditionally part of the progression he might have hoped to follow toward a romantic or physical conclusion, or physically satisfying for its own sake. For the British woman it could be taken as a signal of the start of a path toward marriage. "As a result," wrote Mead, "the Americans in search of dates find themselves misunderstood, their breezy opening lines rejected or sometimes accepted as advances of an order which they did not mean to make. Many a few gay, stereotyped contacts have broken a heart on which they merely meant to pin an expensive flower."

Whatever the nuances, they could be figured out and dealt with over time, but they were further complicated by the particular state in which British women found themselves in those years. The more reserved British men were mostly gone to war and the more brash American men were everywhere. They had money, generally earned twice as much as their British counterparts, and they represented what had been attractive about American culture from a British distance. And the necessities of a society in an existential war had forced women out of the structure of their traditional lives. Whether in work, the demands of family, or in the intricacies of male/female relationships, they were in new territory.

They were at work in the factories, offices and farms of the war effort. If they were mothers and wives their husbands were probably gone and their children were more likely to be latchkey. Hundreds of thousands of British children were living in foster situations inland from the bomb-prone cities, or otherwise unaccompanied. Many of the younger women no longer lived within the boundaries of their childhood homes and hometowns and had been liberated by employment. That number included teenage girls, who were allowed to leave school at age 14 and were without the supervision of soldier fathers and working mothers. Their attraction to the cultural difference of American GIs was an identified problem. A 1945 study by the Home Office attempted an explanation.

> The girls brought up on the cinema, who copied the dress, hair styles, and manners of Hollywood stars, the sudden influx of Americans, speaking like the films, who actually lived in the magic country, and who had plenty of money, at once went to the girls' heads. The American attitude to women, their proneness to spoil a girl, to build up, exaggerate, talk big, and act with generosity and flamboyance, helped to make them the most attractive boyfriends.[6]

It would turn out that the urgings of Burgess Meredith and Gen. Lee that white American soldiers accept the British attitude toward race would fall on deaf American ears. Racial conflict among Americans in England would be as angry as anywhere else in Europe. But Meredith's observation about the openness of the British to African Americans would prove out to be mostly correct at the civilian level, if not always at the official level, and especially among British women.

In 1939, England was a nearly fully white country with the exception of approximately 8,000 Blacks who were mostly concentrated in the port cities from Liverpool to London. That had not changed by 1942, and the government wished to keep it that way. When it began to appear that the country could benefit from the expertise of subjects from British Honduras, as an example, the Foreign office consulted with other offices of government and proclaimed, "the recruitment to the United Kingdom of coloured British subjects, whose remaining in the United Kingdom after the war might create a social problem, was not considered desirable."[7]

Nor, at the highest levels, did the British want the arrival of troops from the United States to include African Americans. They made that clear to the U.S. Army liaison there, Gen. James. E. Chaney, who passed the sentiment on to the War Department in Washington, which replied that they would indeed be included "in reasonable proportion for any type of Service Units."[8] The expected one million Americans would include the required ten percent of Blacks. Racial attitudes aside, part of the British inhibition about Black Americans in their small and crowded country was the understanding that American Blacks and whites would require segregated housing, social and health facilities.

The government would be at pains to not actually say so, but the largest fear was racial friction. It was a distinguished American of the time who perhaps had better license to articulate the problem, and he took it to its sexual core. Arthur Sulzberger, the publisher of the *New York Times* and an unofficial observer in England, suggested to the head of U.S. Information Services in London that African Americans should not be stationed in the rural areas of England, but concentrated in the port areas. "Rural populations," he was reported to have said, "which have no experience with foreigners, let alone colored people, particularly the girls, do not know how to take the negroes [sic] and, as a matter of fact, are very much attracted to them," but in the ports where Blacks were a known quantity "there is not so much danger."[9] Given the personnel needs throughout urban and rural England, it was not a practical suggestion.

The whole matter was a constant dilemma for a current and future president, and a president's wife. Gen. Eisenhower was constantly trying to puzzle it out. England, he suggested in a letter to Gen. Alexander Surles of the War Department's public relations bureau, was a heavily populated country without a consciousness of race.

> They know nothing at all about the conventions and habits of polite society that have been developed in the U.S. in order to preserve a segregation in social activity without making the matter one of official or public notice. To most English people, including the village girls—even those of perfectly fine character—the negro [sic] soldier is just another man, rather fascinating because he is unique in their experience, a jolly good fellow and with money to spend. Our own white soldiers, seeing a girl walk down the street with a negro, frequently see themselves as protectors of the weaker sex and believe it necessary to intervene in the event to the extent of using force, to let her know what she's doing.[10]

Importuned by organizations like the NAACP, Eleanor Roosevelt responded to the problem with the observation that white men and officers seemed very indignant that Black soldiers were "not looked upon with terror," by British girls. "We will have to do a little education among our Southern white men and officers, emphasizing the fact that every effort should be made to prevent marriages during this period but that normal relationships with groups of people who do not have the same feeling that they have about the Negro cannot be prevented and that it is important for them to recognize that in different parts of the world, certain situations differ and have to be treated differently."[11] President Roosevelt was asked by the War Department to intervene with his wife, was said to be sympathetic to the request and said that he would do so.

While deeply engaged in the fighting of a European war, Gen. Dwight Eisenhower had to keep working on the problem of race, but what he came up with was a continuation of a circular policy that could not sustain itself, at least with the British public. He declared that any discrimination against Black troops was firmly forbidden, but that the American doctrine of separate but equal must be followed in England, except where it was not physically or practically possible. If a separate facility for recreation could not be created, for example, it would have to be available to both groups. Even then, it would have to occur with all efforts possible to reduce racial friction. Eisenhower suggested that passes for each group be given on alternate nights, but the result should always follow "the guiding principle that any restriction imposed by Commanding Officers applies with equal force to both races."[12]

The burden of responsibility for enforcing the basket of directives about segregation that should become integration, or segregated integration, when necessary, fell to Gen. John C.H. Lee. One of his actions would be to engage Burgess Meredith and an anonymous Black soldier in a film, and to no effect. But, privately, Lee would be as cautious about the matter of Black men and white women as anyone else, and directed that social events in which the two might mix should take place unofficially by "organization," which would offer artificial segregation. Officially, the reasons given for such planning should be related to limitations of facilities and personnel.[13]

The British *seemed* to wash their hands of the whole thing.

By September 1942, the Home Office arrived at a conclusion with police forces that it was not British policy that authorities should support any form of discrimination against Black soldiers. If American authorities wanted to restrict their Black troops from use of pubs, movie houses, restaurants and similar settings, British police were not to assist in enforcing those prohibitions.

Eisenhower's response to the Home Office directive was to agree with it fully, as per the enlightened parts of American policy, and in an acknowledgment of inevitability. "Undoubtedly a considerable association of colored troops with British white population, both men and women, will take place on a basis mutually acceptable to the individuals concerned."[14]

In the matter of women, Eisenhower understood that part of the problem was the lack of Black American women in England. The Women's Auxiliary Army Corps (WAACs until July 1943, at which time it became Women's Army Corps, WACs) had been created with the same purpose as the mostly Black Quartermaster Corps: to use women in support positions and free up men for combat. It would never reach the ten percent threshold of Blacks vs. whites, and included just 5,532 members (5.7 percent) in Spring 1943.[15]

In August 1942, Eisenhower put forth the idea or order that several thousand African American WAACs should be used to staff facilities where Black troops congregated, but the WAACs quickly characterized the plan as demeaning to its members and it was abandoned by the general. Attention was then moved to the American Red Cross, which ran many of the social clubs for troops at war. The organization took the approach that all of its facilities were equally open to both races, but their placement near segregated concentrations of men meant that they were, in fact, largely segregated. They were staffed by the Red Cross accordingly with Black or white men and women, but the number of women involved was not significant.

The stated Home Office policy that England should not get involved in American racial issues was also taken up by the British military, which then took it around a corner.

Yes, the racial policy of the U.S. military was its own business, but British soldiers should be told informally to have as little contact with Black Americans as possible. The advice was unofficially advanced with the release of "Notes on Relations with Coloured Troops" by the senior administrator of the Southern Command, Gen. Arthur Dowler. Dowler had consulted with his American counterparts, and echoed the "yes, but" beliefs held deeply within U.S. War Department racial policy. "[W]hile there are many coloured men of high mentality and cultural distinction, the generality are of simple mental outlook,"[16] and that the American attitude about such matters should be respected. Friendships should not be entered into between white and Black men, and white women should not associate with them in any way because such relations could come to no good end. Although the Home Office had stated that it would not go along with the racial policy of the U.S. military, the Home Secretary, Herbert Morrison, felt it necessary to offer his opinion in October 1942. "I am fully conscious that a difficult sex problem might be created if there were a substantial number of cases of sex relations between white women and coloured troops and the procreation of half-caste children."[17]

Gen. Dowler's "Notes" were not intended to be made public, but they eventually became so and would remain controversial in England for some time. To the extent that they were intended to influence the informal thinking and actions of military leadership they also bled into civilian leadership, and with one very definite result: many regular British soldiers and civilians would not agree to them. The "Notes" gained the attention, reporting and resulting public discussion of the political and cultural magazine *The New Statesman* and were, for the most part, not generously considered.

The public view of it was perhaps more popularly reflected in the well-read newspaper *The Sunday Pictorial*. The wife of the vicar of Worle, it reported, had attempted to hand down instructions on the matter. Local shopkeepers were to initially welcome any Black customers, but also to tell them they would not be welcome a second time. If women found themselves seated next to a Black man, they were to get up and move. If they were approached walking down the street, they should cross to the other side. Women should not socialize with them in any way, and a Black man must absolutely not be invited into the home of a white woman. The *Pictorial* accompanied the reporting, on the other hand, with advice to the Black American soldiers.

> Any coloured soldier who reads this may rest assured that there is no colour bar in this country and that he is as welcome as any other Allied soldier. He will find that the vast majority of people here have nothing but repugnance for the narrow-minded, uniformed prejudices expressed by the vicar's wife. There is, and will be, no persecution of coloured people in Britain.[18]

The vicar's wife, however, was seemingly supported by a higher ecclesiastical authority. The Bishop of Salisbury, former Bishop to the King, the Right Rev. E. Neville Lovett, counseled that the division between American whites and Blacks was justified by circumstances, and that white women should stay away from Black soldiers.[19]

If the wisdom of religious leadership was not able to sway public opinion, perhaps a whisper campaign warning of venereal disease among Black soldiers could have an effect. It was said to have been suggested in a meeting of the Bolero Committee, those British and American officials who were charged with managing the American presence in the country, in August 1942. And, of course, it was said to have been shot down; but it was perceived to have then taken place.[20] In early 1944 a similar effort took place not in whispers, but in some local newspapers which talked about young British women as collaborators in crime, trespassers in places they shouldn't be, most often in the company of Black Americans and for reasons that were implied if not spoken.[21]

None of it, the racial policies and musings of military and civilian leaders, warnings of the church, questionable forms of public relations campaigns, were taken much to heart by British women. But at some point in 1943, public attitudes about the problem began to change, and it was British women who bore much of the brunt of it.

The African American soldiers in Britain had and would maintain a good reputation among the public. A public opinion survey in August of that year revealed that 25 percent of those asked had formed friendships with some of them, and just one-seventh of the people opposed the idea of mixed marriages. To the extent that prejudice existed it might have been derived as much, if not more, from distinctions of class than of race. It was an unapologetic part of the story of the American presence in the country that the Black men among them had come from economically and socially disadvantaged circumstances. And there was some sympathy for the situation in which these men found themselves: Black men under the stress of war and dislocation from their normal lives in a place with no Black women.

The first "Brown Babies" began to arrive in the maternity wards of the country in the spring of 1943, just as the kinds of newspaper articles of a year earlier about errant young women had become more numerous and specific. On top of that came the increasingly vocal complaints of white soldiers, both British and American: it was the daughters, girlfriends and wives of one, and the potential girlfriends and wives of the other who were at stake.

The next step in the change of social attitudes began to equate the class standing of the women with the standing of the men involved, or with the prostitutes that the men might otherwise have sought out. As attitudes led to increased social ostracism of the women involved, they responded by withdrawal from their relationships or behavior. That led to an increase in the use of prostitutes, which demonstrated to many the true role that some British women had fulfilled. The social spiral downward accelerated for all involved, and when the Brown Babies arrived, they were the most visible and faulted results of what had occurred.

NINE

Out of England

The American Negro needs to do something about this
whole matter.—*The Hartford Chronicle*, 1946

The German passenger liner MV *Monte Rosa* had been launched in
1930 and set upon lucrative routes from Norway to the Mediterranean.
She and her sister ships of the Hamburg-Süd Line were economical to
operate and expanded the access that most Germans would have to recreational travel. With that advantage, she was operated under the Nazi
regime of 1933 as a ship of the Strength Through Joy program that would
enhance the leisure-time life of the German worker.

With the advent of the war, the *Monte Rosa* was converted first to a
barracks ship, then to a troop ship which participated in the invasion of
Norway in 1940 and saw among its subsequent journeys the movement
of Norwegian Jews toward extermination at the Auschwitz concentration
camp in Poland. In 1945, she would serve as a hospital ship, then as a
transport for 5,000 German refugees from the advancing Russian Red
Army, before she was captured by the British in May of that year. By 1947,
she had been taken into the British Ministry of Transport and was renamed the *Empire Windrush*. "Empire" was the name given to a class of
captured ships, and "Windrush" denoted the location in which she had
been captured, the Windrush River, a tributary of the Thames River in the
Cotswolds. The river would then give its name to a seminal event in the
postwar racial history of England.

The spring of 1948 found the *Empire Windrush* on a journey east
from Australia to England. In stops along the way she collected a variety of
stray passengers: among others, those wishing to return to England after
their dispersal by war, those seeking employment in the rebuilding of London and the rest of the nation, and residents of the old empire who were
curious about the mother country. Her last stop was Kingston, Jamaica
to pick up Jamaican British servicemen who had first returned home, but

wanted now to return to England for better opportunities. Even with those passengers, however, it appeared that she would be continuing on with a lot of unused capacity. A notice advertising a "Passenger Opportunity to United Kingdom" was placed in the local newspaper. A cabin could be had for £48 and a berth on the troopdeck for £28, the equivalent of six month's pay for most Jamaicans.

The opportunity presented for the British subjects of the West Indies, some with their families, was obvious. There was not much to do in the Caribbean, but postwar England needed labor to rebuild. When the *Empire Windrush* moored on June 21, 1948, at the Tilbury Docks in Essex she contained perhaps as many as 1,000 men, women and children from the Caribbean Islands.[1] Others of color had come in smaller numbers from that part of the world before that, and would come over the postwar years from India and Africa, but this arrival was the subject of great interest and news coverage. History would call it the arrival of Britain's Windrush Generation, and its evolution into the 21st century would set an observable tone for the racial integration of England.

Officially at that time, the United Kingdom was proud of the multicultural nature of its reach, and had just passed the Nationality Act of 1948, which gave the right of self-determination to the governments of its possessions while reaffirming the common membership of their residents in the larger dominion. Officially, as the *Empire Windrush* approached the Thames with much public interest, its passengers were to be welcomed. Unofficially, however, it was a concern to some in government. Two days after the ship had landed, a group of Labour Party Members of Parliament complained to Prime Minister Clement Atlee that "An influx of coloured people domiciled here is likely to impair the harmony, strength and cohesion of our public and social life and to cause discord and unhappiness among all concerned."[2]

Atlee responded: "If our policy were to result in a great influx of undesirables, we might, however unwillingly, have to consider modifying it. But I should not be willing to consider that except on really compelling evidence, which I do not think exists at the present time."[3]

The ship's passengers found immediate work, often through government Labour Exchanges and many with London Transport and the National Health Service, which needed female workers in particular. Bureaucratically, however, they were called "coloured colonial labour" and treated as inferior. By 1953, the country's Labour Exchanges returned surveys with characterizations of coloured labor as undisciplined, quarrelsome and physically unsuited for hard work in a cold climate. The descriptions were belied, however, by the underlying situation of many of these workers as having arrived with good employment experience in skilled work that was ignored in favor of the low skilled and undesirable jobs that they were given. By the mid–1950s, the need for skilled and quality labor was such that many employers began to recruit directly in the Caribbean.[4]

The first and following Windrush immigrants settled mostly in Brixton or Clapham, but were quickly met with complaints that they were taking scarce housing from white residents. It did not help that landlords saw an opportunity to raise rents for the new arrivals while cramming too many of them into limited quarters. That, in turn, helped to justify any racist attitudes among white Londoners that already existed. In the following years, newly arriving subjects from the West Indies would also be categorized as Windrush Generation, and, by the 1950s, some neighborhoods of London would become settings of racial violence.

Such was the footing upon which the generation traveled through the following decades, and well into the 21st century. Members of the evolved Windrush Generation and the children of its original members found themselves challenged as late as 2018. By law, the first and following Caribbean immigrants had come to England without the need for immigration papers. In 1962 and 1971, new laws subjected citizens of other Commonwealth countries to immigration control with resulting papers to support their presence in the country but protected those who had not needed papers before that year.

In 2012, new measures to restrict immigration created an environment in which employers were required to take steps to prove that each of their employees had the right of residence in the UK. Politically, the policy was frankly described by Home Secretary Theresa May: "The aim is to create, here in Britain, a really hostile environment for illegal immigrants."[5] In 2017, the policy, now named "Hostile Environment," seemed to take a hard turn into the original members of the Windrush Generation, and their families, who could not prove the right to residency given to them before 1973. They became subject to deportation and the loss of government services, employment and housing, and the government seemed to be relentless in pursuing those ends. A leaked memo from the Home Secretary's office in April 2018 told of the success of 12,800 enforced returns of immigrants as of that month in 2017–2018.[6]

Thousands of immigrants were found to have been unfairly treated, and press reporting on what had come to be known as the "Windrush Scandal" would fuel public outrage in some quarters, but the matter persisted unresolved through 2019.

The number of biracial children of British women and African American servicemen in the immediate aftermath of the war would be similar to the number of those in the original Windrush Generation. They too would take on a collective name, most commonly the "Brown Babies" of England. They were called "half-caste" more than "biracial," and in the United States they would come to be called variously the "tan Yanks" or "wild oats" babies.[7] At times, they, too, would become subject to plans to send them from England and back to their country of (half) origin.

Unlike the Windrush immigrants, the Brown Babies did not have a central event or unifying experience that could carry them through the coming years of their lives. They had been born in the places that Black American soldiers had been posted in large concentrations, mostly in scattered western portions of the country, and in Scotland, and had no sense of community. They did, however, gain advocacy in the last years of the war, and it, too, had Jamaican origins.

Harold Moody had been born in Kingston in 1882 and moved to England to study medicine in 1904. He married a white woman who was a nurse, and the discrimination the two faced led him to form the League of Coloured Persons (LCP) in 1931. He was assisted by the American historian Charles Wesley, a leader of the American NAACP, which offered a model for the British organization.

The Black residents of the Caribbean Islands, men and women, would play an important role in the British war effort, and, in 1942, the LCP was joined by Sylvia McNeill, a member of a wealthy Jamaican family who had attended finishing school in England during the 1930s. McNeill became a quick student of the dynamics of the presence of African American soldiers in the country, especially their relationships with British women. Moody enlisted her to undertake studies and surveys to understand the implications of those relationships, and it most naturally fell on their resulting Brown Babies. Her work in 1945 would be credited as a catalyst for more official British attention to the problems presented and was reported to the Minister of Health.

McNeill had surveyed County Welfare offices where the children were known to exist and arrived at a number of 550 that were known to them. It was not presumed to be a comprehensive result, but the number of those who probably most required the attention of government agencies.

"The League of Coloured Peoples," said a letter from Moody to the ministry, "is of the opinion that this is a matter with which the Government of this country, in cooperation with the Government of the United States, must deal [with] as a 'war casualty.' We would urge the importance of wise and effective action at this stage in order to avoid the emergence of a more serious problem in the course of a few years."[8]

A reader in the Ministry of Health had written a question mark at the term "war casualty," but it would be the position of the LCP that the children were indeed casualties of war. Specifically, it focused on 135 of them who fell into four categories.

- A group of four or five whose fathers wanted them in the United States and whose mothers would be willing to send them. The LCP believed that the government should help to facilitate such a transfer.
- Just a couple of cases in which the mothers wished to keep their children, but wished for assistance in getting money from the United States, a problem, it was noted, that applied to all children of American troops.
- Those who wanted to keep their children with only minor assistance as needed.
- The fourth group was the largest by far, and predicted what would become a tragedy for many of the Brown Babies.

Those whose mothers want to put their children into homes. This comprises the major number of the priority group. There are certain possible evil results which must be safeguarded against in dealing with this large group. If they are put together in one large home in one place, then too much will be known about them in the neighborhood, they will be considered a public disgrace and difficulties will arise about employment later on and thus there will be an aggravation of the Colour Bar [the latent racial discrimination in British society].[9]

With that warning, the LCP urged that children who were unwanted by their parents be dispersed with white children to homes throughout England, and be attended by those who could help to mitigate the "psychological shock attendant upon their origin and their lack of maternal affection"; and that the possibility should not be overlooked that some might be sent to homes in "the Southern States of America or in the Colonies." That may not have been the most desirable outcome in the view of the LCP, but it allowed that it would offer the children an opportunity to "grow up in a more congenial racial atmosphere than they may find in this country."[10]

In December 1944, a "Conference on the Position of the Illegitimate Child Whose Father is Alleged to be a Coloured American" was held in London. Its purpose was to help welfare agencies to understand and deal with the problem presented. In attendance were representatives of perhaps 75 social service organizations ranging from the American Red Cross, to the National Baby Welfare Council, the Waifs and Strays Society, the National Children's Home and Orphanage, and the League of Coloured Peoples. Predominant among the attendees were Catholic dioceses from throughout the nation. As discussed through the prism of the welfare of half-caste children, the conference offered a unique view into the past, present and predicted future of racial attitudes in British society.

At the outset, the group was reminded by a representative of the Church of England Moral Welfare Council that the discussion was about babies who "are babies first of all, with the child's need for security and affection, which is a primary need of every child, and plans made for this child must be based on recognition of that need: the child's colour is a secondary consideration."[11] Further, the premise of the discussion was set as a consideration of illegitimacy as much, if not more, than it was of race, and it carried an undercurrent of the perceived American responsibility in helping the children. It was agreed without argument, however, that these were British subjects due the assistance of their own government.

Different agencies in different parts of the country described different problems.

The Gloucester Diocesan Association for Moral Welfare Work represented a rural area with twenty biracial children. Six were children of single girls whose parents would no longer support them. The rest were of married women. In most cases, their husbands were away at war and yet to be confronted with the additions to the families they had left behind, "and we just don't know what is going to happen with these children."[12]

In urban Bristol, eight of the children had been born of mostly married women. Two of the marriages had ended, however, with just one of the involved children remaining in the family. Two of the eight had been placed in a home for children by the Bristol Moral Welfare Association. There remained four children "for which no provision has been made, and where we do not know what we can do."[13]

It was the position of the representative of the Church of England that all effort must be made to keep mother and child together in all cases of illegitimacy, and more so in the case of biracial children, although welfare agencies might be tempted to create special provisions for their care. It was admitted, however, that there might be problems with that approach: in already existing families where the biracial child stood in the way of marital reconciliation, and in "particular rural areas and small towns, where workers found it difficult to find foster mothers for any children, and impossible to find for the coloured child. In a small village there is often a prejudice against coloured people for they are not accustomed to seeing them."[14]

This would not be an issue in London. According to a representative of the Crusade of Rescue of the Catholic Child Welfare Council, it was a problem that had "been with us for all time that I know, and has not been aggravated by the presence in our midst of our American friends; I regret to see the association of this problem with them, as though they had introduced it." Nor was it really that much of a problem for the children involved, up to a point. Black and white children could get along very happily. "There seems to be no need of any special provision in my own opinion. These children should be treated simply and solely as illegitimate and in no way segregated."[15] It was when they grew into job-seeking young adults that the problems would present themselves. The warning reflected the truth of a problem that was acknowledged by others in the conference: economic and social discrimination against colored people in Britain. "[W]e should do what we can now to influence it upon this matter, so that the colour problem is not a bar to employment in this country. We have sixteen years in which to do it and we must begin with the very first relationship that we establish in dealing with these cases, in the attitude we set as to whether we regard colour as the problem, or a more fundamental thing, that the child is born illegitimate with no home or father of its own."[16]

Indeed, the children might offer a step toward a less prejudiced British society, and especially if they were not set apart and segregated as they grew. But that would require resolve in the matter of children's homes and orphanages. Some felt that the lives of the children should not be made more difficult by placing them in integrated living situations, but some of the larger organizations, like the Waifs and Strays Society, said that they would continue to offer space when it became available, regardless of race, so that the children could learn to live in multicultural communities. Dr. Barnardo's Homes, founded by an Irish philanthropist in the late 19th century, was receiving an application for a biracial child every other day, half of them from married women. Its policy, too, was to take them without regard to race, but, in its view, with the purpose of maintaining an equality for white children. "We don't want to load ourselves with a lot of coloured children, and to admit an illegitimate child simply because a woman has associated with a coloured man does not seem quite fair to white people."[17] Most of the children in their experience were boys, which could be attributed to an extra prejudice against boys on the part of the landladies of the white mothers. They, too, worried about what would happen to these boys when they met social and economic prejudice in their working years. But the Barnardo Homes also had a history of trying to export children it deemed not fit for British purity to the British colonies.

Adoption was briefly considered, but to the extent that it might occur it would be among colored couples only and not in a significant amount. Adoption agencies were said to be reluctant to even make the attempt, though that may have been a prejudiced judgment. Adoption to American families would be prohibited by the Adoption Act which forbade the removal of adopted children from England except to British subjects. With those impediments, adoption seemed to be a closed subject, but, instead, became controversial in both countries.

In England, the American civil rights activist W.E.B. Du Bois led an effort by attendees of the Pan-African Congress of 1945 to create awareness of the problem and to enlist the NAACP in finding a solution. Other Black leaders based in England undertook similar efforts that would consider overriding the Adoption Act out of necessity and promoting adoption of the children to American families. The efforts came to nothing, and among Britons who cared about the matter the discussion ranged from the undesirability of sending the children to a country they knew to be discriminatory in law and behavior to how doing so might reflect on the country's challenged relationship with the African and West Indies colonies.

Then, in August 1947, the London Daily Mail reported sensationally and wrongly that a chartered ocean liner was being prepared to transport "5,000 'dusky problem babies' to America."[18] The story was repeated in the American press and served the rhetoric of those in the U.S. who had been talking about the children from racist and right-wing positions. Their tone was often virulent and promoted through pamphlets like "20,000 Little Brown Bastards," distributed by a disciple of the segregationist Huey Long. In the U.S. House of Representatives, Mississippi Congressman John E. Rankin talked of the "illegitimate half-breed Negro children from England ... the offspring of the scum of the British Isles."[19]

Another, and most natural, step toward bringing some of the children to America lay in the very fact of parental connection, but it was blocked in at least two respects. Some African American fathers were willing and wanted to bring their children to America, but British law did not recognize them as their legal fathers, and the U.S. military was not interested in helping. Many of the men would be willing to marry the woman with whom they had a child (and the sense of the conference on the children of Black Americans was that Black men were more willing than white men to step up to that obligation), but they would have to live in the U.S. where sex and marriage between the races was forbidden by the anti-miscegenation laws of most states. Eventually, an official figure from the U.S. Immigration and Naturalization Service of 37,789,[20] and an unofficial but widely estimated figure between 50,000 and 100,000 "War Brides" would come home with American servicemen by 1950, but the brides of Black servicemen could not be legally welcomed in most places, although some of such marriages did occur.

For most of the Brown Babies of England, growing up would require the dual task of arriving at one's own individuality while overcoming seemingly endless implications of their otherness as children who lived just outside of the usual nurture of society.

The most fortunate were those who stayed with already existing families formed by the mother, her husband and other existing or future children born of the couple. To get to that result, however, the child would have to survive a temptation by some families to choose the easier path of adoption out. That accomplished, the next hurdle was the husband's acceptance of what had occurred and the way in which it would affect his own relationship with the child. Without a lot of documentation, most writing about the era suggests that many men did indeed accept the responsibilities of fatherhood in extraordinary circumstances, but many did not or did so grudgingly, or used the child as a recurring weapon in a troubled marriage. If the family did ultimately succeed in staying together, the biracial child would always be a reminder and a sign within a circle of friends and family, and within the larger community. In some cases, the biracial baby became darker as the years passed, and many would find that the perception of "cute" novelties as young children wore off as they became teenagers. Ultimately, the children of white American soldiers would blend into British society; the children of Black American soldiers would always stand out, as would their mothers and stepfathers.

Although it may have been the position of the Church of England that the children should be kept with their mothers and socially supported whenever possible, the lack of the apparent sanction of a family and the implied shame of unwed pregnancy left many of these women on the margins, with children who pointed to the quality of their character that had begun to become associated with prostitution during the coarsening of attitude about white British women and Black American soldiers in 1943.

Some of the children had been abandoned in the hospitals at birth, and others would eventually become abandoned in various ways at some later age. The next resting place would be residence in children's homes and orphanages, and all the concerns that had been voiced about such places in the London conference on children of African American soldiers were at play. It would be the Holnicote House at Minehead, Somerset that would offer the best example of what could be done for the children. It would also help to bring attention to the problem in the United States as the war receded.

As the war came to an end, the decision was made in Somerset County, 150 miles west of London, that all of the Brown Babies of the county would come into care. The move was prompted by the attention of the Ministry of Health in 1943 to the growing presence of illegitimate births in the country, and the number of such children in Somerset in the following year. By the end of 1945, the county's nurseries held 37 of the children, of which 27 had been born to married women. The operating premise was that, realistically, the children would not receive parental care and were not likely to be adopted, therefore they would be taken into the home as early as the age of two weeks, irrespective of the marital status of the mother. There was no reported resistance to the plan, which was eventually accompanied by a change of opinion: with aggressive and thoughtful work it could be possible to find good adoptive homes for the children both in England and America. The country's Children Act of 1948 had slightly and briefly eased the prohibition of international adoptions, and Holnicote was able to make some small headway in both countries.

In 1946, the Brown Babies of England seemed to show up in the African American press for the first time. Under the headline "England's Brown Babies in Trouble," the *Hartford Chronicle* reported and editorialized that the mothers of the children were living in difficult circumstances, and "The American Negro needs to do something about this whole matter. It is not a question of taking the child away from the mother and bringing it here for adoption, but there are more than enough churches, lodges, fraternal organizations, etc. to send a regular stream of funds to England to protect and help raise these youngsters."[21]

In 1947, the *Detroit Tribune* reported that a number of American fathers were trying to bring their children from England to America against the resistance of both countries, but that the more difficult problem was the expense of passports, visas, travel companions and transportation costs, which made the prospect impossible. The article went on to assert a claim by the League of Coloured Persons that unnamed U.S. officials had been taking surveys on the numbers of illegitimate children of American servicemen abroad, but stopped the process when results in England and Japan showed "that the figures do not sustain the charge that Negro soldiers are less moral than white soldiers, despite the illegitimacy that is forced by regulations forbidding interracial marriage."[22]

Later that year, the subject broke further into the American press with an article about the "Brown Tiny Tims" in *Newsweek*, and, in 1948, the country's largest pictorial weekly magazine, *Life*, devoted a full page to "The Babies They Left Behind Them" with a large picture of seven children sitting on the lawn at Holnicote House behind radiant smiles. They were described as half-Negro and "conceived in war and orphaned by peace."[23]

The article described nearly idyllic lives for the children, which were, however, in jeopardy by the inability to find adoptive homes for them in Somerset. Their mothers faced disgrace and economic hardship.

> Uncle Sam has shown virtually no interest in her problems…. Nor will the Army consider romantic damage claims although it has paid out $9 million for broken

palm trees, soil damage and even miscarriages among English sheep unnerved by American artillery fire....

Although it is the more dramatic, the dilemma of the half-negro children is only a small part of a worldwide problem of illegitimacy. In Britain alone, 22,000 children were born out of wedlock to white U.S. soldiers. There have been no surveys in France, Italy and many other countries, but it is estimated that U.S. forces have been responsible for 30,000 to 50,000 illegitimate births in Germany; for 1,000 to 4,000 in Japan; and for 2,000 to 4,000 in the Philippines.[24]

TEN

Occupation Babies

What might some future Hitler do to rid the nation
of this dark minority?—*The Pittsburgh Courier*, 1948

In the matter of orientation films for U.S. troops entering new countries, England was one thing, but Germany was quite another thing.

The film that was shown to American soldiers of the occupying force of postwar Germany was short and to the point. There were no movie stars flitting about from pub to train station to encounters with pretty girls, and no stilted vignettes with admonishing generals. *Your Job in Germany*, 1945, was an unrelenting ten-minute condemnation of Germany and its people, delivered under the premise that if you, the soldier, did not take it seriously, America, and your sons, might be fighting with this historically evil nation once again.

It opened with the Liberty Bell ringing beneath the Ode to Joy of the German composer Beethoven's Ninth Symphony (one can't know whether the choice was meant to be ironic) and the headline in bold type "WAR WITH GERMANY ENDS IN VICTORY ... VICTORY LEADS TO PEACE," followed with "SOMETIMES NOT." It would be the conduct of the American soldier that would determine the direction at the current fork in the road. Hitler was gone, propaganda was off the air, the concentration camps were empty, but ...

> You'll see ruins, you'll see flowers, you'll see some mighty pretty scenery (over folks in lederhosen in pretty scenery with jaunty music). But don't let it fool you. You are in enemy country. Be alert, suspicious of everyone. Take no chances. You are up against something more than tourist scenery. You are up against German history. It isn't good.[1]

A history of Germany's 19th century conquest by force of other nations follows with note of its operating slogans: "Our God is blood! Germany over all!"

More pretty scenery and farmers working their fields to happy

In the training film "Your Job in Germany" shown to American soldiers who would occupy Germany and Austria, the message was to be suspicious of people with a history of war and violence (U.S. Army).

German music. "Europe relaxes. The danger's over. Nice country, Germany. Tender people, the Germans. Very sweet music." Then comes World War I, and, when occupying forces enter the country upon Germany's defeat, the narrator's solemn, deep voice becomes high-pitched and mocking. "Why, these people are okay. It was just that Kaiser that we had to get rid of. You know, this is really some country!" Then comes the World War that the audience has just experienced. The German folk are once again dancing in their traditional costumes.

"Ah, Hell. This is where we came in. Yeah, this is where we came in."

The ultimate message intended to be given to the occupying soldiers was that they should not, under any circumstances, consort with the German people. "In battle you kept your wits about you. Don't relax that caution now." Nazi beliefs were not gone; they were just undercover. They were out of uniform now. "You won't know them, but they will know you. They're still watching you. And hating you."

> You are soldiers on guard. You will observe their local laws. Respect their customs and religion. And you will respect their property rights. You will not ridicule them. You will not argue with them. You will not be friendly. You will be aloof, watchful and suspicious. Every German is a potential source of trouble. Therefore, there shall be no fraternization with any German people. Fraternization means making friends. The German people are not our friends. You will not associate with German men, women, or children.... They cannot come back into the civilized fold by sticking out their hand and saying "I'm sorry." Do not clasp that hand.

Your Job in Germany was directed by Frank Capra and written by Theodore Geisel, who worked in the Army's animation and film department during the war before returning to his better-known identity as children's author Dr. Seuss. Ultimately, the film had no discernible effect on what would occur in Germany in the following years.

The order had been a tall one. After the U.S. entry into Germany in September 1944, approximately 1.6 million U.S. soldiers were stationed in the country, reducing down to 135,000 after 1947. They were enemies occupying a hostile country, and the non-fraternization rule made military and security sense. But it made little human sense, especially on the scale of the number of humans involved. Friendly encounters quickly occurred in spite of themselves, and to the extent that reporting about them appeared in the American and British press it became censored by military authorities.[2] Though human interaction was inevitable on the ground among similar people who spoke different languages, it was unthinkable to people at a remove from those interactions, and whose countries had just endured years of war with each other. They must not be told about it.

By June 1945, military leadership on the ground was ready to give up on a policy of non-fraternization in Germany and Austria. On a social level, it was just not being observed, and attempts to control it were leading to a breakdown in discipline. On a sexual level, it was a nonstarter. For all of its stern certitude, *Your Job in Germany* had mentioned women almost in passing, and not at all with the relish that Burgess Meredith had considered a pretty girl on a bicycle in *A Welcome to Britain*. A pamphlet passed out to soldiers, however, cast German women as potential killers, and, in doing so, told a tale about Dutch women.

> Your attitude toward women is wrong—in Germany. You'll see a lot of good-looking babes on the make there. German women have been trained to seduce you. Is it worth a knife in the back? In Holland, girls belonging to the resistance made dates with German soldiers. Just after dark they walked their dates along a canal or river. At certain places, Dutchmen waited. Then, a wallop with a sock full of sand from behind, and another unconscious German soldier was shoved into a canal to drown.
>
> One Dutchman now serving with the Ninth Army teamed with his sister to drown 15 Germans in canals during the German occupation of Holland. Altogether hundreds of German soldiers were "liquidated" this way. A French resistor says: "From my experience during five years of occupation, I know that German women are often used as underground workers, and sometimes they are slyer and more fanatic than men."[3]

There were no discoverable reports of American soldiers knifed in the back by German women, but the military command's recommendation of the removal of restrictions on fraternization pointed to the sudden rise of venereal disease among the troops in Germany. If sex was forbidden with German women, prophylactics could not therefore be provided for illicit sex, or soldiers would not indicate that they were breaking the rule by seeking them out. And the available women were omnipresent, according to the *New York Times*.[4]

The distinguished war reporter Drew Middleton ventured out of the cities and found women standing outside of forested areas near the occupied towns and villages in search of what the soldiers called "fra' bait," cigarettes and candy. In urban areas, the ruins of war offered a seclusion that was impossible to breach. If caught, one of the dodges might be an insistence by the soldier that the woman was not German, but a displaced person of war. As tenuous an excuse as that might have seemed, some commands countered the ploy by identifying displaced women and requiring that they wear a corresponding button

At the bottom line, soldiers and command insisted that the rule was foolish and impossible to enforce. One soldier complained that he and his fellows had taken losses across Europe and could not now enjoy themselves. "What the hell's the matter with those guys up top..." At the top of the command, however, Gen. Dwight Eisenhower could not agree because "in view of the horror that newspaper stories and pictures of concentration camps had aroused recently in the United States and Britain he did not think that that was the time to ask for the relaxation of the rule."[5]

The non-fraternization rules that had been so firmly enunciated in a film at the beginning of 1945 were gone by the middle of the year. It was not just the impossibility of their enforcement and their effect on morale and discipline that did them in, but a growing realization that if the Germans were to be brought back to proper civilization, that could best be accomplished through positive social and human relationships between the American and British soldiers and German citizens. It would take another year for the removal of the prohibition of marriage between German women and American soldiers. Over the following three years, more than 20,000 German women would immigrate to America as wives and fiancés, but for some of them the journey may have been an attempt to escape the condemnation of German society.

Drew Middleton's reporting had not been without compassion for the women involved. Nazi philosophy had encouraged procreation without regard to the social structure of marriage as a contributor to the strength and numbers of the Aryan race. The implication was that sex without marriage had become socially acceptable. And, as in England, German women had undergone a social and economic evolution as regards their role in society. Their men were permanently or temporarily gone; in the age group 20–30, the ratio of women to men was 167 to 100 in 1946.[6] They were now more in charge of their own lives and liberated in that way. But the liberation had brought with it the need to do what needed to be done for their own survival and that of their families. Different women reacted in different ways, but it was a characteristic of the occupation that many German women were not inhibited about presenting themselves as attractive and desirable to the American soldiers, for whatever reason.

On the other hand, many of them were raped, either violently or with their passive resignation.

Rape is a condition of any war, and particularly of the aftermath of war. Accounts need to be settled, standards of morality have long been ignored, violence is a way of life. The best of what it is to be male is called for and the worst is often allowed. And most wars offer examples of rape that is encouraged, facilitated and even institutionalized in the form of enforced prostitution. World War II was far from an exception to the rule, nor was the incidence of the rape of European women by American soldiers. Statistics, however, are vastly wide ranging and will never be definitive.

Officially, the records of the Judge Advocate General (JAG) for 1942–1945 put the number of *reported* rapes in the three largest European countries at 552 in Germany, 181 in France and 121 in England, totaling 854 (there are no reliable figures for the Netherlands).[7] That's one set of figures. Another viewpoint put the number of German women raped by Americans between 1945 and 1955 at 190,000. This was the assertion of

Dr. Miriam Gebhardt in the German book *Als die Soldate kamen (When the Soldiers Came*, but changed for the English edition to *Crimes Unspoken*). Gebhardt was a historian in the field of women and education. The book was controversial, though based on extensive research, and considered credible by some.

Another controversial book, because it, too, severely challenged the figures of the JAG, applied those figures to a formula that is considered approximately reliable in criminology. It noted that rape is among the most underreported of crimes, and for very complicated reasons, especially in war and its aftermath. It had been the opinion of the distinguished Cambridge criminologist Sir Leon Radzinowicz that only 5 percent of rapes were ever reported. In his book *Taken by Force*, American criminologist J. Robert Lilly multiplied the JAG figures by a factor of twenty and arrived at 11,040 rapes in Germany, 3,620 in France and 2,420 in England. Many of the crimes committed were gang rapes of a single woman, so that over the period of January–September 1945, as an example, the U.S. Army convicted 284 of its soldiers in the rapes of 187 women in Germany.[8]

The number of those rapes committed by race of the rapist can't be known, nor would they be able to predict the incidence of rape by race during the occupation. Though the military population ratio was ten percent Black and 90 percent white, the conviction rate on rapes in England, France and Germany during the nine-month period was 65 percent Black, 32 percent white and 3 percent other. Lilly's research found that of American military prosecutions in France, Germany and Belgium, 1944–46, 59 percent were for rape and 87 percent of those executed for all crimes were Black. At the time of World War II, the lynchings of Black men for perceived sexual transgressions against white women were still a feature of American society, and they would continue after the war.

Whether the results of willing, passive or violent sex, an estimated 94,000 children were born of German women and occupation soldiers of all nationalities by 1949. As in England, the women were likely to find themselves judged poorly by others, and their children were vulnerable to guilt by association. Three thousand of them were fathered by African Americans by 1950, and another 2,000 by 1955.[9] They were born into difficult lives with a lot to overcome.

It was not the first time that Germany's goal of racial purity through war would be thwarted by its failure in war. With the defeat in World War I, the occupation of the Rhineland region of West Germany had included thirty to forty thousand African members of French forces. Though hardly in a position to complain, Germany's military, social and political leadership demanded that the Black troops be removed, and asserted in a petition to Parliament that "these wild people are a dreadful danger" to every German man, woman and child, whose "honor, life, limb, purity and innocence are being destroyed. More and more cases are coming to light in which colored troops have defiled German women and children, injuring, even killing resisters."[10] The soldiers, in this view, were certainly sexual predators and carriers of disease, and their progeny would be the same.

Biracial children were inevitably born of the Occupation after World War I and would come to be known as the Rhineland Bastards, or, more formally, *Besatzungskinder*, Children of occupation. Their number was no more than 600 and, for the most part, they had been born of consensual sex in and outside of marriage, but they would become symbols of Germany's shameful failure in war.[11] Adolf Hitler would inveigh against them in *Mein Kampf* as contaminators of the white race. They had most certainly been brought into Germany by Jews "with the ultimate idea of bastardizing the white race they hate and thus lowering its cultural and political level so that the Jew might dominate."[12]

Under Nazi law, biracial children and their mothers were not protected citizens of the state. They could be subject to forced sterilizations under the direction of the *Sonderkommission 3* based on information about each individual child developed by the Interior Ministry. Some were placed in concentration camps where they were subject to medical experimentation and physical and mental abuse (it is believed by some, but not proved, that many were murdered).[13] Thus was set a German predicate for the treatment of its mixed race residents that would underlie yet another humiliating defeat in war, but in this case met with occupation forces which were themselves racially discriminatory by national custom and military policy. Both countries were about to embark on new and difficult, though positive, eras of their identities in matters of race, and the children of each would be catalysts for that change. But in the immediate postwar German years, the newly born biracial children were symbols of failure and miscalculation—for both sides.

For Americans, they were the products of an impossible social construct of racial integration, at best, and of the sexual violence of American men, at worst. For the American military, they were a sign of the breakdown of command. For Germans, they were visible symbols of a humiliating defeat in a war that had been tragically premised on white Aryan superiority—yet again. For white German and American men, they were a suggestion of emasculation. Indeed, the two groups came to form a bond of sorts that was premised in part on anger at Black American men in this regard. It was encouraged by the German press and not discouraged by the American Military Police, who seemed to go along with a need to defend white women against seduction and monitor their activities.[14]

In Nuremberg, as an example, the so called "Neger-clubs" were watched by police for German women who seemed to socialize with those within. In November 1945 more than a hundred women were said to have been taken into custody each day and sent to jails or workhouses. As justification, officials talked about the danger of racial sexuality combined with criminal and materialistic sexuality of the women involved. American officials eventually intervened with the police, but not with much apparent urgency. The significant book on the subject, *Race After Hitler*, pointed to an undated survey of the early 1950s of 552 women who had consorted with African American soldiers after the war. Just more than half said that they had done it for the material benefit of food, clothing and money. One quarter pointed to genuine romantic motivation, and one fifth to sexual interest and desire, along with the wish to keep up with friends who were attracted to Black men for any reason.[15]

Whatever their motivation, they were more likely than not to be condemned and vilified by German society. Women with white American soldiers often had it difficult enough with the public, and especially with German men, but those with Black men would hear epithet accusations like *Schokoladensau*—chocolate pigs—*Amihuren*—Ami-whores, and *Negerliebchen*—nigger lovers. They could be subject to head shearing, other forms of violence and mandatory testing for venereal disease. They would be classed with common prostitutes, despite a survey of mothers of biracial children that would yield 134 from the upper classes and 180 deemed to be middle class. The vast majority had come to motherhood from long term relationships ranging upward in length from several months.[16]

Individually, the children born of these women may have been symbols of various kinds of perceived failures of order and society, but, worse, the mothers who would most naturally be their chief nurturers and protectors had no rights in determining their care. By West German law of the time, mothers and their immediate families were legally responsible for the children, but could not be their legal guardians. That power fell to government through appointed male guardians, or to the woman's husband, even if the child was not his. The husband could challenge his own paternity, and do so easily if the child was biracial, but, if he could not prove the fact, he was otherwise required by law to support the child until age 16. American men, however, were not controlled by the law until 1949, when U.S. law was changed to allow German jurisdiction over Allied servicemen. It offered conditions and exceptions, however, that made it ineffective in the lives of most of the mothers and children, and the U.S. military would take no responsibility for them at all.[17]

Another effect of laws that gave the mother no rights in the raising of her child was their tacit support of a pregnant woman who might quietly disappear to a home or program that would support her until the birth of a child, which she would then leave behind to the care of the state. From a practical perspective, it would be easy to do.

On July 23, 1952, a short, cryptic article appeared at the bottom of page 5 of the *New York Times*.

NEGRO CHILDREN STUDIED
Offspring of U.S. Soldiers are a Problem in Germany

A conference had been opened in Bavaria to discuss "the problem of 3,000 Negro 'occupation children' in West Germany, now old enough to enter elementary schools. The article did not explain what exactly the problem was, but it did observe that the children were 'well up to the average standard in intelligence and physical fitness, and added that most of their mothers had reared them with a devotion greater than that shown by many mothers of white illegitimate children.'"[18]

By now, the symbolic nature of the children had become more complicated and contradictory. Inevitably, they were a reflection of the moral failings of their mothers, and in many minds, they were children of the enemy. In a society that had to deal with grievous crimes born of the drive for racial purity, discrimination against Jews that had led to the Holocaust could now evolve into discrimination against the Black people which the children represented. Good intentions of studying and understanding them so that they could be better served could smack of the German penchant for anthropology and defining the worth of a people through their body types and facial features. And the quantification and census of them could be used to fulfill supposedly well-intended goals of helping them to live and grow up with their own people—to send them away, and remove them to America.[19] Contrarily, and yet to come later in the 1950s, they would be seen as offering a positive path into a rethinking of the nature of Germany that would turn out to take it into the next century.

The problem that was talked about in the *Times* article was probably related to anthropology and the fact that the first of the children were becoming school age, the reason, perhaps, for the notation in the *Times* that they were found to be no less than average in mind and body. Indeed, a number of academic studies of the children took place at this time. One in particular was probably representative of most. "Analysis of Somatic and Mental Development of European-Negro-Half-Castes of Preschool Age with Special Attention to Social Circumstances" was the 1952 work of the young anthropologist Walter Kirchner. It found the children to be in good shape, even more advanced than most others, but predicted that their fortunes would become harder as they grew older. It was not that the inherent physical, sexual and mental attributes of biracial children were problems unto themselves, but they would eventually come into disharmony with German education and society. He advocated for continued study and pedagogical training reflecting their "peculiar nature."[20]

Depending on one's viewpoint and interpretation of history, Austria had either been conquered and occupied by Germany in March 1938, or happily reunited and merged with its northern neighbor through annexation. Germany had needed Austria's natural resources, and a rising tide of Austrians were drawn to German National Socialism. The deal was sealed with a triumphant German march into Austria, largely met by cheering Austrian crowds. Adolf Hitler returned to the nation of his birth on the same day.

The event and the years that followed were called the *Anschluss*, and featured the same cruelty, dictatorship and persecution of the Jews that marked daily life in Germany itself. It lasted without much incident until the Moscow Declaration of 1943, in which the Soviet Union, United Sates and United Kingdom asserted that the annexation had been without legal effect. Austria had been taken by aggression and it must be liberated from Germany. An unspoken goal of the declaration was to return the idea of independence to the Austrian people and support the evolution of a resistance effort. It had the intended effect and, by the time of the Allied occupation by zones of the nation in April 1945, many Austrians were inclined to think of their country differently once again.

As it was elsewhere, precise numbers of resulting liberation or occupation children of all Allied forces could not be determined. By one account, 8,000 were registered in the federal states of Austria between 1946 and 1953, but, beyond those registered, the actual number might have been 20,000,[21] or it might have been 30,000.[22] A consensus from many sources, however, puts the number of biracial children at 350 to 500, with most narratives resting on 400. They had been conceived in a gentler sexual environment than had been the case in Germany. The rape of Austrian women by Russian forces during the liberation/occupation of the country would be one of the most notorious examples in the history of warfare. The American forces, subsequently, were seen as protectors against Russian behavior, and supporters and employers of a society and economy that were trying to return to normalcy.

A modern narrative of the Brown Babies of Austria, sometimes called *Mischlingskinder* (mongrel children), was created with the research project "Lost in Administration," directed by Philip Rohrbach of the Wiesenthal Vienna Institute of Holocaust Studies. The premise of the title was that the children had disappeared into the history of the time, as had the government's attention to them, during difficult lives. In 2016, Rohrbach curated an exhibit at the Folklore Museum Vienna, "Black Austria. The Children of African American Occupation Soldiers." It was reported upon generously in the Austrian press and, as had occurred in the Netherlands with the history project that is the source of this book, offered a forum for community for the remaining children of that time.

The exhibit brought together the stories of twenty of them. Their documented and actual relationships to their fathers were tenuous. The same military rules and attitudes about marriage and American state laws against miscegenation applied. Fathers who may have been emotionally and psychologically present, although at a geographic distance, would eventually fall away. The research estimated that 70 percent of the group had been raised by a single mother, 15 percent had grown up in a more normal extended family and the rest in foster homes and orphanages. As elsewhere, some were abused, and some were used as free labor. And racism was always present in the backgrounds of their lives.

During World War II, some of the biracial citizens that had resulted from World War I had been subjected to Nazi anthropologists and used to make the case for the necessary purity of the Aryan race. Many in postwar Austria wanted to remove the new children from their midst. They were sent to orphanages that could be nurturing or terrible; the Vienna exhibit offered stories, similar to those in the Netherlands, of physical abuse in Catholic facilities. Or it was perhaps best that they be sent out of the country, which led to the work of one of their most important advocates.

Trudy Jeremias had been born in Austria in 1925, and had fled the Nazis with her family in 1938. She grew up in America, but wanted to return to Europe after the war. The only way she could find to do that was to become a stewardess with Sabena Belgian Airlines. At the time, the migration from Europe of white and biracial children of American fathers had become intense. In Austria, they had been pushed through a cycle of displaced lives that had started with the Army's banishment of their fathers to other places like Korea, or the official disapproval of marriages that would support them, then to welfare offices that favored orphanages over single motherhood. The mothers often became social outcasts, and could only give in to the removal of their children. The mothers of biracial children, in particular, were pariahs in their own families, and the Austrian sense, in any case, was that their children needed to be with their own kind—in America.

Sabena was a busy carrier of children to the United States, most between the ages of four and eight. Jeremias spoke German, and as she started her new career, she asked her employer if she could be given special responsibility for their welfare. She came to know them well and it became her job to bring them to the ground of a new country. "Many thought that they came to their mother and I tried to explain to them that they were not waiting for them here."[23] Instead it would often fall to her to introduce them to new mothers and fathers, and she remembered that with the biracial children the differences in skin tone and relative blackness made the introductions sometimes awkward and angry.

Trudy Jeremias could only sustain the work for one year. A successful artist in New York City in the 21st century, she could barely remember the blur of the time, but she wondered what had become of the children, and her curiosity was a catalyst for the Vienna exhibit. The exhibit and the underlying research, in turn, then served as a form of originating documentation of what the researchers called "The first generation of Schwarzer in the Second Republic of Austria."

In the 21st century, Niko Wahl, co-curator with Philip Rohrbach of the Vienna exhibit would refer to the adopting out of Austrian children to American—rather than to Austrian—families as human trafficking.

In Germany, as in Austria, the most intense attempts at problem solving with the children focused on adoption, either within the country or in the United States. The most famous of the adopted children in 1952 was a young girl named Toxi. At the beginning of the 1952 school year, large throngs of the German public would attend to her story, and she would eventually play a role in the coming discussion of what Germany should be and how it should proceed in the postwar era.

"Toxi"[24] was a movie, and the little girl it depicted was played by an actress, Elfriede Fiegert. In the lore and publicity of the film, Elfriede was only playing a version of her real self. She had been the child of an African American soldier and a mother who had put her into a home and disappeared (later discovered to have been a doctor who emigrated to America soon after giving birth). Unlike most others, she had been adopted by a loving couple who, themselves, became part of her story. As Russia was becoming increasingly a postwar burr in the west German saddle, the Fiegerts were refugees from Nazi occupied Silesia, which had been most notably the location of the Auschwitz concentration camp. The liberation of Silesia by Russia in 1945 had created a different kind of problem for its residents and, sadly, the flight of the Fiegerts from Russian menace to American protection in Germany had resulted in the death of their own two-year-old daughter. Then they adopted a half-American child. They also had experience in the movie industry.

The choice of Elfriede to play Toxi was told in the language of movie marketing and the ascension to stardom. The film's director was the famous Robert Stemmle, who wanted to create a moving and positive film about the experience of the Brown Babies. He had reportedly auditioned 400 little girls for the role to no avail. Elfriede then appeared to him as "a small brown thing" wrapped in traditional German clothing. "My name is Elfie," she said to him. "No," he replied, "you are Toxi."[25] Indeed, the movie's marketing paid generous attention to the similarities between its protagonist and its star. It was the perfect vehicle for Stemmle's goal of bringing the plight of the children into the warm light of social good.

In the 1952 popular German Film "Toxi," Elfriede Fiegert, a "Brown Baby" herself, plays an orphaned child who comes into the life of a multi-generational West German family. The film is a consideration of where Germany has been and where it is going through the different shadings of response to Toxi from four generations (Wikipedia).

In the film, the little orphaned girl is left on the doorstep of a financially and intellectually prosperous family home that is constantly abuzz with the comings and goings of four generations. A boy and girl her own age will eventually become her friends. The young adults who have come of age postwar, and their father and grandfather represent different shadings of past, present and future. They are all good people. As the film plays out, it is the father who most resists the inclusion of Toxi in family life, while the grandfather and young adults seem to represent pre- and post–Nazi viewpoints. Thus, in Heide Fehrenbach's interpretation in *Race after Hitler*, the onus of responsibility for the child is removed from the errant mother and the past history of a failed war of racial atrocity and delivered to the consideration of a new German society.

The film's pivotal and most emotional scenes often involve the grandfather and the little girl. In the most important, he visits her in an orphanage where, with other children like herself, he hears them sing a song of lament:

> I would like so much to go home
> To see my homeland once again
> I can't find my way on my own
> Who will love me and take me along?[26]

Though a happy film with jaunty music and funny moments, *Toxi* is relentless in this message: these children are being held apart from the society into which they've been born.

As relentless in German society of the time was the strain that wanted to send the children "home" to America. And, in America, the movement to receive them home reached a crescendo that had been orchestrated by the African American press since the late 1940s. Many in Germany thought that it was an American problem to solve and the Black press in America pretty much agreed, sometimes to the extent of excoriating the Black fathers who had left their children behind. They asked their readership to send assistance to children in orphanages, or to those living with their single mothers.

The Pittsburgh Courier was particularly aggressive in its coverage of the Brown Babies, both of England and Germany. "Brown Babies Turned into Sideshow Attractions," it headlined on July 17, 1948.[27]

> The most cruel aftermath of the most brutal war in history is the fact that "Brown Babies" have been turned into side show attractions. For twenty cents curious neighbors can see a "Brown Baby." For 15,000 marks you can BUY a "Brown Baby."
>
> These international orphans ... in the European Command of the American occupation forces ... are being given away, abandoned, killed because their mothers cannot care for them. And there are 1,435 recorded births (unverified) in the Munich (Germany) area alone.

The writer, William G. Nunn, had traveled Europe as an observer for the Army and was now managing editor of the newspaper. The babies were in desperate need of help, he said. He had received letters from all over the country asking how families could adopt the children, but there seemed to be no clear path to getting that done. Some of the fathers had been trying to help from America, he reported, and the mothers in Germany were organizing for strength in numbers. Black American women already in Germany through marriage were being enlisted in helping others to understand how to care for the children.

As urgent as he felt the need for American adoption, Nunn also gave voice to a sentiment that had been held by some in Germany, England and the Netherlands: from what was known about racism in America, it might be the case that the children would ultimately have more fulfilled lives in one of the European nations. "The European attitude on race in Germany allows for a fuller development of a non-white, these people say."[28]

A year later, the *Courier* found the problem to be even more dire. The headline asserted that "German Brown Babies Really Need Your Help,"[29] and the article beneath it pointed to a prospect of genocide. As the children grew older, they would become symbols of the occupation of the country. There were just perhaps 10,000 of them, but there had been 700,000 [*sic*] Jews.

> The Germans were led to the path of exterminating these 700,000 Jews. What might some future Hitler do to rid the nation of this dark minority, which belies the claim of the purity of the German people? Would this minority be exterminated? The German people have demonstrated that they are capable of such an act.

Printed beside the article were the names, birthdates, mother's name and German address of 40 of the children, part of a continuing list kept by the paper. Readers were urged to write directly to the mothers or children and offer their help. "The forgoing children are living human beings."

One of the Black American wives in Germany who were drawn to the children was civil rights activist and reporter for the *Baltimore Afro-American* Mabel Grammer. She and her husband Oscar, an Army warrant officer in Mannheim and Karlsruhe, would eventually adopt twelve of the children on their own. Most of them would grow up to serve in the U.S. military and one of them, Nadja West, would become the U.S. Army Surgeon General in 2017. Beyond that, Grammer developed and wrote about the Brown Baby Plan. It started in the mostly Catholic orphanages, and followed with writing in America that sought to overcome the notion that Black families were too poor or disadvantaged to take care of children not their own. Grammer managed to master the German bureaucracy and create proxy adoptions for American families that could not come to retrieve them. She pushed and pulled the paperwork back and forth across the ocean, and enlisted Scandinavian Airlines System in the cause.

The effort was met with resistance from some who felt that it was Black children born in America who needed the most help, especially those living in the South. And it would emerge that some of the children she had helped to move to America had gone into abusive homes. But it was believed that she had helped 500 children to find their lives in America, and, in 1968, she and her husband were honored by Pope John Paul VI for their humanitarian efforts.

As in England, a portion of those who advocated for the children believed, rightly or wrongly, that if they could not be sent to families of their own kind in America they should be raised with their own kind in segregated institutions. Perhaps the true nature of the philosophy could be seen in the most famous of the orphanages, the Albert-Schweitzer Home in the Edersee region of North Rhine Westphalia. Just as Mabel Grammer was a successful advocate for the American adoption of the children, Frau Irene Dilloo was the force behind nurturing, albeit segregated, homes in which to grow up.

The wife of a minister, Dilloo applied Christian principles to a genuine effort to help the children and was widely admired in the German press for the effort. Early on, she asked for and received a letter of support from the German Doctor Albert Schweitzer, accompanied by the tenets of his philosophy on the matter. At the time, Schweitzer was internationally admired for his humanitarian work in the deepest reaches of Africa. In later years, and in a time when thinking about African people would reach more enlightenment, Schweitzer was seen as a benevolent though paternalistic force in the lives of people whom he thought to be inferior. The assessment was most often supported by the quote from his writing "With regard to the Negroes, then, I have coined the formula: 'I am your brother, it is true, but your elder brother.'"[30] Visits by journalists to his African facilities in 1953 found them to be substandard and unhappy places.

In practical matters, however, Schweitzer and Dilloo had much to offer that was constructive. It was important to both of them that as the children grew into adults they be encouraged as citizens of the larger world. It would accrue to their chances at financial success and, not incidentally, send them out into the world as ambassadors for a West Germany that was re-entering the world as a positive force. In that regard, Frau Dilloo sought out international connections between her charges and their contemporaries in other nations. As late as 1959, a suggestion of the work that was yet to be done with the German media and public came in the coverage of a visit to the Schweitzer home by the youth of a similar home in Dakar, Senegal. A feature of the event was a ceremonial dance exhibition which was headlined in the press as "dances to the Beat of a Jungle Drum at Edersee," appealing to stereotypes of Africans as exotic and primitive. The biracial visitors and dancers were depicted as coming from a "Home for Toxis."[31]

"Toxi" was by now a seven-year-old movie, but it still resounded in German society. As well, it had made its way to America in 1954 as a "real treat," in the words of the *Pittsburgh Courier*.[32] It was used as a fundraiser by the NAACP.

After the grandfather's visit to the orphanage, and the singing of the song of lament, the film continues with an intergenerational struggle between the father who does not want the family to engage with Toxi, the grandfather who is drawn to her and the young adult couple who decide to marry and adopt the little girl. The young man is employed in advertising, which allows the film to go into a consideration of the imagery with which the children should be portrayed in society: as a caricature of prevailing stereotypes or a real, individual person.

The marriage does not take place, however, and the grandfather suffers a heart attack, giving the father the opportunity to make good on his desire to remove Toxi from the family. He quickly gathers her up to return her to the orphanage … but this is a movie, after all, with a movie's requirement for a happy ending—or two.

On the way to the orphanage, and through a series of events, Toxi becomes lost in the city. As the father searches for her frantically he comes to realize his affection and responsibility for the child. After rescuing her from a Gypsy caravan that is about take her away, she is happily returned to the family home.

And it is Christmas Eve, thus a second happy ending. As the children of the newly united family perform a Christmas pageant for their elders, in which Toxi has worn whiteface makeup (and one of the white children wears blackface), a knock on the door brings Toxi's real African American father. He is a very handsome and well-dressed man given an intellectual bearing by fashionable eyeglasses, and he has come to take her home to America. She wipes off her white makeup, a reprise is heard of the tune of the song of the orphanage—"I would like so much to go home"—and all live presumably happily ever after.

"Toxi" offered a mixed message at a time when Germany was beginning to actively determine which of the competing generations would take control of the future, and the plight of the Brown Babies became an inevitable and powerful part of the discussion.

It was not lost on the German people that their own racist agenda in the prosecution of war had led to defeat and occupation by a country and its military that were themselves racist. As in England and the Netherlands, the people could see that racism in action every day. The idea began to evolve that neither the United States nor the German past offered a usable example of the way forward, with one exception.

The National Conference of Christians and Jews had been formed in the United States in the late 1920s to work against American strains of anti–Catholic and, eventually, anti–Black bias and violence. With encouragement from U.S. occupation forces, it became the model for the Society for Christian-Jewish Cooperation (SCJC) in 1948. As the Brown Babies became a "problem" in 1952, the SCJC gained an influential and educational role within the governments and agencies that had to deal with it. Among its most important contributions was the development of social science that could effectively understand the nature and practice of prejudice.

The treatment and welfare of the biracial children would be the method and the test for Germany's way out of the past, and, in August 1952, many of those who played a role in dealing with them met in Wiesbaden to deliberate over a premise that the children demanded and enabled a necessary German reform of the thinking of its white population. Indeed, the children were a German problem (and not an American problem), that required German attention and compassion, that would eventually lead to German progress. The conference ended with a large portfolio of recommendations about the care, education and inclusion of the children in social agencies, schools, churches and charities, and the reminder that the children were equal under the law, should not be treated as different or "specimens in a side show."[33]

As reporting from America during the 1950s continued to describe sometimes deadly racial conflict in its society and schools, those who sought a proper place for the Brown Babies now growing toward adulthood could suggest that Germany was now surpassing America in this regard. In November 1960, the popular magazine for an African American readership, *Ebony*, published an article about 1,500 of the Brown Babies who had been effectively educated and made a "frictionless move" into the German workforce. Once hidden away, they now had the acceptance of a public "awakening to the realization that Negroes are in Germany to stay, ready to take their rightful place as first-class German citizens."[34] A youth social worker in Nuremberg pointed to the determination to help the children to grow up in communities that did not isolate them.

> The incidents in Little Rock (Ark.) [resistance to school integration by armed force] have caused much indignation in Germany. I hope that no one will ever have reason to tell us Germans to clean up before our own door. It is essential that our colored children can expand and develop their talents and abilities so

that they will be firmly rooted in our community and will not some day constitute a source of unrest. They can help us make good some of the guilt we have laden upon us in the past.[35]

One of the Brown Babies whose life would never quite work out was Elfie Fiegert. She had not been given a credit in her real name for the film *Toxi*, but had been named only as Toxi in the list of properly named cast members. Whatever the intended message of *Toxi*, it was further confused in Fiegert's next film, three years later. *Der dunkle Stern* (*The Dark Star*) was not to be considered a sequel to Toxi. It told the story of a little biracial girl, Moni, who lives in the rural, iconic and culturally defining Bavarian Mountains, which she considers to be home in the powerful sense of the German concept of *Heimat*, or homeland. This is a home she cannot go home to, however; one in which she cannot live because there will be no future for her there when she grows up. Instead she becomes a circus star of the trapeze, and, as the film ends, she sets off on an international tour that will take her everywhere else in the world but home to the farms and mountains of Bavaria.

Fiegert had dwindling success as an actress as she grew older, and at one point attempted to change her legal name to Toxi, but, like Moni, she found no future in that wish, and disappeared from view in her twenties.

ELEVEN

Adulthood

What would these 20,000 dead that we buried, what would they think if they could speak?—Jefferson Wiggins, 2009

If the fictional Toxi were to have a counterpart little girl in the real life of the biracial children of postwar Germany and the Netherlands, it might have been Maria Andres. Unlike Toxi, however, she would not find a real home until her seventy-second year, and it would be a sometimes dark journey that took her there.

Maria's great grandfather had at one time been the mayor of the village of Gleisenau in northern Bavaria. In a village that numbered houses by the order of their construction his was number 13, in which her grandmother, also Maria, and mother, Sofie, were born. At the end of the war, the two lived in Altdorf bei Nürnberg.

The Nuremberg rallies of 1935 had given public proclamation to Nazi policies of condemnation of Jews and Roma. The related Nuremberg Laws forbade marriage, sex and other kinds of relationships between pure blooded Germans and Jews. The Nuremberg trials of 1945–1946 led to the conviction and execution of many of those Germans who had pursued those policies and prosecuted the war.

The Battle of Nuremberg in April 1945 had marked the certain end of the war. It had been Adolf Hitler's order that the city not be taken under any circumstances. Its place at the heart of Nazi belief and policy gave it the added protection of the willingness of its most passionate adherents to give their lives to the cause. A civilian militia complemented regular German forces and several divisions of the Luftwaffe. As Allied forces headed east into Germany in February 1945, they marched toward the geographic and spiritual heart of the country. Nuremberg sat between Berlin and Munich and it came into the sights of the U.S. 7th Army as it captured Aschaffenburg, then Heilbronn.

149

The frantic German fortification of the city that embodied the soul of Naziism predicted the ferocity and destruction of the five-day battle that followed. A German force of perhaps 7,000 would not have a chance against 45,000 U.S. troops, but the fight was desperate and door to door. The American tanks reached the rallying grounds in which the tenets of the Nuremberg Laws had been proclaimed in 1935, and the city was surrendered on April 20. It was Adolf Hitler's birthday and he would be dead by his own hand ten days later.

All that was left of Nuremberg were the facades and skeletons of what used to be the beauty and character of a Bavarian city, rising from the foundations of rubble pushed to the sides of ruined streets. The occupation of the city by American troops brought with it the same social and sexual conditions as in the rest of the country, with the addition of infrastructure and materiel support required as the world focused its attention on the eleven-month span of the Nuremberg trials starting in November 1945. Maria Andres was born in July 1946 of a father whose identity would never be revealed by Sofie, but whose name she had once seen on one of the many adoption papers that would be generated in her childhood.

Sofie had lived on the margins of German society during the war. She had been herself a child without a known father and Maria would be one of four born without benefit of a father who was spoken of. A brother born in 1940 had died in infancy and her own birth was followed by two sisters, Regina and Christine. As with many children born into mysterious circumstances, her curiosity about unknown and missing members of a nuclear family would eventually be activated and stay with her in a relentless pursuit of whatever small details could be discovered through the following decades. If asked about spare memories of her mother, she could fall to tears. "She was a desperate woman. She did her best. She couldn't do any more. I still see her face. She was a tiny person."

At one point, Sofie gave up Maria and Regina to the Nuremberg Home for Children. The rule was that a mother who had done so could have no further contact with the child. "I remember her once in a church, and I was there with another family, and there's my mother, and I was not allowed to go to my mother. That's what I remember. Because she gave me away. She was not allowed to have any contact with me."

Then Sofie and Christina were gone from Germany on a Scandinavian Airlines flight to New York. In Maria's adult view of it she had no choice. "Mothers with Black men were hunted down. She ran to America."

In an orphanage run by Catholic nuns, Maria and others like her, were convenient scapegoats, perhaps something even more immoral than the racist war of a now devastated country. They did not have proper food, and they were kept barefoot. "They did not know what to do with those kids. All of them [the brown babies], not just me. They did some cruel things to all of us. They were still [in the frame of mind] of the Holocaust, with the Jews. We were inferior. And so they thought about Jews and they thought about us. And maybe also about our fathers."

Maria was very familiar with the story of Toxi, "but it's not reality." The orphanage was always frightening. When she wet the bed at night, she was lifted out painfully by her arms. "What did I do? Was I not good? What was wrong?"

"And I remember. Because I was doing something naughty they put me in a box, a wooden box, and they sat on it. And I was so scared. For too long, too long I guess. I gave up crying. I just gave up. And okay. That's it."

And it was at that time that Maria came to one of the most frightening events of her childhood: a meeting with *Krampus*, also known to children in the Netherlands, where she would be going next, as *Zwarte Piet*, Black Pete.

As it had been presented in the movie, the Christmas pageant that had been performed for the grownups by Toxi and the other children was more complicated than it might have seemed. It had further challenged the notion of who should be who in this new postwar society by turning a custom of the German Christmas season on its head, then putting it back on the shelf with a different face. The custom was that German and Austrian children went door to door at Christmas to ask for contributions to charity in costumes of the Three Wise Men. Because one of the visitors to the birth of Christ was believed to be African, one of the children would be in blackface. In this case, however, a white child had been in blackface as per custom, but the brown child in the group had worn whiteface—then wiped away at it when given the confirmation of her true identity in the person of her father.

The point made by the film was obvious, but it can't be known if the filmmakers intended also to comment on another centuries old custom that had been sometimes problematic throughout much of Europe. It would continue to be so, at least in the Netherlands, into the 21st century. In each of the cultures it was a slight variation on a simple theme: there was a kind and benevolent St. Nicholas type, the giver of gifts and candy; but he often had an assistant, the carrier of switches, who traveled with him to track down the bad child, and who was often a dark and frightening character, dramatized by a white person in blackface.

The German version of this character that had been visited upon Maria Andres, and presumably the other brown children of the orphanage, was more fearsome than most. His dark skin portended violence and danger, and he was in some beliefs descended from a Black slave, Knecht Ruprecht, a servant to St. Nicholas. In German lore, although

The presence of St. Nicholas in a Viennese home in 1896 is overpowered by the children's fear of his assistant, Krampus (Wikipedia).

Krampus (and similar entities with different names) was associated with St. Nicholas, he acted autonomously from the benevolent saint. He was his own final arbiter of who was good and bad and could give treats to the good children while beating the bad children if they were deemed to be deserving. In real life, he was often portrayed by large and threatening grown men who wandered the countryside in the first dark days of December.[1]

In modern times, St. Nicholas became increasingly associated in popular culture with the celebration of the Christmas holidays, but he was, in history, a separate and unrelated presence, a 4th century bishop of Myra, Greece (now Turkey). Over the centuries he acquired the denotation of the patron saint of children and of other classes of people, including sailors, which gave him prominence in the seafaring Netherlands. A common oath for the start of a journey was "May St. Nicholas hold the tiller." One interpretation holds that he was brought to American culture by the Dutch of New Amsterdam and eventually renamed through stages of translation as Santa Claus, although the two are distinct characters who are often blurred erroneously into one. In the Netherlands proper he became Sinterklaas, and, by the 14th century, he was established as the bringer of gifts to children on the annual occasion of the anniversary of the eve of his "birth into heaven" on December 5. With the gifts he also left behind switches to be used on children who misbehaved.

Over the years, artistic renderings and celebratory recreations of his annual journey increasingly depicted a man in flowing bishop's robes and a long, white beard, assisted by a servant who led his horse or performed other tasks of the Saint's benevolence. In his book *Blacks in the Dutch World*, Allison Blakely suggests that it was a convergence of Christianity, ancient Dutch paganism and the time of winter that produced a servant who was dark and black. In Pagan lore, after all, winter was a time of death and darkness and it was marked in events that saw darkened men roam the villages in a noisy and threatening manner, seeking gifts and treats door to door. In some interpretations, the servant was the embodiment of a Moor who would have been part of the history of the Spanish Netherlands of the 16th through 18th centuries. In others, he was a former slave who had been freed by St. Nicholas and repaid the favor by becoming his trusted assistant.

As in Germany, the servant became a fearsome blackfaced character, sometimes depicted as hairy and horned and wearing chains connected to St. Nicholas, but which could be dangerously rattled. Finally, in 19th century Netherlands, he became Zwarte Piet. He could be a welcomed servant who helped Sinterklaas better distribute his gifts and candy, but he was always the carrier of the switches. And sometimes he carried a sack, in which he could place bad children and take them away.

Black Pete would become an indelible and often controversial presence in Dutch culture, and the way he was seen and used could be seen as a reflection of the course of the journey of Black people in Dutch society. When they were a curious and rarely seen presence, Zwarte Piet could be recreated as a Sinterklaas cookie to be eaten. At one point, he became a card game similar to the English-speaking game of Old Maid, at the end of which one did not want to be holding his card. The card could depict him in any kind of caricature, from respectful to clownish, even as an animal or inanimate object.[2]

By the first quarter of the 21st century he had become perceived as a symbol of the ridicule or trivialization of Black people in much the same way as the use of blackface was still a matter of controversy in American culture. Leading up to that time, the Netherlands had evolved through the relative racial calm of the postwar years to the heavy immigration of those from other cultures and races of the 1970s, accompanied by strains in the economy and housing.

Zwarte Piet became quickly controversial for the U.S. Army when an American officer offered his jeep for a Saint Nicolas parade in Breda, in the province of North-Brabant. It carried both St. Nicholas and Black Pete, which African American soldiers interpreted as Jim Crow. The newspaper *De Stem*, February 2, 1945, reports that a riot ensued. The Dutch responded with the assurance that Black Pete was "no more than a harmless little joke, but they were told that some jokes were never harmless." The protestors were then promised that "as long as there are any Negro soldiers in the Netherlands, no person, male or female, would ever be driven around in black makeup." The newspaper drawing is by Wim Boost. (Breda City Archives, by permission of Marjon Boost).

At its best, the social response to change reached back to the historic Dutch nature of accommodation of differences as a positive constitution of the whole. That had always worked well for the Netherlands within itself and within the larger world. Beginning in the 2000s, however, the stresses resulting from immigration, changing technologies and an increasingly complicated world became harder edged in most respects. For his own part, Zwarte Piet remained a marker of society throughout it all. To those who paid close attention to the Netherlands from abroad, and with the expanding technologies of communication throughout the world, he could be a signal to some of a particular kind of Dutch racism. In 2013, he received the condemnation of the United Nations Commission on Human Rights. "The working group," said its chairwoman, Verene Shepherd, "does not understand why it is that people in the Netherlands cannot see that this is a throwback to slavery, and that in the 21st century this practice should stop."[3]

At the time, the vast majority of the Dutch people did not agree that Black Pete was a racist symbol, and Dutch schoolchildren were said to see him only as a clown, but not as a Black person. A minority disagreed, however, and annual holiday celebrations in the cities where most Blacks lived were met with demonstrations against the character that could border on violence, but which were never ultimately dangerous. By 2019, a national television program for the Christmas holidays was set to replace the traditional Black Pete with a character whose face was only covered in smudges of soot collected while bringing gifts through the chimney.

"This is a beautiful, historic day," said a leader of the Kick Out Zwarte Piet movement. But he vowed that the effort would continue until the Netherlands was Zwarte Piet free. "Where Zwarte Piet is still there, we will fight for change."[4] Two months later, pro and anti Zwarte Piet demonstrations took place in Den Bosch, followed by Zwarte Piet songs sung to ridicule the playing of a Black player of the Dutch Football Association. The player left the nationally televised game, which was temporarily stopped.

In June 2020, the Netherlands began an examination of its own history in reaction to protests against "institutionalized racism" within the United States. American demonstrations in response to the death of an African American, George Floyd, at the hands of Minneapolis police had spread to European cities including Amsterdam and Rotterdam, then become a matter of debate in the Dutch parliament. Prime Minister Mark Rutte, who had earlier in the year apologized on behalf of the nation for the Dutch role in the Holocaust, admitted to a qualified change in his own opinion about Zwarte Piet.

For his own part, he said, Black Pete had always been a Sinterklaas character who was simply Black, and without special meaning. But he had increasingly spoken with those who felt personally discriminated against by the use of the cultural figure, who, he agreed, could be attributed to "structural racism" that existed in the country. He would not be anxious, however, to involve the government in removing Black Pete from Dutch life, but preferred to leave it to cultural influences over time.[5]

The middle ground journey of Zwarte Piet through the attitudes, perceptions and beliefs of the Dutch people might describe the adult experiences of the children of the Zwarte Bevrijders, the Black American liberators, since coming of age in the 1950s and early 1960s. For many, they were present, but not entirely so. Their identities were confused. Some struggled for most of their lives, and most would look for their fathers, or whatever they could at least learn about their own identities, with varying degrees of success.

For Maria Andres, childhood would seem a relentless trial. After the encounter with Krampus, she was moved to a home on a farm where she was kept barefoot with two other Black children. She received no schooling, was put to work on the farm, and she was awakened each morning by an older white boy who treated her roughly. Then, as was part of the German effort to deal with the Brown Babies, she was evidently advertised for adoption in a magazine and taken in by a childless couple in the Netherlands. As she would understand in adulthood, the adoption, which was formalized in 1954, was to make a point within a Dutch-German family that had been split by the war. The grandfather of the family was a German historian and had been a Nazi sympathizer. The grandmother did not understand how her son could have adopted a colored child. It would eventually occur to Maria that the adoption had been intentionally provocative.

Her adoptive parents were Dutch intellectuals and for some years she lived in Sweden, where her mother was a university professor and she was treated well by others, but she understood that to be more as a curiosity than the person that she was. When they returned to the Netherlands at her age of nine years she attended Montessori schools in Bilthoven and Oostburg, but there she was made to sit at the back of the classroom though she had obvious trouble with her eyes, incurred upon birth from her mother's venereal disease, and could not see well. At that age she had begun to seek out a social life for herself and to look for people who looked like her, but those she found, Ambon Moluccans from Indonesia, would have nothing to do with her.

In adulthood, Maria would not lose the child's need to find people like herself. Zwarte Piet would stay with her, but she would remember him as a kind of betrayal. The Zwarte Piet she had known in the Netherlands had not been nearly as frightening as Krampus in Germany. And he had looked like her—until at some point she had realized that he was only a white person wearing a blackface that could be wiped away.

Then, when her body began to change, the stepfather she had come to love began to molest her "so you can get used to it for when you do it for real." She stayed away from home as much as she could, and she was eventually placed in an expensive boarding school. As her adoptive parents receded from her life, she began to think about who her real parents might be. She was fifteen years old.

Like Maria, Wanda van der Kleij would not fully recover from the sexual abuse suffered at the hands of her stepfather, and his admonition that her blackness made her unworthy of education and training put her further adrift. She became married and gave birth to a daughter, Birgitte. As Birgitte grew, she began to ask about a grandfather, but Wanda had nothing to offer. It wasn't until her mother and stepfather divorced in 1985, that Wanda was told briefly that she was "of an American," but her mother would say no more than that. The women had never been close and became less so after that.

Nothing seemed to be right. Birgitte became an unwed mother herself, much to her grandmother's anger. Wanda would be married and divorced, then married and widowed. Despite occasional stretches of therapy, she could not overcome a restless nature, but perhaps best grounded herself in volunteer advocacy for the interests of the physically and mentally disabled. It would not be until the chance meeting with the daughter of Rosy Peters at a Maastricht bus stop that her life would take on a firm bearing.

Rosy and Wanda had sexual abuse in common, but that was not all of it. Rosy had married in 1966 while already pregnant, but the pregnancy then ended in a miscarriage. Her husband could not be with her and the nuns took the dead child from her before she could resolve her situation. Four children followed, though a daughter moved away to the family of a friend at age thirteen. The home, a small apartment with six people, had been too unhappy for her. When Rosy focused on her work in home health care she was able to be happy, and the family eventually found a spacious, detached home near Maastricht. Her husband, Conny, had become a fairly successful popular musician with the group The Walkers, which had an international hit with the song "There's No More Corn on the Brazos," based on a prisoner song of the American South.

As the children drifted into their own lives, the large house seemed to become

Wanda van der Kleij with her daughter Birgitte, undated (courtesy Wanda van der Kleij).

Rosy Peters with her four children on the pond in the Schuttersveld neighborhood in Brunssum, undated (courtesy Rosy Peters).

darker. Financial security had come with her husband's success, but the cost was his long periods of absence. She could not overcome the memory and effect of her stepfather's abuse starting in young childhood. She was subject to anxiety attacks, became afraid of the dark and claustrophobic. She was not yet forty years old, and she attempted to kill herself.

Her nights in the psychiatric ward of Annadal Hospital in Maastricht were sleepless, but she developed a friendship with one of the night nurses, a kind man who talked with her quietly. He helped to bring her through the tunnel of her life at that moment, and into a new time in which she would try to understand the mystery that had always been with her: who was she, and who was her father.

The kind nurse had been Huub Schepers. Remarkably, however, he had not burdened her with his own very similar troubles. Huub had done well since his time at St. Joseph's Children's Home, but he had only buried his memories. Work in a Catholic nursing home set him on the career course that would eventually take him to meeting Netty, whose parents and nine brothers and sisters accepted him readily, giving him the first real family of his life, but reminding him painfully of the family he had come from.

By the law of the day, marriage under age 21 required the consent of both sets of parents. The intervention of a priest and social services

Netty Schepers with her three children with Huub Schepers, undated. Though she and Huub would divorce, she would care for him until the end of his life (courtesy Netty Schepers Wanders).

agency could not get the cooperation of Huub's estranged stepfather, and his mother could give him no moral support. He had to meet with her and burst into tears upon seeing her. She would only say "please don't blame me for anything." He would never see her again, and when she died Netty just happened to see her obituary in a newspaper. It mentioned as survivors the three children she and her husband had, but it did not mention Huub.

After the children were grown, and despite a happy marriage with Netty, the memories of St. Joseph eventually began to emerge and had the effect of nearly immobilizing his life. It was the time of the Deetman Report investigation into the sexual abuse of children in the Catholic church, and that gave him license to begin to talk about his experiences. He would be one of those whose grievances would be accepted and compensated, but by opening up his past he seemed only to fall deeper into its dark chasm. He could no longer live comfortably among other people. He and Netty were divorced, though she would care for him for the rest of his life. He was hospitalized in 2009, then moved to an assisted living home where he found the companionship of a service dog, Boedha, and some measure of peace in long bike rides by himself in the hills east of South Limburg.

Although he had spent only three months in Limburg performing the sad labor of the establishment of the Margraten cemetery, it would be Jefferson Wiggins who would set off a series of events that would bring about an enhanced quality of life for Huub Schepers and the others. Finally, well into the 21st century, they would become known to each other, to the rest of the country, and, in many respects, to their own selves in a new way.

As she had done for Wiggins before he went to war, Anne Marie Merrill of the Stapleton public library on Staten Island would help to set the course of his life in the years that followed the end of the war. The first day of his homecoming to the docks of New York City had been satisfying. In this city, he was a free man who had served honorably in a war that had properly ended. He could go about and ride the subways, held in the esteem due any other man who had survived those last few years.

> Then when I traveled back to my hometown in Alabama, as soon as we got into Washington, DC it started again. Here I am, a decorated military officer, one who had helped to bury almost 20,000 people, and on the train I was riding I saw a sign that said the front of the train (the sootiest part) was for Blacks and the back of the train was for whites.
>
> What had I done to deserve all this? What would these 20,000 dead that we buried, what would they think if they could speak? It was very devastating to me.[6]

Finally home in Dothan, Alabama, he found that the German prisoners of war who had been shipped inland but not imprisoned were allowed to ride in the front of the city buses while he was still relegated to the back. He felt, and he saw the feeling in others, that it was a situation that was once accepted but was now ready to explode. He returned to New York and sought out Mrs. Merrill, still on Staten Island. "What should I do? What should my task be now?" he asked.

Her response was a basic lesson in the equal rights espoused in the Bill of Rights of the United States Constitution.

> *"All men are created equal. They are endowed by their Creator with certain unalienable rights..."*
>
> And she said, "Ask yourself if this is what you really believe, if this is what your task should be and if this is not what your task should be. Then you must begin to understand that no changes will be made unless you make them."

To the last years of his life Jefferson Wiggins would think of Mrs. Merrill as an angel who had been sent to him at just the right time. He had said that to her once in a little Italian restaurant on Staten Island, and she had leaned over the table to say "Whatever you think I am, that is exactly what I am." The moment would stay with him through the following decades.

He wanted to be a teacher, but after four years of college he was turned down by the schools in Dothan. He thought that, given his experience in the war and his determination to be educated, they were probably afraid of him. Instead, he was hired by the Veterans Administration to teach in a school meant to give another chance to mostly Black high school dropouts. His career eventually took him to New Jersey and Connecticut where his contribution to education would lead to a statewide day declared in his honor in 2005.

The career was activist in equal rights and multicultural education. It came to Wiggins, and many other Black men returning from service, that the first step in asserting their rights to equal treatment was to start to believe and act as if they expected and were due those rights, and in no less a measure than any white man. Wiggins was alarmed, however, at what he saw as an inclination toward violence in that pursuit. He had seen enough of that in the war, and, instead, he joined with those who saw the core of the problem as the suppression of voting. Those who voted determined what would happen and gave their consent to those with bad intentions. Those who could not vote had no power of consent.

Legally enforced voting rights in the United States would eventually come to pass in fits and starts, but they would always remain in need of support and reaffirmation, and well into the 21st century. Not long after the conclusion of World War II, however, the U.S. military began a process to move away from its historic segregation of forces. It had turned out that the necessary policy near the war's end of converting Black soldiers from quartermaster duties to platoons that would fight alongside white platoons had had some effect on attitudes. In mid–1945, the Research Branch Information and Education Division of the European Theatre conducted a survey of white officers and sergeants on their attitudes about the Black rifle platoons. The group had been initially opposed to the platoons by a margin of two to one, but after their work with the soldiers three-quarters of those surveyed were more favorable to the policy. Both groups agreed that they had worked well together.[7] Similar results came from groups of enlisted soldiers.

The changed attitudes, however, had not evolved into full integration. Majorities of white officers and soldiers would welcome working *alongside* Black platoons, but only a very small number would accept full integration. It would be President Harry Truman who would take the final steps to end the policies of military segregation that had so hobbled the effort of World War II. In 1946, he created the President's Commission on Civil Rights with the directive that it recommend "more adequate means and procedures for the protection of the civil rights of the people of the United States."[8]

Those recommendations included laws against lynching and poll taxes, which restricted voting, and the creation of a civil rights division of the Department of Justice. They would eventually lead to Executive Order 9981 directing the end of all segregation in the U.S. military. As with voting rights, the effect of the order would be both positive and not always consistent, but by the end of the century the military would be seen as a good model for what could occur in the larger society.

For Jefferson Wiggins the mission was clear. The Black man had gone into the countries of Europe to liberate the people (and bury the dead); now it was time to go into their own country to liberate themselves. One Sunday morning in 1955 his mother awoke him before dawn and demanded that he drive her the ninety miles to Montgomery so that she could hear a new preacher she had been told about. Wiggins resisted; he had heard enough speeches during these years of anticipated change. But this would be Martin Luther King, Jr., and the church was full to overflowing.

> I think I expected too much, expected to see an angel of some kind. But when the choir lowered its tone a little bit, Dr. King walked out and to me he was just an ordinary looking man, nothing special, kind of short, with a little bit of stomach, and I said to myself "So this is who I came to see and hear."[9]

Appropriately for Wiggins, King had chosen this morning to address Black veterans of the war. He acknowledged that they would be angry. They had seen death and destruction and fought against the evil of fascism, and any nation that would deny its people their basic rights was evil. But, he said, "Don't expect changes overnight. It takes time." He quoted from *Proverbs*.

> "There is a time and a place for everything." He was saying there is a time to kill and a time to refrain from killing, there is a time for joy and a time for sorrow.
>   At the end of all this, he said "Now is the time for your freedom. It is not going to be easy, it is not going to come overnight, it might not come in your lifetime, it might not come in my lifetime, but it will come." And it did.

Wiggins would continue to believe, and to live his life, in the steady and incremental moderation of progress that was envisioned in that statement. With his wife, Janice, he had created the Wiggins Institute for Social Integrity and the Wiggins Fund, programs and organizations that promoted multiculturalism, civil society and education for the disadvantaged. He had written two books. *White Cross, Black Crucifixion* resulted from his work as a director of community programs in New Jersey in the 1960s. *Another Generation Almost Forgotten*, in 2003, was an autobiography, but it had nothing to say about his time at Margraten, nor had he ever talked about those three months with anyone.

Then, in 2009, he received a phone call from the Netherlands that surprised and angered him with its effrontery, but which would open the door to a piece of history that the people of that country had forgotten about, or, more likely, not really known. That included those whose lives had been most effected by what had occurred when Black Americans had come to liberate their country.

TWELVE

Settling Lives

It suddenly felt like I belonged to something.—Huub
Schepers, 2015

Perhaps it was the Christmas Eve service at the church in Margraten
in which the people of the village and the American soldiers came together for the first time to hear the priest urge them to "Be stout of heart,
be courageous, be prayerful, my beloved..."

Or it might have been the moment when the American captain
Shomon came to the Dutch mayor, urgently. "Can you help us? We need
men. We need men with shovels. Can you issue a call to all able-bodied
men of Margraten to report to the cemetery at once?"

The common cause of the American cemetery, the men who had
built it, the men buried within it, the people of that part of Limburg, the
farmers who had sacrificed their good land to it and the families who
would watch over its graves through all of the seasons, years and decades
yet to come would make the Margraten cemetery a beloved place. Right
at the center of south Limburg, 7 miles from Maastricht and 13 miles
from Aachen, Germany at either end of Route NL 278 / 1 DE, it placed
a trapezium of rich, green grass and more than 8,000 white crosses and
Stars of David in the middle of very productive farmland that stretched
to all horizons. The hard-working village of Margraten sat just more than
a mile to the east.

It had certainly been the sacrifice that the buried and memorialized
Americans had made for them that made the cemetery a sacred place
within the region. The Memorial Day observance on May 30, 1946, had
been preceded by the appearance of twenty trucks holding flowers collected from sixty surrounding villages. At that time, the cemetery held
nearly 19,000 American and some other dead, including Germans yet to
be moved. Twice that number of Dutch citizens lined the roads and pathways to their graves. Many were dressed in their best clothes and some of

164

On the American Memorial Day, May 30, 1969, the American Cemetery at Margraten prepares to receive the Dutch and Belgian people who live in the countryside, villages and cities that surround it (National Archief of the Netherlands).

the men wore top hats out of respect. An international press covered the event, and airplanes flew overhead to gain the best photographs.[1]

The celebration of the American Memorial Day at Margraten would not fade away with the passing of postwar years. If anything, it became a more powerful annual touchstone with the liberation of Limburg into the next century. In 1945, a town clerk in Margraten had suggested that the citizens begin to adopt each grave so that it might be watched over and its occupant remembered. Eventually, the adopters were listed from throughout Limburg, Belgium and from Dutch residents in nearby Germany. Relationships were formed between the adopters and the American families of the dead, and adoptions were handed down from generation to generation. Seventy years later, all graves and the names on memorial walls were still adopted, with a waiting list of those who would take up any adoptions that might fall away with time.

In 2008, the realization occurred that those who had been associated with the creation of the cemetery in the mid–20th century were dying, and taking with them a vital part of Limburg history. With the support of the nation's Legacy of the War Heritage Program of the Ministry of Health, Welfare and Sport, the *Samenwerkende Heemkunde Organisities Margraten* (Association of Margraten Local History Organizations)

Dutch citizens observe the American Memorial Day at the Netherlands American Cemetery at Margraten, May 31, 1947 (National Archive of the Netherlands).

embarked on the oral history project *Akkers van Margraten* (*Fields of Margraten*). The project would talk with Limburg citizens, especially farmers, who had been present during the time, those who had played a role in the cemetery's construction, and some of the American soldiers who had been involved. The result would be the book *From Farmland to Soldiers Cemetery* by current author Mieke Kirkels and Jo Purnot, published in 2009. A television documentary, *Akkers van Margraten*, based on the project would follow in 2010.

As the oral history project began, and up until that time, there was little remembered and known about the role of African American soldiers in the liberation of Limburg. There was a memory that the cemetery's first graves had been dug by Black soldiers, but no records available to know much more than that. It was only by chance that the project was able to learn the name of the First Sergeant who had led a unit of the gravediggers, and eventually to find him in Connecticut.

Jefferson Wiggins was unsettled and angered by the call. He had never talked about his time at Margraten. His autobiography published in 2003 had barely touched on the struggle of existence in a segregated military. His wife, Janice, would later describe forty years of restless nights and frequent nightmares that he would not explain to her. The phone call from a stranger in the Netherlands was an unwelcome intrusion on his life, and he couldn't understand its motivation. "I can't believe that someone wants to know about this after so many years, that someone has questions about something that has never been talked about."[2]

He told Janice that he remembered being there when it was very cold. "But I think," she said, "the emotions came in layers and they were in a deep place right then. He was trying to deal with memories that came back and that were clearly not pleasant. I think he was resisting letting the memories come to the surface. He wanted to know about the project but was still very reluctant to let these memories express themselves." Eventually, he determined that the necessity to tell the story of what he and his fellow Black soldiers had had to do was paramount and he agreed to be interviewed. A documentary production crew that had already returned from interviews in America was sent out once again.

A few years later, Wiggins would learn about *Crosses in the Wind*, the book about the building of the cemetery by Capt. James Shomon, for the first time. Shomon had been a good man and a friend, but under the heading of *Negroes and Corpses* Wiggins read:

> They looked and looked; then suddenly a few made a break for the latrine. Back they came, however, and looked again. I heard one mutter, "Gruesome, ain't it? Sho' is gruesome. Ah can't stand working hyar. Ah's gonna dig graves. Yassuh, give me a shovel. You kin handle him. Ah's gonna dig graves."[3]

There was much that only Wiggins could describe about that time and place, and his place in the autobiography and documentary would bring new depth to the knowledge of what had occurred in Limburg. The publication of the book in 2009 took place on the occasion of the 65th anniversary of the Liberation of south Netherlands and a friendship that had developed between Wiggins and Mieke Kirkels led to an invitation to be part of the planned celebrations and memorials. He knew that it was something he needed to do, and he agreed to her suggestion that he give a speech during the event.

Wiggins had been a public person for much of his adult life and giving a speech would be nothing he wasn't used to. But this one was at first confounding. Janice watched over his anguish. "He started several months ahead of the speech and it was a very difficult process. The topic was very difficult. I think he was going back and forth between the burden of the memories and having to deal with those memories in order to talk about what happened there. He also was internalizing the fact that he had the responsibility to tell a story that no one else could tell. He felt the weight of that responsibility. He would write for maybe 15–20 minutes and would say, 'I can't do any more today.'"

His preparation for a return to the physical cemetery that had been hidden in his mind for all of those years was as deliberate and careful. Arriving in the Netherlands with Janice in September 2009, he was one of a number of Americans who would have their own reunion, but of them all he was the most sought after by the Dutch press. All of them would be engaged and thanked by officials and members of the public, but the story told nationally about the event seemed premised on this one Black man who had emerged from a book and video documentary of the time and returned to the place in which he had dug the graves of his fellow Americans.

Jefferson and Janice Wiggins had been to a few of the war cemeteries in Europe over the course of their marriage, but without acknowledgment by him of his own role in one they would not visit. It sat before him now, and Janice watched him pause and take a breath. "Okay, we are here," he said.

"Then, when we finally got to the graves," Janice remembered, "you could really feel him reacting. He was trying to take it all in. You just could imagine that all these memories were going through his head. It was raining a little bit and we got into the tent at the beginning to get out of the rain. There were photographers, a TV reporter was there, so there was a lot of activity. And all wanted to talk to him; it was just too much."

A friend who had joined them on the trip to watch out for his failing health cleared the tent. "I used to be a tough soldier," he said, "but I'm not anymore." After a respite, he went back out to talk with a television reporter, then asked Janice to just walk with him out into the graveyard of which he had turned the first earth.

His speech was given in Maastricht on September 11, 2009, excerpted:

> Sixty-five years ago, I was a nineteen-year-old farm boy who had never been more than three miles from the cotton fields of my home in Alabama. I had never seen more than one death in my life—that was the death of my sister, who died at age eleven.
>
> I remember very vividly that she was dressed in her Sunday best.
>
> The people who came to mourn her death were friends and neighbors. They all

Jefferson Wiggins (*center*) returned to Margraten in 2009 with his wife Janice Wiggins (*left*) and retired German Gen. Egon Ramms (*right*), then Commander of the NATO Allied Joint Forces Command, Brunssum (NL) (U.S. Army).

agreed that her passing was tragic because at age eleven that was too much, much too soon.

The brave soldiers that we laid to rest here at Margraten were a little older than eleven, but we can all agree that their passing was also much too soon.

I recall that Friday morning long ago when we disembarked from the Army vehicles, looked out across the plains of Margraten and saw the vehicles loaded with the dead.

It shook me that these dead had no friends or relatives here to mourn their passing. There were no relatives, no friends who would stand at the graveside and say a final "goodbye."

There were only two hundred sixty African American soldiers whose sole task it was to bring some dignity and some respect and to say, inaudibly, "goodbye."

We had been commanded to give respect to those we could not even associate with in life.

But on that first day, we realized that whatever life experiences we'd had as African Americans, this was our obligation—to set aside our prejudices, our colors, and our fears and give to these young Americans the honor, the respect and the dignity that they so well deserved.

———

It seemed to me that everyone in the little country church where my sister was eulogized and buried was in tears. But who was there to weep and to mourn each of the soldiers we laid to rest?

It seemed as if the trucks bringing in the dead were always one step ahead of our ability to dig their graves and to give them the proper burial that they so much deserved.

After several days, someone said, "Don't worry, you'll get used to it."

What a cavalier attitude that was!

We never got used to it. And sixty-five years later, it still boggles our minds. We were Black Americans, detailed to bury white Americans. But in our lifetime, we couldn't eat in the same mess hall or go to the same social clubs. And yet, we could bury them.

In life, we couldn't associate with them. The ultimate irony was that in their most sacred moment—the moment of death—we were given the most sacred task.

———

War affects all of us and it occurs to me that we all have a role to play in a conflict of the magnitude of World War II.

The people of the Netherlands—especially those in Margraten and Maastricht—know this all too well. When the dead were buried, we, as soldiers, went on to other duties and we finally went home.

But the twenty thousand [in 1945] who were buried in the Netherlands remained.

Who was it that took on the responsibility of managing such a huge cemetery?

Who took on the task of remembering those who had given their lives to a cause that was intended to give us all our freedom?

The people of the Netherlands took on that task.

So I believe we owe a debt of gratitude, especially to the people of the Margraten area who, each year place flowers on these graves. In doing so, they say, in effect, "Thank you. We remember you and we honor you."

And I say, to these gallant people who care for these graves, "Thank you. We respect you and we honor you."[4]

The September trip to Margraten had been preceded by an August letter to Wiggins from American President Barack Obama. It had come about at the suggestion of Connecticut congressman Chris Murphy and was meant to be the acknowledgment by a president of the extraordinary contribution of a citizen who was, in this case, about to represent a piece of little-known American history in a foreign country.

"As a veteran," said Obama, "you were part of great milestones in our Nation's history. Your generation stood for the triumph of freedom and liberty over hatred and intolerance, and your story is an important piece of the American narrative."[5]

The letter was not a direct reference to the particular aspect of racial history that had been manifest in Wiggins' experience of the war, but it was perhaps a marker of the beginning of a new contribution on his part. The speech in Maastricht had gone on to conclude with the hope that the experience of 65 years previous would help to prevent a similar experience 65 years hence, that bridges would be built "that span the chasms of hate, prejudice and misunderstanding. Sixty-five years from now we should be able to look back on these events and know that it is, indeed, possible to live in a world free of violence."

The speech had also been firm and assertive in describing the circumstances and effect of American military racism in World War II, and when Wiggins returned home he determined that he could not let the subject go. Indeed, as far as he knew he was the only member of the 960th Quartermaster Service Company left to tell the story of its work at Margraten and the racial context in which it took place. The liberation commemorations had placed him in the Dutch public eye, and a friendship with author Mieke Kirkels had been formed. The two of them then set out to produce a book about the creation of the Margraten cemetery in the context of his life and experience. *Van Alabama naar Margraten* (*From Alabama to Margraten*) was published in the Netherlands in 2014.

"Jeff placed a high priority on completing this book," wrote Janice Wiggins in the introduction, "ensuring that history recorded the contribution of his company at Margraten, a record written from the perspective of one of their own." She noted that his health had not lasted through the completion of the work. He had died on January 9, 2013. Then, in the years since his death, his experience resounded in her own. His return to Margraten, and the repeated retelling of the story to interested audiences had seemed to diminish his ability to experience joy and his personality had changed. The emotional burden had become part of her own memory of their many years together until she was eventually able to put it back into its proper proportion within their lives and a marriage well-lived.

For Huub Schepers and others, *Van Alabama naar Margraten* was the first complete and written explanation of their blackness in a white society. It was an explanation of who their fathers were, why they had been there, and what their experience had been.

Schepers sought out author Mieke Kirkels at a book signing and took her hand. "My father was a Black soldier," he said. "I am so happy with your book. I looked for information about my biological father for such a long time."

Kirkels would subsequently be sought out by others of the children, now in their seventies. But it would be Huub Schepers who would offer them the example of how they could unlock the mysteries of their lives and affirm the efforts by some to solve the ultimate mystery of a father's identity. His story was told in an article in the national newspaper *de Volkskrant* under the headline "The Battered Life of a Liberation Child."

As told, the story was both happy and profoundly sad. "It suddenly felt like I belonged to something," he said of the Wiggins book. "Something opened inside. One of those boys could have been my father."[6] But the words came from a man described as brittle in appearance and living in the shelter of a care home in Gulpen with an emergency call button in his living room. "His tongue is Limburgish, his skin is dark and he has frizzy hair."

Netty was still a presence in his life, still caring for him at a distance and helping the reporter to understand. She had left him because she could not get close to him, but she was still there as close as she could get. The story of his time at the Saint Joseph Home was retold more darkly. He had been forced to spend hours on his knees with his hands in the air, forced to eat salt bread, to brush the floors with a toothbrush. His pants would be pulled down as a prelude to punishment. His long-term escape from all of that had been to become a nurse. The patient was now the vulnerable one. "They ask for help from you, nothing else. I also liked that."

And now, said the article, he might finally gain some resolution. "Huub Schepers would now like to find out who his father was. He believes he is really ready."

Van Alabama naar Margraten had also been a revelation to Ed Moody, and the *de Volkskrant* article compounded the effect. He had not known about the segregation of the American army during the war and it was difficult for him to comprehend. He sought out Huub Schepers and the two began a friendship. They had more than their African American fathers in common. Huub had been a child in Saint Joseph, but Ed had been

Huub Schepers, seen at Margraten in 2015, would become the central figure in the forming of community of the adult children of African American liberators in Limburg (courtesy Johannes Timmermans).

an employee there years later and late in his working life. He had seen the basement "prison cells" and "thought certainly that horrible things must have taken place" within them. Huub confirmed his imagination.

Ed had lived a good life. After his years a boy musician, he had married Annie Grotheus in 1967, then sought and received full Dutch citizenship just in time for the birth of a son, Richard. Grandmother Lenie Wetzel helped to care for him. She had not remarried, and when the occasion arose it became necessary for her to seek a divorce from Edward Moody in the United States, but he had disappeared from view. He had moved on from the address attached to his letter of many years earlier asking if Ed could visit him in America. Ads were placed in newspapers where he had lived in New Jersey, but he could not be found. After a period, he was declared legally missing and Lenie was allowed to marry.

As an adult, Ed was a successful upholsterer and, as in his childhood, his obvious biracial nature was never a problem. When he turned forty, his daughter Esther began to search the internet for the whereabouts of her grandfather as a gift to her father, but Ed was not happy with the effort. He did not feel the need to know any more than he already knew, and he thought of his father's possible predicament. He may have been married, and the information could be damaging to his American family.

Ed's dilemma was ultimately no different from that of most of the other liberation children of the Netherlands, Black or white. He had always wanted his father to seek *him* out. Whether it was expressed or hidden, he was left incomplete by the father's failure to do so.

Upon the fiftieth anniversary celebration of the full liberation of the Netherlands in 1995, Esther began again to search for Edward Moody. This time she found his address and called the related phone number. The call was answered by his widow, Bessy. She had always known of his child in the Netherlands and she received the call graciously. Edward had had a successful career as a truck driver, a son who had preceded him in death and a daughter who was semi-estranged from the family. Esther formed a good relationship with Edward's stepdaughter, but it ended with her unexpected death. Ed regretted that he had not looked for his father years earlier. The discovery of his death had seemed abruptly final.

By the time of Ed's reading of *Van Alabama naar Margraten* and his new friendship with Huub Schepers, he and Annie had five grandchildren. The identity of their grandfather was well known to them and a point of pride. All were regular visitors to the Margraten cemetery, and they had adopted the grave of a Jacob G. Moody, a white soldier from Arkansas.

The friendship of Huub Schepers and Ed Moody would become the core of the experience going forward of the known Limburg adult children

Huub Schepers (*left*) and Ed Moody (*right*) meet for the first time at Margraten on May 19, 2015. Author Mieke Kirkels sits between them (courtesy Johannes Timmermans).

of the African American soldiers of World War II. The article about it in *Dagblad de Limburger*, in turn, led to the creation of the oral history project that is the basis of this book and became a social exchange for those involved.

Rosy Peters' attempted suicide had been followed years later by a move to Spain with her husband, Conny, and a determination on her part to know her father's identity. Her first effort took her to Surinam in search of a man who had once been legally designated as her father, but who, it would turn out, was not actually so. Then, finally, when she was fifty years old her mother, Roos, took her aside privately to tell her about the Black American soldier who had grabbed her in the woods. Implying that she may have known his identity, she said that she did not remember his name, and she would say no more than that. She died in 2002. Rosy was at least relieved and happy that she had been a child of the liberation rather than a child of the war.

In 2015, Rosy's daughter Maureen was approached by a co-worker who speculated that she must have received her noticeable tan during a visit with her mother in Spain. Maureen was not shy about her origins and told the man matter-of-factly that she was the granddaughter of a Black American soldier. The co-worker referred her to the article about Huub Schepers in *de Volkskrant* and Maureen sent it to Spain. Her mother asked that she immediately get in touch with Schepers, and it was only then that Rosy learned that he had been the nurse who had held her hand through the long nights of hospitalization. They would meet again in October 2015, and she asked him why he had withheld his own story from her. "I felt I should not burden you with my problems," he said. "I was there to help you."

Then, the line of connection would extend through the bus stop in Maastricht when Maureen came across Wanda van der Kleij and put the two older women together, bringing Wanda into the oral history project.

She, too, had never given up on learning more about her father. She knew that his name was Edward Brown, and she had talked with a neighbor of her mother who had seen him during the liberation years. "Your father looked exactly like you," she said, "but with a moustache. He had

a slight build and was not very dark." At one point in 2001, Wanda enlisted the help of a "Quest for Fathers" feature of *Dagblad De Limburger*, but he would never be found.

It was the comment made decades earlier that schoolmates Petra and Robert Joosten would probably marry because of their similar skin colors that brought them both into the fold in 2015. Another child from the school who had been a friend of Petra's was made curious about that time by the Schepers article and looked through old photographs to find a picture of Joosten. He emailed it to Petra, but the two old friends did not know what had become of him. That would not be learned until after Schepers' death.

After Toos had died,

The friendship formed after a chance meeting by Wanda van der Kleij (*left*) and Rosy Peters (*right*) became part of the larger forming of community among the adult children of African American liberators of World War II (courtesy Rosy Peters).

Petra had looked all over the house for whatever else she could find about her father, but to no avail. With the help of a cousin, however, she had already learned his address in Chicago, but she was reluctant to intrude on his life. Her need to know more about him seemed unavoidable, however, and she turned to her stepfather. They were close, and at one point he told her that if Jimmy Harbut had come back he would be able to give up Toos, but not to give up her child. She replied that her own children had always seen him as their real grandfather. But he could offer her no more information.

Finally, she wrote a short note to Harbut saying that she was a villager who wanted to know more about his experience and that she would be calling. Later, fortified by brandy, she dialed the number in America and the woman who answered, upon hearing "Netherlands," immediately handed him the phone. They talked generally about his time in Limburg, but when she mentioned names, including her mother's, he could not remember it. He was now in his nineties. As promised, she called him again a few weeks later. She got the impression that his wife was not happy with the call, and the conversation she had with Harbut was brief. She sent him a Christmas card, but without a response. They had not yet broached the subject of their relationship, and they would not talk again. He died in Bowie, Maryland, in December 2015.

In the following year, research for the Dutch version of this book led to the discovery of a niece in Chicago who was happy to be helpful to a child that the American family had known nothing about. Cynthia had the same pictures of Jimmy Harbut as had been given to Petra by her mother. The two were able to talk over the internet and to develop a friendship. Petra was relieved to learn that Jimmy had been divorced when he met her mother, a fact that was important to her. Cynthia had known her uncle well, but she set out to learn more about him on Petra's behalf. His inability to remember her mother may have been due to his age and infirmity— he lived in a wheelchair and required constant care—but it may have been because after he returned from the war, he and his new wife were not able to conceive a child.

They had met in a Chicago church choir and lived in a nice apartment in the comfortable African American neighborhood of Chatham. He had worked in a toy factory and as a public-school janitor, was a good cook and kept a neat garden. He had always made Cynthia feel special, and he loved his Buick automobiles, first a Wildcat and then an Electra 225. He was a volunteer at church and contributor to its community charities. His daughter from his first marriage, Priscilla, had died in 2012, however, leaving him with two grandchildren whom he barely knew.

Like Petra, Huub Habets had been blessed with a stepfather who was unflinching in devotion to the child who was not his own, but he, too, had always felt incomplete. He was a quiet, trim man with a smile that seemed to welcome anyone and anything. His wife, Evelyn, often compensated for his shy nature and, upon reading the article about Huub Schepers and Ed Moody in *Dagblad de Limburger*, she urged him both to join the oral history project and to look for his real father.

After public school, Huub had wanted to go to art school but could not afford it and ended up in a vocational school that led him to work as a mechanical fitter, eventually to a career with the technical services company *Imtech*. He had two children from a previous marriage, and one from his more than 40-year marriage to Evelien. In their final years, Huub had tried to open the subject of his father with his parents, but his mother could no longer communicate, and his stepfather fell silent, while indicating to Huub at the same time that the question would not affect his love for the younger man. At one point, Huub considered and passed on an attempt to go to America to see what he could find. He had looked at the racial discrimination that was visible there and decided that, as a Black person, his travels would not be safe.

Of all of the known Limburg children of the African American soldiers, it would be Cor Linssen who would come to know America professionally and well. The spirit of his mother's good natured introduction of her children and "our Huub, our Jo, my Cor, our Herman" was carried

Huub Habets in 2015 (courtesy Paul Koenen).

through a childhood in which he had always been the different child in the village, the school or the family, but never unhappily so and often as a point of pride. As he got older, he questioned the difference, but his parents would not address it with him. Eventually, he took on the role of speaking up on their behalf when questioned about their dark son by parrying the question with his own sense of humor.

But Cor was destined to move out into the larger world, and it was in coming to know African Americans in the Netherlands postwar that he began to understand himself through a job with one of his brothers at a bar in Roermond that was used by members of the U.S. Air Force Central Command in Brunssum. That led to an interest in the hospitality industry and he was easily hired by the Holland America steamship company where his outgoing nature and countenance made him popular with passengers. One time, he received a hundred-dollar tip from a woman who thanked him for his "million-dollar smile."

He had never had reason to be aware of racism, but his experiences with an international work force and travels to the port cities of America gave him an education. He had once been reprimanded for a perceived racial slight against an Indonesian co-worker. He had not even known enough to intend the slight, but he learned about racial sensitivity. Once, when the ship stopped in Savannah, Georgia, he was advised to not to go ashore and face the reaction he might find there. He had not been aware that there would be a problem for him in America and he went ashore in any case. There, his only confrontation was with another Black man. While waiting in a cashier's line he let an elderly white woman go in front of him. The Black man behind him told him forcefully "That was not done."

"Where I come from," he told the man, "we do let older people go ahead of us."

It was not until age fifty that Cor began to think seriously about his American father. His mother would say nothing about it and a former neighbor could only tell him that he had been "a gorgeous, dark, tall man who was visiting your place at Knevelgraafstraat day in and day out." At one point, he thought of approaching the Dutch television program *Spoorloos* (*Without a Trace*) which searched for lost family, but his mother told him "If you do so, I'll jump out the window."

Cor eventually came ashore to work as a caterer. He and his partner, Truus, each had two children from earlier marriages. At the age of seventy, he began to feel overly tired and not well. He was diagnosed with sickle cell anemia, a particular disease of African American families, but remained stabilized in the following years.

Donna Bastiaans would become part of the social group that resulted from the newspaper articles about Huub Schepers and Ed Moody. Her

Cor Linssen in retirement from a life that took him all over the world with the Holland America Line, then into hospitality and catering (courtesy Hans Heijnen).

unsettled life as a young woman would never quite change. She had lived for a time with a man of color she had met in Belgium who became the father of her son, Hamady. The mother and child eventually moved to Spain where she married the man who would give Hamady his last name of Aguilar.

Hamady grew up with the constant tension between his mother and grandmother over the older woman's refusal to wait for the return of her father, Adolphus Graves. Donna's experience as a young woman had caused her to move from Maastricht to Liege where her color was not as much as an issue, but Hamady's experience as a young man had been a good one with multiracial friends in the social life of Maastricht. Donna had raised him on the low wages of a seamstress or domestic worker. In retirement, she sometimes still had to deal with a restlessness, which could best be addressed by driving alone in the Belgian Ardennes. "I come back very quiet and relaxed from a trip like that."

The regret about the lack of her father was always in the background of her life. By 2020, Hamady, a mechanical engineer, was the father of a five year old son, and Donna had suffered setbacks in her health. She continued to live with a prominently placed photograph of Adolphus Graves.

Upon the death of Huub Schepers, his memorial service brought together a number of the children and included Trudy Habets. She had often wondered why more was not known about the African American liberators who had come to Limburg.

After a particularly difficult childhood centered around the Catholic Institute for Girls, she took a job as a live-in housemaid with a couple in Schaesburg. The Lamers treated her respectfully and supported her ambitions by allowing her to attend evening classes in a fashion design school. And they helped to get her out from under the jurisdiction of Child Services and the Catholic home. She did not stay with the fashion school, but she was able to reach an autonomous adulthood with the Lamers' help and would stay in touch with them throughout their lives. At age twenty-one, she married a man who had been born in Belgium of an African American father, but the marriage failed. She had a son with a man in Germany in 1973, and the two of them moved to Weert to be near her once estranged mother, Maria, with whom she hoped to reconcile.

Starting in the 1980s, Trudy Habets became a community activist and volunteer worker in social and educational agencies in and around Weert. In the Netherlands, recognition of extraordinary contribution is often given in the form of Knighthood as an award for valor. In 2014, Trudy received a knighthood from the Dutch King, awarded by the mayor of Weert, Joseph Heijmans (courtesy Marjo Daniels).

But Maria died in 1980 and Trudy was not able to make friends with others. Her loneliness was compounded by the hostility she found in those around her. She was once yelled at on the street: "Go back to where you came from." Eventually, she came into contact with members of the Dutch Antilles community in the town and would travel to Aruba frequently later in life. She returned to school to study social work at a time of the positive discrimination (affirmative action) movement in the Netherlands, but it was still difficult to find lasting work. She sometimes felt that she was either too Black or too white depending in the nature of a given job, and eventually became a teacher of social work.

Robert Joosten with his friend, the Dutch comedienne, singer and television actress Adèle Bloemendaal, for whom he was a caretaker in the last years of her life. She called him "The Negro with a soft 'g,'" a reference to his Limburg accent (courtesy Robert Joosten).

Late in the 1980s, however, she became a member of the Emancipation Committee for Equal Rights and Treatment of the Weert municipal government and would receive a knighthood from the mayor of the city in 2014, an award for extraordinary civic engagement. Over those years, she raised four children with her partner Jan Janssen. In retirement she became a Dutch language teacher in the immigrant community.

Robert Joosten had been the only one of the Limburg children who had moved out of the province over the years, and would first be exposed to the information about the Black liberators that had emerged from the lives of Jefferson Wiggins and Huub Schepers through an obituary for Schepers in a Rotterdam newspaper. After a childhood spent watching out for his mother's safety he had, like many of the others, headed first to a career in nursing. Life events had then taken him to Rotterdam where he studied at the Rotterdam Dance Academy, then on to Amsterdam as a member of the traveling youth-centered Scapino ballet. As an adult, and with his husband, he became an integral member of the Amsterdam theater community.

The obituary of Huub Schepers that had drawn Joosten into the fold of the adult children of the Black liberators in Limburg was also published in the national newspaper *NRC Handelsblad*. Written by reporter Paul van der Steen, it was as much a traditional obituary as it was the telling of a story that had played out just beneath the veneer of Dutch society since the middle of the previous century.

His mother could have slept with the Black Americans soldier "out of warm feelings or out of financial need." One could not know the true answer. The sexual abuse as "punishment" at Saint Joseph may have been intended as punishment for the color of his skin. Thoughts of suicide as a teenager had given way to a countenance of peace and softness that had brought him through marriage to a large, accepting family and a father-in-law who simply explained to others that he had been "baked a little longer than other people."[7]

But he and his wife had had to face discrimination that refused to rent them homes and slashed bicycle tires. Despite everything, he had become a psychiatric nurse. His wife remembered that some of his patients would even come to their door to thank him for his help, though he could express no feeling within his own home and fell to a reliance on alcohol. It could only be the Deetman Report that could begin to set him free, and the story of Jefferson Wiggins that had made him the catalyst of the finding of community among the other children. They had had their first meeting in the International Museum for Family History in Eijsden "I finally have brothers and sisters," he had said afterward. A month later, to the day, his new family would conduct a memorial service for him in the same place.

As he lay beneath the American flag, his ex-wife quoted from a Dutch translation of the *I Have a Dream* speech given by Martin Luther King, Jr., in 1963.

"Finally free! Finally free! Thank God almighty, we are finally free!"

THIRTEEN

International Families

I wish he'd known me. I really wish.—Maria Andres,
2019

The principles of Gestalt had risen out of the work of 19th century European and English philosophers and psychologists and been formulated into an understanding of the conditions of human perception by German psychologists in the early 20th century. It held, among other things, that the human inclination was to perceive a whole that was more than the actual sum of its parts. Thus, when trying to understand and deal with one's life, it was necessary to be aware of its conditions in the "here and now," and to see it in its actual and current parts, rather than allowing it to be perceived as a result of what Gestalt called The Law of Closure.

The Law of Closure held that when looking at parts of a thing, like the arcs of a broken circle, the mind filled in the gaps and completed the thing. Based on its life experience of perceiving and applying full circles, the mind was habituated to see them even if they were not really there. The task of Gestalt therapy was to perceive reality correctly and productively. If life was perceived as chaotic in some way, it was necessary to see it in its actual and disconnected parts, and to see it in the here and now rather than past and future.

Maria Andres would spend her life trying to calm its chaos, to find the real parts of her family and to form them into a completed circle. And as a child with a complicated and difficult life, she had always been subject to the psychological theories, practices and dictates of others. "How frightening it is," she thought "that your psyche is filled with unsolicited [diagnoses]." As a young woman, she was drawn to the study of Gestalt theory, and would become a practicing Gestalt therapist in the city of Groningen until 2006, when she would move on once again, as she had repeatedly since the sexual abuse committed against her by her once trusted stepfather.

The boarding school had removed her from that problem, but replaced it with another. She was different, and she had a German name, so she was bullied and without friends. Virtually alone at age 15, she decided to look for the mother that she had not even been able to approach after her adoption. It was then that she learned that her mother Sofie and her half-sister Christine had moved to New York in 1954. Then, a half-brother, Nikolaus, had been born in 1956. Maria wrote to Sofie and asked if she might visit her in New York, but the reply was that she should stay away. An unstated reason may have been that Sofie's German passport had not mentioned the two children she was leaving behind when she fled Germany, and she did not want that known. In a letter, she told Maria not to tell anyone of their relationship. After a few more letters back and forth, correspondence stopped.

Eventually, Maria formed a relationship with a Dutch air force sergeant. Marriage would be a way of moving on in her life and changing her Germanic last name, always a problem for her, and to get a Dutch passport, but the law requiring parental permission before age twenty-one was a roadblock. Her now estranged stepparents would have to be brought back into her life, but then it was realized that the lack of adoption law in the Netherlands would not allow them to give their permission based on an adoption that had taken place in Germany. And, far beyond the law on the matter, Maria would understand many years later that the damage done to her by her stepfather had always been a burden on her relationships with men. In childhood sexual abuse, she said "you did not know what was going on. And of course you have sexual feelings. Of course. And you don't know what is right and what is wrong."

The marriage took place when she became of legal age and the couple moved to Beekbergen in the province of Gelderland where the first of two sons was born. It was the time of the beginning in the western world of the counterculture movement that would bring revolutionary change to civil and women's rights, human sexuality and the use of drugs. A challenge was put to the traditionally established rules and norms of the way people should live, the authority of governments and the interaction of nations and cultures. The so-called "hippy movement" of the 1960s could trace its origins back to Western Europe at the turn of the century, and particularly to the *Lebensreform* era in Germany and Switzerland that had moved toward a return to naturalism in the way one went about one's life, and a veering away from the strictures and dogmas of religion and increasing industrialization.

By some interpretations, the more extreme strains of lebensreform had been corrupted into the rise of Naziism in Germany. Maria had then been born of its defeat and now, as a young adult she would be carried away by its evolution into the hippy movement of the United States as it spread back to the young people of Western Europe. She and her husband entered the hippy community of Sloten in Friesland province. "I loved the hippies. It gave me some freedom. Of course it did. It was an escape for me."

But she was the only Black girl in that small society. "It was strange. I bluffed it out until I could not bluff it out anymore. Of course I was different. Even in the hippy culture I was an exotic." When the community was joined by émigrés from the Dutch Antilles her skin color became more normal. Then, they too, began to treat her as different. "Even those Caribbean people, they said to me 'You have no tribe.' And it hurts." A hitch-hiking trip with friends during this time, down through Spain and across the Mediterranean to the African continent would offer no further help. A second son was born in 1970, but the marriage was failing and her husband's problems with drugs and alcohol were ended with his suicide and the destruction by fire of the boat on which they had lived. The fire took most of the papers that she had been able to accumulate as carriers of her identity.

Maria's next recovery would take her to the study of Gestalt as she worked in social and economic welfare organizations in Groningen and Assen. Her practice as a therapist was opened with a partner, then closed with the partner's subsequent death. But her attempts to know the parts of her origins that would close the circle of her life would only go into abeyance until the final efforts of the adult children to find their fathers in 2015–2016.

Of all of the children, Els Geijselaers would be the most quietly persistent and ultimately successful in closing the circle with her father. That had to do with the woman she became, the son she had raised in Berg en Terblijt and the family he had created in turn. Most certainly, it was the result of the very nature of her father, Henry Van Landingham, and of the nature of the family that surrounded him in America. And the full story of it was physically centered in the marl caves of the hamlet of Geulhem, just as they had been in the history of the Valkenburg region of Limburg for centuries.

By the time of World War II, the corridor system connecting the caves that had been dug out of the sandstone beneath the hills that looked toward Maastricht to the west approximated fifteen miles in length. The recorded history of Berg en Terblijt dated back to the Early Middle Ages, and the caves—the *Geulhemmergroeve*—evolved out of the mining of sandstone for the buildings of the region beginning in the 16th century. As they expanded, they kept track with the course of history that surrounded them.

The French Revolutionary Wars of 1789–99 had brought Limburg under French domination as part of the Batavian Republic. It would create a generally benevolent relationship between the French and the Dutch, and a time of modernization for Dutch governance. But changes in the authority of the church, and the unwillingness of many clergy to pledge allegiance to French rule led to the creation of a chapel deep within the caves as a place of refuge and hidden rituals.

As they were mined, the caves yielded the fossils of dinosaurs and sea creatures and were converted to homes and businesses. By the turn of the 20th century, they were popular with tourists from all parts of Europe. Rock dwellings built into the caves were rented at very minimal cost into the 1930s. Then came World War II, and the cave systems throughout the Maastricht region found new and vital purpose. Most obviously, they could be places of refuge and protection from bombs and armament for all parties to the war, including German munitions factories that could not be found by Allied bombers. In August 1944, the Bavarian Motor Works (BMW) started the development of a 27,000 square foot airplane engine factory that would employ 700 people in another cave system not far from the Geulhem caves, but it was abruptly interrupted by the subsequent liberation of Limburg.

With the arrival of the Americans in September 1944, the wartime commerce of the village that had been hidden in various parts of the caves could come out into the open. A black market for food and goods soon developed and was largely supplied by whatever might "fall" from the American trucks. The upper command of the U.S. military knew all about it, but.... This was a place that had been stripped by the Germans of all of its animals and produce. Most of the men had been sent away to forced labor in Germany.

Henry Van Landingham had arrived with the liberation at the same time. "When we got here, the women were all alone trying to figure out how to feed their children." The caves became central to his work as a driver for the Red Ball Express. In 2019, his grandson, Marc Geijselaers, with his wife, Sonja, took a visitor through some of the outer caverns that were only peripheral to the vast network of dark rooms and corridors deep within.

The outer religious spaces of the time of the Batavian Republic were now candle-lit altars of faith, and preservation efforts of the 21st century had formalized one of them as a baptismal gallery for the children of the region. At Christmas time they were now the sites of village celebrations. Artwork etched into the walls during the French Revolution depicted the cannons of that era and the proclamations of those who had gone into hiding and resistance. A turn of a corner took the visitors into an art

A room within the Guelhem caves contains a wall lit by candlelight "In memory of the liberation of Berg en Terblijt 14-9-1944." Flags of both nations are accompanied by the signatures of those involved who have returned to the caves over the years since the war, and at least one former United States ambassador to the Netherlands (author photo).

gallery of work etched into the walls in 1905 and known to tourists as the Orange Gallery in honor of the Dutch royal family. In another room, the Dutch and American flags had been etched and painted into the sandstone in 1944 and 1945. "A tribute to the liberators of our little town," said Marc Geijselaers. The flags were surrounded by the signatures of many of the white American soldiers of the liberation. Those of some of the Black drivers of the Red Ball Express came later, including that of Henry Van Landingham.

The visit was joined by the modern-day supervisor of the caves, Frans Bergsteyn. In the candlelight that bathed the signatures and flags, it was important for him to tell a story that he had, no doubt, told many times about the African American soldiers who had come to liberate a village, most of whose residents had never before seen a Black person. Geijselaers paraphrased from Dutch to English.

> One time, the trucks were driving through here in very bad weather. A child was looking at the GMC trucks, and he had a little teddy bear in his hand, and it fell

Caves supervisor Frans Bergsteyn (*left*) and Marc Geijselaers (*right*) pose at the memorial plaque at the Geulhem caves in honor of those killed and wounded in the liberation of Berg en Terblijt. The house across the road in the background is the family home into which Els Gejseillars was born in 1945 (author photo).

down. A lot of the trucks ran over it. The Black soldier stopped the convoy, picked up the bear and started washing it in his helmet. And the kid was standing there, like "What's going on?" The next day, when the bear was dry, he gave it back to the kid.

It was a story that had taken its place in the lore of the village and, no doubt, been remembered by some when Henry Van Landingham returned to Berg en Terblijt for the first time, in 1996. The origin of that journey had been in the letters that Marc's mother, Els, had sent to Henry

A Chevrolet tow truck left behind from the Red Ball Express shares the residential garage of the Geulhem Caves with Frans Bergsteyn's modern Opel (author photo).

in 1995. And the letters, in turn, had been preceded by her determination ten years earlier to learn to speak and write in English so that she might find him.

In Van Landingham family stories, Henry had left the war with a long walk. A return home seemed to have been held up for his unit, but he was sick and feared death if he couldn't get home. "So my father actually left his own unit," as his daughter Arzheyma would recall the story, "and walked to the coast to find a ship. He was going to get on the first ship moving, but they wouldn't let him on the ship." Then he heard that the ship needed someone who knew how to run a movie projector. He told them that it was something he knew how to do, "so they let him on the ship and he didn't, really. So they showed the same film over and over and over again because he didn't know how to change the film."

Upon returning to Buffalo after the war, Henry Van Landingham headed into the rest of his life with the same seeming confidence and élan with which he had driven his truck, "out running [sic] the convoy now, but I can't help it." He and his wife, Mary, had a daughter, Arzeymah, born in 1943. A son, Philip, would be born in 1946. He had been interested in aviation before the war, studied mechanics in high school, and became a mechanic for the Curtis-Wright Corporation postwar. The following years would see him involved in the small businesses of construction and gas stations, and his most enduring work as a housing inspector and manager for the city of Buffalo. Through all of his life in Buffalo and retirement in Florida, he would be active in the Episcopal church as a choir boy, vestry member, Men's Club leader, church warden and a Lay Eucharist Minister LEM.

During Arzeymah's growing up the story of the walk to the coast and the projector would be one of the few things he would willingly say about his time in the war. Another was how cold he had been in the Battle of the Bulge. He had never been so cold in his life, and he could still feel the cold when it came to mind. "I think he was like a lot of World War II soldiers. They put it in the background. Whatever horrible things happened, they didn't talk about it." That silence extended into his general bearing as a father who did not express much to his children, and Arzeymah had learned a trick. It was one of her first memories of childhood, at age three or four. He had brought home a small pair of souvenir Dutch wooden shoes. "I guess I noticed that when I put on those shoes and ran around he would sit back and get a funny look on his face." It was the way that she could get his attention.

Then, many years later, his silence began to break. The first of two letters came from Els.

The *Vereniging Bevrijdingskinderen*, the Association of Liberation Children, had been founded in the Netherlands in 1984 to support the children of the Canadian soldiers of the war. Eventually, it broadened its scope to England and the United States and, in 1991, Els asked for its help in identifying her father.

Her life in Berg en Terblijt had continued to be a good one for the most part, and her marriage to Haike Geijselaers at age 18 had produced her son Marc, born in 1965. But no one would talk about the obvious secret at the center of her life. She had put it in the background for a number of years, but the insistent question began to return after the death of her mother. "The uncertainty about my origin, the anger that no one told me anything," she told the Dutch magazine *Libelle*. "I was sure there had to be someone who knew.... Where was I supposed to start looking? This became a big problem again after my son got married. I felt thrown back on my own resources. Who was I? I became stressed, nervous, lost my sense of self-worth."[1] Els knew, however, that those who loved her were well intended in their silence. A pact had been made between her mother and older sister and brother. "Something like, make it clear, she is one of us. They have always been very nice to me, they protected me."

The closest she had been able to get to her father's identity was a handful of memories of others in the village. Some remembered him but could give only a vague description. He might have been shorter and younger than her mother. Someone said that he had a name that was something like "van Landingen." One day, a neighbor told a now grown Marc, matter of factly "When I see you walking around, I see your grandpa walking around."

The request to the Association of Liberation Children was followed by a casual phone call from an old friend who had been the child of a white American soldier. The friend asked if she was interested in knowing the name of her father; it was something that her aunt had written down on a piece of paper years ago. The name was not precise, but when Els showed it to her sister, Maria, she was surprised to learn that the name and its correct spelling had been known to Maria all along. Els was upset, but Maria could not understand why. "Why do you want to know who your father is? Didn't you have a good life with us? You were always the pampered one. What will you be stirring up?"[2]

A list of three Americans named Van Landingham arrived from the Association of Liberation Children, coincidentally, on Dutch Liberation Day, May 5, 1994. A series of letters back and forth was begun. Marc and Els decided to proceed cautiously, and the first was from Els to each of the men named Van Landingham saying that the 50th anniversary of the liberation of Limburg would be celebrated soon and the occasion had reminded them of a soldier named Van Landingham who had "visited my family quite often. He brought my family extra food supplies and helped getting through a very tough time."[3] The letter seemed to ask Henry Van Landingham if he knew an address for a Henry Van Landingham, but that may have occurred in a mistranslation. It also offered to reimburse its addressee for any postage costs he might incur.

Els received two responses; one from a man who proved to be white and a very gracious response was returned from another, though the letter gave no clue as to his race. This Henry had been very surprised to receive the letter. It had been such a long time, and he had had to read it many times to bring back the memories.

"My time in the Berg was most peaceful. I remember the caves where so much was done. Do you still grow mushrooms there? The old church were [sic]our company headquarters were located…. I am pleased to have been able to have helped in some way to help make this war time less painful. I hope we will hear from you again. God Bless you and your friends."[4]

Els thanked him for his response in a returned letter. She told him that the church had been torn down and that her current home had been built on its site. The caves were now a museum and were very popular during Christmas, when thousands of candles were lit. And mushrooms were still grown within them. The liberation celebrations had been very good this year with many American vets in attendance and a parade of old Army vehicles. It was a pity he had not been able to attend. She concluded:

> Maybe you still have some pictures of you in your uniform, and send us one of those, and of course you and your family.
> Please do it, and send us fotos.
> I am looking forward to your next letter.
> God bless you and your wife.[5]

In their marriage, Marc and Sonja would become regular travelers to visit friends, and relatives of hers in the United States. In 1995, they traveled to Florida, where Henry Van Landingham and his second wife, Hazel, had retired to Ocala. Marc contacted Henry to say that he wanted just to visit with him and thank him for his help in the village a half century earlier. The Van Landinghams readily agreed.

"We stood at the front door," said Marc. "And a little Black woman opened the door, and we right away felt at home."

"Goosebumps," said Sonja.

Henry would later say that his first reaction was "What are these two young people doing on their vacation visiting two old Black folk."

"This was my grandpa," Marc recalled. "I recognized things, like the way he spoke, the way he moved."

Marc and Sonja talked generally about the village,

Henry Van Landingham at the time of the war. He did not return the picture then in response to Els's letter, but it would become an important photograph in the family's history of the time that its American and Dutch members were brought together (courtesy Marcus Gejseilars).

his late grandmother and his mother. They and Els had believed that her father had been aware of the pregnancy before he had moved on in the war, but that appeared not to have been the case. Marc did not feel that it was his place to be the one to confront Henry with the full story and the conversation went on pleasantly, about "The Berg" and especially the caves. Henry had enjoyed the time there and the warm hospitality of the people, but he had gotten very sick and still carried the consequences of that. And he talked about his life in Buffalo after that.

When Marc and Sonja returned home, they told Els what they had found and showed her pictures. It was then that Els wrote to him and revealed the true reason for her previous letters and the visit of her son. His response was as gracious as it had been when he was first approached, and this time it was not by a letter, but by a phone call across the ocean. "Child," he said, "it has to be you, you are the spitting image of my younger sister. Why didn't your son say anything?"

In the fall, Els, Marc and Sonja traveled to America and Henry Van Landingham met them at the Orlando airport. He took Els into a bear hug and would not leave her side for the rest of the visit. He put her luggage in one of the bedrooms and said "This is your room, and it will remain your room." He took her to his church and introduced her to the congregation.

He wrote in her journal. "Dear daughter, may this be the beginning of a new family life."

In 2019, Arzeymah, sat at the table in the same house in Ocala and spoke of a family that was still strong many years later, though it had entered into new generations. Els and Henry were no longer alive, but there were grown children now. Marc and Sonja had two teenaged sons, Marciano and Delano. Arzeymah's grown daughter, Atiyah, would stop by to check in on her mother and a visitor who wanted to know more about Henry's life.

The Dutch daughter Els and the American daughter Arzeymah had become very close. For Arzeymah, the father who had been something of a mystery to her had been unlocked by the arrival of Els. Arzeymah had not had the best example of her parents to teach her how to interact with others. Her father had been "emotionally unavailable" in the parlance of the time. "There were no hugs and kisses, no quiet conversation."

"I had to learn—and I never learned it thoroughly—how to show feelings, how to show affection. And I loved Els so much because she was able to do that naturally with him. And it was something that he was missing."

The first visit to Florida by Els, Marc and Sonja had been followed by a return visit to Berg en Terblijt by Henry, Hazel, Richard and Arzeymah six months later, in 1996. The occasion was the christening of grandson Marciano in the Geulhem caves. It seemed a glorious time for them all.

Henry revisited the places he had known, including a hotel where Arzeymah and her brother quietly speculated that Els had been conceived. He and Hazel would make a second trip to Berg en Terblijt in 2002.

Sonja watched Henry during the first visit. He was still quiet and would not show his feelings easily. "But he was the head of the family. The guy everyone listens to. And what he says, everyone has a deep respect for him." He and Els, though, could talk and listen to each other easily. An iconic family photograph was taken as they sat in a jeep outside of the caves, dressed in their best, as Els looked to the sky, smiling radiantly.

Having found her American origins, Els would not then fall away from her continuing mastery of the English language. She kept working on it so that she could better talk to her new relatives, and she and Arzeymah talked about a lot of things over the years. It may have been that their conversations, bringing their own individual life experiences to the formation of a new, international family, took them to the core of the story of the Dutch children of African American liberators: it should not have been a story at all, and in many respects it wasn't, but in the end, of course, it was.

On the occasion of the first Communion in 2004 of Marciano Geijselaers, the full American and Dutch family was able to meet just once, and less than four months before Els' death. Left to right: Sonja Geijselaers, Delano Geijselaers, Henry Van Landingham, Hazel Van Landingham, Arzeymah Raqib, Philip Van Landingham, Marciano Geijselaers, Els Geijselaers, Penny Van Landingham and Haike Geijselaers, husband of Els (courtesy Marcus Geijselaers).

Henry and Els sit together in a World War II Jeep during the 1996 reunion of the family in Bergit en Terblijt (courtesy Marcus Geijselaers).

Arzeymah had adored her father and watched how he conducted his life all through her growing up. Racism was always there to contend with, but it did not seem to be one of his concerns. Instead, his great effort was in getting himself out of poverty. Life was to be pursued with ambition. Hard work, good behavior and ethics would get him through,

"He was part of a group of young Black people," said Arzeymah, "they didn't want to be boxed in by being Black. So they did a lot of things that Black people never do. They went horseback riding, they played golf, all that stuff, and not just once. He was good at it. So he didn't let the fact of being Black stop him from doing what he wanted to do. In fact, he made a point of it not stopping him. And he learned about money, and he invested his money."

His family had come out of the South, and he had rejected their lifestyle. His first wife, Arzeymah's mother, had come from a well-to-do Jamaican family, and he took them as an example. His sister had been ambitious, as well, and become one of the first Black civil service office workers in Buffalo. Henry and some of the other young men in his family and among his friends had first established themselves financially as Skycaps at the Buffalo airport, working for tips. But it paid well, and it was at a time in American racial history that Black men were establishing themselves financially as railroad porters, by which they were gaining political power through unionization, and contributing to the first stirrings of the Civil Rights Movement beginning in the 1950s and 1960s.

From that starting point, Henry had moved to the postal service, using the points he had acquired as a soldier and driver of the Red Ball Express in the formulation that qualified him for civil service. He ended his career as an official of the city of Buffalo and a civic leader in that city.

Racism had always been part of the mix, but as a motivator. Arzeymah, had learned it from her father as a matter of course. "That's how I was brought up. You had to be twice as good to get the same results out of the system, because you were Black. You have to put effort into it and realize that just because you have the credentials and can show them that you know more than they know, really, you have to be able to handle that diplomatically. You, as a Black person, just become bicultural. You're kind of *this* person in *your* community and you're *that* person in the white community."

And in her community the biracial situation in which her family now found itself was also of interest but not ultimately important. "You have white people in your family and your community, and that's okay. The fact that they're half white or all white is irrelevant. It doesn't come into play. You mention it, you talk about it. It's in your conversation, but not in a negative way."

Els had been born into circumstances that had no history, no traditions that were spoken or unspoken, and no pathways to success or failure. There were no guidelines toward a biracial concept of herself. She was not supposed to seem different from others, but she was. She was loved by her mother, and by her stepfather, who accepted her as the child of his wife's infidelity—"Haike was really a beautiful person," said Arzeymah. She was accepted in the village of Berg en Terblijt, and the hairdresser's comments about the difficulties of dealing with her hair were an observation, but not a complaint.

Her brothers had always protected her. When she persisted in searching for her father and finally came close to finding him, however, one of them, for whatever reasons, demanded that she drop the pursuit, and he cut off contact with her when she would not. After that, they would never talk again.

Though Els had told Arzeymah before she died—and years before the coming together of the rest of the adult children of African American soldiers in 2015 and 2016—that she thought she had been the luckiest of them all, she had always struggled. When she was growing up she could be in a room with others, feeling that she did not belong there. She wasn't supposed to be there, and she needed to disappear, but she couldn't because of her skin color.

"You'd see a picture of her with her brothers and sisters and you'd say 'Who is this child?' So she wanted to make herself disappear, either physically or psychologically. And she said she thought that people were going to come and take her away.

So it was very important to her to figure out who the hell she was. She spent time and effort. I mean, you don't go to the army, and several departments, and rejections and letters and calls and all that if it's not important to you. I think she was more comfortable here, that she had a family here and we loved her and accepted her. And it wasn't like we were pretending."

A few weeks after her last visit to Buffalo, the call came from the Netherlands that Els was dying of ovarian cancer. Arzeymah and her sister-in-law hurried across the ocean to see her one last time. She was told that Els had been waiting for her to arrive, and she recognized Arzeymah, but could say no more. She died that night.

Talking about it years later, Arzeymah wept in the same way that she had upon the thought of the orphans of war.

"Somebody comes and enriches your life. And then ... they're gone. You know?"

But the generations of the family carried on. Arzeymah's daughter, Atiyah, made a point of describing her grandfather by addressing her mother for a visitor's benefit. "You know, my grand dad was very influential in being in the community, and I think this contributed to you, as far as you being out in the community, and your protesting. We're talking about somebody [Arzeymah] who's been there when Martin Luther King did his 'I Have a Dream' speech, you know right on the front lines, and I think that came out of the home you were raised in, and it kind of carried through."

And it had carried across the ocean. Els's son Marc spoke of Henry Van Landingham with great reverence. He was not "my grandfather," but "Grandfather" as a proper noun. Marc had been born in the house across the road from the *Geulhemmergroeve,* and in which his grandparents had met during the liberation.

"I'm proud of my heritage. I always knew that there was something, because I looked different from all of my cousins. And I never felt unwelcome, or racism; maybe a couple of times in Maastricht."

When Henry Van Landingham had finally been found in 1995 and Marc could show pictures of him to friends, and to Sonja's cousins, it was taken as unremarkable. Their frequent travels to the United States, however, had occasionally resulted in events that could only be seen with a sense of humor. Once in a restaurant with *Opa* and *Oma,* grandfather and grandmother, they had been asked about the nature of their relationship by a waitress. The question had been perhaps impertinent, but not hostile. Once, as the family visited Canada, the Canadian border agent questioned the relationships he saw within the car with some suspicion, and an indication that he thought something was amiss.

Marc thought such things were funny. Henry could be mildly annoyed by them, but his wife, Hazel, who had grown up in Georgia during difficult times, did not respond to them well. Like her daughter, Atiyah, Marc pointed to his aunt Arzeymah as a quiet force, in Marc's view "the rebel of the family." They had visited with her once and found a box of pictures that placed her right in the center of some of main events of the civil rights movement, on the Mall with Martin Luther King, Jr., in marches with Jesse Jackson.

"I thought it was great," said Marc. "My aunt with Jesse Jackson. But she never said anything about that."

On one of their trips to the United States, Marc and Sonja took their two sons on a long drive from north to south. They noticed that the further south they traveled, the more they would experience odd looks and sometimes clearly racist reactions. They stopped at a hotel in Atlanta and when the clerk asked why they had come to the city they told her they were going to the Martin Luther King memorial. She seemed surprised and asked why they were doing that.

"We want to teach the boys about Martin Luther King," said Marc. Again, the clerk's question seemed more curious than antagonistic, and she helped them to get the most out of the visit.

Years later, sitting on the terrace of a nice restaurant overlooking a city square in Valkenburg, the visit to the memorial was remembered as a natural thing to do. And for Marc it seemed little more than a logical progression from what had occurred in his little village in World War II.

"I consider it the same as the American soldiers who liberated the Netherlands and our village, who were dedicated and gave love, sometimes the ultimate price—their lives. That's the same thing that Martin Luther King did. He gave his life for the freedom of Black people, the freedom of speech, the freedom to go and vote."

In 2019, Maria Andres still had the sparkle in her eyes and smile that had lit up a picture of the person she had been seventy years earlier. Apparently used for a newspaper ad putting her up for adoption, it was a photograph of a dark-skinned little girl perfectly posed in a perfect world, down to the placement of a smiling, white little girl doll beside her, just so. At the time, she was about to head into a life that might have permanently damaged any child, followed by an adulthood lived often on the brink, and without the firmament of a known family and heritage. When she got to the other end of it, seventy years later, she had managed to survive and to be able to keep moving toward the connection with whomever of her family she could find.

As she had grown older, questions about her mother began to return to her—inevitably. Sofie had disappeared across an ocean with one of her sisters and told her not to speak of it again. Now, decades later, what had become of her? And what had become of Maria's sister, Christine (Regina had been adopted by an American couple in the 1950s)? And the brother Nikolaus who had been born to her mother in New York?

Maria had moved to Limburg and joined the oral history project of the children of Black American fathers. Aside from the now shared resolve of the children to make one last effort at finding their fathers and families, it was a time of increased use of genealogy and consumer DNA testing in the unraveling of family puzzles. She thought that she learned that her mother was still alive and living at an address in New York City, but received no response to a letter to that address. On the internet, she found a picture of the address on Google maps and the phone number of an adjacent laundromat. When she called it, the person who answered did indeed know her brother and told her that he would have Nikolaus call her, but the call never came.

Early in 2019, Maria was finally able to talk to Nikolaus by phone and email. She had already learned that Sofie had died and been preceded in death by Maria's sister,

Maria Andres was advertised for adoption in Germany with this picture evidently placed in a magazine and was adopted by a Dutch-German couple in the Netherlands (courtesy Maria Andres).

Christine, in 2009. Among her first questions to Nikolaus was an attempt to solve the mystery that had been at the center of a young child's life: why had her mother disappeared to another country without her. The move had been paid for by Nikolaus's father, with whom he had never spoken.

Of their mother, Nikolaus told Maria that she had lived a loveless life and that the child born and died in 1940 had probably been the child of rape. Sofie's death had come in the throes of dementia at age 94. Christine had spent years as a homeless addict and died in a nursing home of diabetes at age sixty. Nikolaus himself was in poor health and living in the same rent-controlled apartment on upper Broadway into which he had been born in 1956. The space was shared with the ashes of his mother and sister. He was living on spare retirement income, and resisting the gentrification attempts of his landlord to make him leave the place. As of 2019, Maria had not been able to travel to New York to meet him, though their long-distance relationship would continue.

Separately, she had been trying to know her mother's family in Germany and had contacted them. But they had firmly resisted her and would not co-operate. "They did not want to know that they have brown in their family. So I dropped it."

Her sister Regina had grown up in Texas and died of cancer, leaving behind a daughter who Maria would be able to meet for the first time in a subsequent trip to Florida

But it was the Black side of her in which Maria knew that she would find her resolution.

She had always thought that her father's name was Charles Humphrey and that he was from Florida. It was information she had once seen on some adoption papers, but they had since been lost, perhaps in the fire that had accompanied her husband's suicide. It was based only on a memory, and that was all she knew. She had nothing to back it up as she grew older and enlisted the help of others in her search.

By 2018, the intricacies of genealogy, DNA, newspaper archives and research for this book had led to the discovery of the Charles Humphrey who was her father, and to his obituary. Charles "Charlie" Humphrey had died of cancer on March 2, 2000. He was a retired cement worker, Army veteran, and member of the Shiloh Baptist Church of Orlando. He had been survived by two children, four grandchildren and two great grandchildren.

The larger family of which Charles Humphrey had been a part was extensive and spread throughout Florida. He had been born into a farm a family in Greenville, near the Georgia border, died in Orlando to the south, and Maria had found cousins in Clearwater, further south, who then had welcomed her joyously when she made her first trip to the United States and arrived at the Tampa airport. She had come to them from Europe as a relative they might not have even conceived of had she not contacted them just a month before. And it was still a remarkable thing to think about, but the falling into each other's arms had been immediate, satisfying and constantly repeated. The next evening, cousins Lillian and Ruth Mae would take her to the church that had been founded in Clearwater by their father. They told her that she would meet more of her family there, and the larger family that was not of blood but of church.

Before that, they sat around the kitchen table in a family home on Water Street and shared experiences of the lifetimes that had preceded the moment.

"It is a sort of healing," said Maria. "To make you complete. To know your family. To see them and to feel them. The circle is now round. All the parts are together now. I know who I am, and I take myself as I am, but there was a piece that was missing, and now it is not missing. I can just live on with it."

A few days later, the cousins took Maria further into Florida and toward the cemetery where her father was buried. They visited more cousins along the way, and the woman who had lived with Charles Humphrey for many years after the death of his wife in 2008. She met her half-sister just briefly and perhaps awkwardly; she would later learn that it had been the day before she was to have heart surgery.

On they went to the Woodlawn Memorial Park in Gotha, west of Orlando. The day was overcast, windy and cold. The long walk across the bare grass of winter and

Maria Andres finally arrives at the Florida grave of her father, Charles Humphrey, in January 2019 (courtesy Maria Andres).

hundreds of grave markers set flush with the ground was difficult for Maria, but she kept up with the pace of her cousins. The grave was fully sheltered by the lowest branches of a very old oak tree.

Maria stood above it for a very long time, her hands in the form of a prayer, looking down at it, then up again at her cousins, then down again.

"I wish he'd known me. I really wish," she said, mostly to herself.

"It's okay."

Sitting, left to right: Wanda van der Kleij, Rosy Peters, Maria Andres. Standing, left to right: Marcus Geijselaers—son of Els Geijselaers, Birgitte van der Kleij—daughter of Wanda van der Kleij, Maureen Peters—daughter of Rosy Peters, Huub Habets, Cor Linssen, Ed Moody, Huub Schepers (courtesy Paul Koenen).

Afterword
by Sebastiaan Vonk

Maria Andres' father was a member of what America has come to see as The Greatest Generation, ordinary men and women from all walks of life who rose to greatness in extraordinary times, helping to free the world from evil. According to author Tom Brokaw, they formed "the greatest generation any society has produced."

But where does the African American contribution to the war effort fit in that picture? That the country was engaged in a world war was extraordinary. African Americans, however, found themselves fighting under the same conditions that they faced at home. As the late American historian Stephen Ambrose has written, "the world's greatest democracy fought the world's greatest racist with a segregated Army." Nothing out of the ordinary there. It complicates the dominant narrative surrounding the war today.

The harsh reality of Jim Crow in wartime became painfully apparent to Corporal Rupert Trimmingham and eight other African American soldiers, who were travelling from Louisiana to Texas. After great difficulty in finding a lunchroom in which they would be served, they were allowed in the kitchen of a railroad station to grab a bite to eat and get something to drink. What then happened caused Trimmingham to send a letter to *Yank* magazine, published April 28, 1944:

"11:30 a.m. about two dozen German prisoners of war, with two American guards, came to the station. They entered the lunchroom, sat at the tables, had their meals served, talked, smoked, in fact had quite a swell time. I stood on the outside looking on, and I could not help but ask myself these questions: Are these men sworn enemies of this country? Are they not taught to hate and destroy ... all democratic governments? Are we not American soldiers, sworn to fight for and die if need be for this our country? Then why are they treated better than we are?"

205

Trimmingham and his fellows would likely continue to be hidden away in the war, and in ways that continue up to the present day. The contributions of African Americans are still largely absent in Hollywood productions. At the former sites of war in Europe, these soldiers continue to be largely omitted from the picture. Contemporary representations make one believe that an essentially white American army liberated Europe, even though 900,000 African American soldiers served in Europe alone.

Jefferson Wiggins, whose story forms the central thread of this book, was one of those soldiers. Today, little reminds visitors to the American War Cemetery and Memorial in Margraten, where he dug graves for weeks, of both the chaos of war and the circumstances of segregation in which men and women like Wiggins served. The serenity and grandeur of such cemeteries today stand in sharp contrast to the reality of battle. The uniformity of the endless rows of crosses and Stars of David ensures that every soldier is remembered equally. After all, death knows no color. All are praised for giving their lives for the same cause, even though that cause was an ideal that was not fulfilled for them at home.

One could spend countless hours reading the names that have been etched into the white marble grave markers, as many do. They will tell you the soldiers' names, their ranks, and their units, but they will offer little about the person the name belongs to. It was only in recent years that it became known that among more than 10,000 soldiers buried and memorialized in Margraten there are 172 African Americans. One hundred sixty-nine of them found their final resting place beneath the earth; three others are remembered on the Walls of the Missing.

That number could be established because the army kept meticulous track of the race of individual soldiers and units in its records. The burial certificates of a soldiers did not name the race of the individual, but included a code. Race code "2" indicated that the soldier was African American. The Quartermaster division of the Ninth Army kept track of "colored" units by marking related documents with an asterisk.

The majority of African American soldiers, including those buried in Margraten, were not permitted to serve in combat and had been placed in positions of support. In the Quartermaster Corps, the soldiers were deployed as truck drivers, or they worked in bakeries, laundries, and bathing facilities. In the Ordinance Corps and the Engineer Corps, African Americans offered other kinds of vital support for the war effort. Many thousands of them are believed to have resided in the Netherlands for a prolonged period of time during the war. The exact number remains unknown.

There were some rare exceptions to the non-combat rule. Most notable were the so-called "negro infantry volunteers." As war casualties mounted by the end of 1944, in part because of the German counterattack that has become known as the Battle of the Bulge, supreme commander Dwight Eisenhower decided to temporarily desegregate the army. That story is told in Chapter Six of this book. Just over 2,000 African American volunteers were added to combat forces during that time and, today, 35 of them rest in Margraten.

African American soldiers also found themselves fighting in tank and artillery battalions. The 745th and 761st Tank Battalions are the only African American units known to have fought in The Netherlands. The former played a vital role in liberating the Dutch city of Venlo in early March 1945, together with the 35th Infantry Division. The 969th Field Artillery Battalion gained notoriety because of its role in defending the perimeter around the Belgian city of Bastogne during the Battle of the Bulge. In that same battle, eleven African American soldiers of the 333rd Field Artillery Battalion were massacred in Wereth; many more were taken prisoner of war.

While knowledge about who these men were, whether in combat or support, and what they accomplished continues to steadily expand, much remains unknown still. Identifying the names of the 172 African American soldiers at Margraten has been the starting point of a long quest to learn more about a group of soldiers whose stories have been lost to history.

Over the years, members of the vibrant remembrance community in Margraten have made a tremendous effort to know the stories of those buried and memorialized in the American cemetery. The first of them were those, beginning in 1945, who adopted the graves of the fallen, bringing flowers on special occasions. The adoptions became a great comfort to the soldiers' families back at home in the United States, especially those who would not have the opportunity to visit the graves of their loved ones. Long-lasting friendships have been created between families on both sides of the ocean, and exist to this day. Soldiers' photos, when they have been available, have been displayed prominently in the homes of the adopters, as if they depicted relatives of their own.

The Fields of Honor Foundation is a group of volunteers of all ages who work to preserve the memory to U.S. soldiers buried and memorialized all over Europe, and I am fortunate to be able to head it up. It maintains tribute pages to tens of thousands of soldiers in an online database, and has sought to decorate each of their graves in Margraten with a personal photograph. The ongoing project *The Faces of Margraten* allows visitors to the cemetery to look into the soldiers' eyes, highlighting the human cost of war. At the time of the 75th anniversary of the end of World War II, about three quarters of all 10,000 soldiers remembered there were matched with a photo.

But for more than eighty percent of the African American soldiers no photo could be found.

One can think of a number of reasons they are not available. The socio-economic position of many African Americans in the 1930s and 1940s might not have enabled them to have their photo taken. Records traditionally available to white Americans, like school yearbooks, were less so for Black Americans. Poignant, for example, is the letter that the father of John Mitchell, one of the 172 African Americans in Margraten, wrote to the War Department, notifying them that he wished to have his son's remains permanently interred in Margraten. One of the reasons was his financial situation. "I am very poor. I don't have any money to carry out the burial. No way." He ends his letter inquiring about the death insurance, pointing out to the bad situation he is in since his son's death.

It is a painful reminder that we would not fully comprehend the unique experiences of African American soldiers if we were only to focus on their military service. As a historian of memorial and sacred spaces, Edward Linenthal has written, "too often, in too many ways, the enduring legacies of slavery, the Civil War, Reconstruction, Jim Crow, and even the modern civil rights era stick like a fishbone in the nation's throat." Only by thoroughly engaging with these histories can we truly appreciate the experience of African American soldiers. Linenthal calls it "conscientious remembrance." As he rightfully argues, "It is an act of moral engagement, a declaration that there are other American lives too long forgotten that count."

There is no time to lose. Events, once again, have painfully reminded us of that. No African American was awarded a Medal of Honor, the highest military award for valor, during or after the war for actions in World War II. A 1992 study commissioned by the U.S. Department of Defense and the U.S. Amy found this was the result of systematic and racial discrimination. The study recommended several awards given to African American soldiers to be upgraded to the Medal of Honor. In January 1997, President Bill Clinton awarded the Medal to seven soldiers, all but one posthumously.

Private First Class Willy F. James Jr., was one of them. He was one of the aforementioned "negro infantry volunteers," serving with the 413th Infantry Regiment of the 104th Infantry Division. He was killed in action on April 8, 1945, and found his final resting place at Margraten. Although he was finally recognized for his heroic deeds, he was still in a sense forgotten. By the time of the medal ceremony, his widow, Valcenie, had started to suffer from Alzheimer's disease. She was no longer fully aware of what was going on. Beyond that, the personal belongings, including photos, of Willy had been lost during a move. A drawing of him is all that remains today. As more veterans and soldiers' close relatives pass, memory is at risk to be lost to history forever.

A resolution to bring change has brought communities in the Netherlands and African American communities all over the U.S. together through chapters of the African American Historical and Genealogical Society. A story like that of Maria Andres tells us that we still can find answers. Of course, we will perhaps never fully be able to understand what their lives entailed. As veteran Matthew S. Brown said during his first return to Europe in September 2019, and in a memorial event at Margraten: "I don't have the time to tell how hard it was to live in a segregated community. Two bathrooms, two fountains. Two this, two that."

However, that does not mean that we cannot try to be empathetic to their stories. Neither does it mean that we cannot say "Thank you for what you have done." It would be a recognition long overdue.

Sebastiaan Vonk is a Dutch historian of American Studies at the University of Groningen interested in their shared history, especially World War II. He is chairman of the Fields of Honor Foundation, *which manages* Faces of Margraten, *that seeks photographs of each of those buried in the cemetery as part of the Dutch effort to honor those Americans who liberated them in 1944 and 1945. The original Dutch version of this book was a result of that attention and a subsequent project seeks to tell the stories of 172 African American Liberators buried at Margraten, first identified in the work of author Mieke Kirkels, which was joined by Vonk.*

About the Authors

Mieke Kirkels was appointed an *Officer of the Orange—Nassau* by the Netherlands in 2017, a designation conferred on behalf of the Dutch King or Queen for those whose contributions have "earned special merits for society." Her career has included the role of a National Ombudswoman, with attention to equal treatment for women in the labor market in the 1980s, followed by work in communications and Human resources management. In 2009, she became a Public Historian, focusing particularly on the role of African American soldiers in the Netherlands in World War II. That interest was derived from her family's history in farming and her work to tell the story of the development of the American Cemetery at Margraten through an oral history project, the documentary "Bitter Harvest," and a book, with co-author Jo Purnot, *From Farmland to Soldier's Cemetery* in 2009. The project revealed the little-known history in the Netherlands of the role of African Americans in its liberation in 1944 and 1945, and was followed by *Van Alabama naar Margraten*, written with former African American grave-digger the late educator Jefferson Wiggins. Published in the Netherlands, the book helped to reveal the lives of the children of African American soldiers and Dutch women to the rest of the country and to each other. The Dutch version of this book, *Kinderen van zwarte bevrijders*, followed to tell that story further and has led to a current project that will document the lives and contribution of 172 African American soldiers identified through her efforts, with others, as buried in the Margraten cemetery. She lives in Leiden, South Holland, Netherlands.

Chris Dickon is an Emmy-winning American public radio and television producer/reporter who has been writing books about unknown aspects of American history since 2005. His most recent books, *The Foreign Burial of American War Dead, Americans at War in Foreign Forces*, and *A Rendezvous with Death: Alan Seeger in Poetry, at War*, have focused on the human elements of war, and developed new information in their subject matter. The writing has been motivated, in part, by his own history as an illegitimate child of World War II whose father was unknown to him. During the course of the writing of this book, his father's identity and family was revealed to him for the first time through the use of DNA analysis. He lives in Portsmouth, Virginia.

The authors give great thanks for the editing assistance of Kees Ribbens and Sebastiaan Vonk in the Netherlands, and Dr. Frances Beck in the United States.

Appendix

Relevant World War II Era Law and
Custom for International Marriage,
Immigration, Birth Status,
Adoption and Assistance.

An understanding of the status of children born of American and Canadian soldiers and the women of various World War II nations requires a survey of laws, norms and customs related to marriage, adoption, citizenship and immigration in those years, and years following. This summary looks at each from the perspective of the nations involved, and at resources available for many children of World War II and their families in searching for unknown fathers. In many cases, this information is fluid and changing and should not be taken as legal information and advice.

Marriage Between American/Canadian Soldiers and Foreign Nationals During World War II and Its Aftermath, by Country

A model for **U.S. military policy** about marriage between Americans and Europeans and Asians might be found in policy related to relationships between American men and women working together in military service during the war. Personnel in the North African, Mediterranean and Middle East theaters were generally allowed to marry without much difficulty. Marriage was possible in the European theater, but when it occurred one of the partners would be transferred at distance within the theater, or beyond. The policy was intended to discourage pregnancy and marriage decisions made in haste. In the Pacific theaters of the war, marriage was not permitted unless the woman was pregnant, in which case, by Women's Army Corps (WAC) policy, she would be immediately discharged from the service and sent home.[1]

Variations in policy occurred. In the Navy, WAVES were forbidden to marry military men until 1942, when rules only forbade marriage to fellow sailors, and that restriction was lifted in 1943. Navy nurses, however, were restricted from such marriages throughout the war, with a brief exception in 1945. In the Marines and Coast Guard, marriage was allowed, but with restrictions against marriage within the same service.

Known and followed policy within the military seemed designed to prevent distraction and conflict within the war effort by romantic relationships and resulting family responsibilities. Spoken and unspoken policy about relationships between American forces and foreign nationals carried similar goals, with the addition of the burden of differing rules and customs within and between different nations.

In the Netherlands, a concern was the legality of a marriage in the countries of both partners, and followed a model developed in adjacent Belgium. A young woman could not be married in any case without permission from her parents or legal guardians, and the young man needed to demonstrate that the marriage would be legally recognized in his state of residence. In addition, he needed to provide a birth certificate which most soldiers did not carry with them, and many had perhaps never received due to lax rules about birth certificates in the United States. Without a certificate, he was required to produce four witnesses who knew him well enough to swear to the circumstances of his birth.

Interracial marriage in this case was further hampered by the state law requirement, and most American state laws forbade interracial marriage.

In Great Britain, marriage between American military men and British women was discouraged at various levels by various commanders, and enforced up to a point by various hurdles placed in the way of those who sought it. It could not take place without official approval that might be gained through the filling out of numerous forms and the expenditure of perhaps a year of effort. For a time until the rise of public disapproval, the British Red Cross involved itself in investigating the backgrounds and suitability for marriage of some of the young women involved. Similar investigation of the young men involved was said to take place in the United States.[2] It would be possible, however, for the couple to marry with the prospect of maintaining postwar residence in England, or common law marriage in the United States.

Marriage between Canadian soldiers and British women met the same general hurdles, but by 1944 the Canadian Department of National Defence had set up Canadian Wives' Bureaus across England, to help to prepare the women for their lives after the war.

For Americans, biracial marriage was not legally banned, but highly discouraged or forbidden at the command level on the premise of miscegenation laws in the United States. In general, command forces would forbid the marriage as "against public policy." Though there was no legal basis for the claim, command usually prevailed.

In Germany, marriage between American occupation soldiers and Austrian women was not allowed by the military command until January 1946, and German women in December of that year. Even then, bureaucratic and command hurdles were significant, and could be made more so in the case of interracial marriage until the integration of the Army in 1948. In all cases, investigation of the woman who had been a member of an enemy nation, and the movement toward denazification of German citizens, could offer further encumbrance and justification for denial of permission.

In Japan, similar military proscriptions applied, combined with family disapproval for most Japanese women, and expected discrimination if they ever went to America.

Status of Children Born to American and Canadian Soldiers and Foreign Nationals

United States

Under the Nationality Act of 1940, a child born abroad of an American father or mother, or both, was a citizen of the United States, with an important provision: as of January 13, 1941, the U.S. citizen parent had to have lived in the U.S. or one of its possessions for ten previous years, at least five of them after the age of sixteen. In 1946, the law was modified to accommodate those citizens who had served honorably in the armed forces by pushing back the five-year requirement to age twelve. Since then, the requirements of age and years in residence have been occasionally adjusted.

Canada

Until 1947, a child born overseas of a Canadian father and brought to Canada attained Canadian citizenship. But Canada's first citizenship act was passed in 1947, and had the effect of removing or confusing the status of citizenship for war babies and orphans, and war brides of Canadian servicemen. In subsequent years, many Canadians who thought of themselves as citizens were surprised to learn that they were not. They became known as The Lost Canadians, and it was not until the Citizenship Act of 1977 that some, but not all, of the limitations of their citizenship were addressed. Continuing problems were faced by pre–1947 women and children, whose situation was similar to that of the Windrush Generation of England who had been allowed into the country before a certain date, but had no documentation to support them in subsequent decades. In addition, the post war years for all nations of the British Commonwealth required a sometimes intricate evolution from their residents' status as British subjects to national citizens of specific nations. In 2020, the definitive structure of Canadian citizenship was still not fully resolved.

England

Under the British Nationality and Status of Aliens Act 1914, anyone born within the Commonwealth was a British subject. The Nationality Act of 1943 allowed dual citizenship.

Netherlands

Before 1984, any child born of a Dutch father, within the Netherlands or abroad, was a citizen of the Netherlands. A child born of a Dutch mother and a foreign father was not a Dutch citizen, but could gain citizenship through an "Option Procedure," which was generally open to all applicants who had been clear of criminal activity or custody for five years. In most cases, any other current nationality had to be renounced.

Germany/Austria

Until 1975, German citizenship upon birth was held only by those whose fathers were German citizens. Postwar, occupied Germany, however, held thousands of children whose origins were unknown or could not be confirmed. Management of their lives and welfare had fallen to the Allied Control Authority (ACA) of the four powers that occupied the country. But the ACA was a military operation not practiced in the welfare of children, and its American officials sought to gain control of the task by creating a structure to determine the legal identity of a child. They adopted these principles, to be used in the American sector of Germany:

1. A person born of legally married parents would be deemed to have the citizenship of the father or, if the father was not a citizen of any state, or not known to be a citizen of any state, including Germany, that person would be deemed a citizen of the country of his/her birth.
2. An illegitimate child would be deemed to have the citizenship of his/her mother, or if the mother was not a citizen of any state or not known to be a citizen of any state, including Germany, that child would be deemed a citizen of the country of his/her birth.
3. A person of unknown parentage who was born in a known

country outside of Germany would be deemed a citizen of the country of his/her birth.

4. A person of unknown parentage born in Germany, or a person of unknown parentage whose country of birth is unknown, will be deemed a citizen of Germany.[3]

An effect of the policy, and other factors, was to eventually resolve most questions in favor of German citizenship, though children of certain American parentage could also be American citizens. With the founding of the West German Federal Republic in 1949, all war children were granted German citizenship.[4]

Policies of Adoption to America for War Babies

On December 22, 1945, American president Harry Truman issued a directive allowing the immigration of displaced persons and unaccompanied children who would be adopted to enter the country for humanitarian reasons, but under the limitations of source nation quotas already in place. Under the Displaced Persons Act of 1948, the United States took in 400,000 of the displaced of postwar Europe until 1952, when the Act was replaced by the McCarran—Walter Act, which severely limited immigration. In 1953, more liberal immigration forces, including now president Dwight Eisenhower, brought forth counterbalancing legislation under the banner of the Refugee Relief Act, which would provide more than 200,000 visas for European refugees (and 7,000 for certain Asian refugees).[5] The RRA, however, exerted strong controls on adoption that included investigations of prospective parents by child welfare organizations that could take as long as a year. And state adoption laws and norms that frowned on interracial families could be another impediment. Prospective parents who traveled to the child's country of origin, however, could return with a child successfully adopted under that country's regulations.

As regards children in Germany, the mid 1950s saw the creation of U.S. military adoption boards which helped an adopting military member to establish his or her suitability and to work with German courts.

Similar American Acts and regulations allowed and regulated international adoption through the Korean War and into the 1950s, but postwar adoptions were often flawed. American citizenship was not automatic for the adopted child, and required separate paperwork in the form of an Application for Certificate of Citizenship. Some adoptees have lived their lives with all of the rights and obligations of citizenship, only to find when applying for a passport or coming under the jurisdiction of law enforcement that they were not citizens. The problem was solved by law in 2000, but not for those over the age of 18, and they would remain in limbo as of early 2020.

Adoption to Canada was allowed postwar with controls that would assure that the immigrant child would not become a burden to the state, thus many came under the sponsorship of non-governmental organizations like the Canadian Jewish Congress or Catholic welfare societies. Those adoptions originated, however, within the rules of the nation from which a child would come.

Netherlands

There was no effective adoption policy in the Netherlands until 1956, and adoption was controlled by the law of the adopting country.

United Kingdom

Until the Adoption of Children Act of 1943, adoption laws and protections were loosely enforced. The 1943 Act forbade the adoptioning out of the country to any adoptive parent who was not a British subject. The Children Act of 1948 sought to further codify the welfare of children, but eased the rules of international adoption. Decisions about individual adoptions of young children not able to make their own decisions would be made on a case by case basis by the Home Office, but restrictions began to appear again in 1949.[6]

Germany/Austria

In the Third Reich, the regulation of adoption had been one of the ways in which the state could manage Nazi practices and beliefs about racial and social purity. All adoptions were subject to approval by Nazi administrators, and families that had been previously formed through adoption could be peremptorily broken up if they were deemed to be unacceptable to government policy. Families were not involved in the process and could one day hear an unexpected knock on the door which would result in the removal of their child, without appeal.

Traditionally, adoption and other practices of child welfare had been the work of Christian organizations in the two countries, but they had been removed from the process and it would take some years before they could regain their authority postwar. In the immediate years after the defeat of Germany, adoption policy and practice was unmoored and improvised. The Federal Republic did not legalize the powers of Christian welfare organization in matters of adoption until 1951. In the interim, however, the American Military Government generally continued to follow adoption regulation that had existed in the Third Reich, with one exception. It enacted a law in December 1947 that allowed parents of adopted children who had been taken from them by the Nazis to petition for reinstatement of their parenthood.

Adoption to the United States was never expressly forbidden during this time, but it was subject to much discussion and debate within Germany (Chapter Ten).

The War Brides Act of 1945

Immigration policy of the United States during the war was driven by the Immigration Act of 1924, which prevented or limited immigration from Asia, parts of Eastern Europe and certain ethnic and religious groups. The War Brides Act of December 28, 1945, opened a three year period in which immigration quotas were suspended to accommodate foreign spouses and children—natural and adopted—of American military members.

The Alien Fiancées and Fiancés Act of 1946, and a 1947 amendment, allowed entry of fiancés of servicemen and removed limitations on Filipino and Asian Indian women. Those who did not ultimately marry after entrance into the country were subject to deportation.

The War Brides Act expired at the end of 1948.

There are no specific, reliable figures of the numbers of war brides who came to the United States. Commonly used estimates are that:

- One million Americans soldiers married women in fifty countries of the world war.
- 100,000 were from Great Britain.
- 150,000–200,000 came from continental Europe, including 14,000 from Germany/Austria.
- 16,000 came from Australia and New Zealand.
- 50,000–100,000 came from the Far East, including Japan.[7]

The Canadian Wives Bureau, was an effort by the Canadian Department of Defense to prepare and welcome the wives of Canadian soldiers. Most coming from England and the Netherlands. An estimated 48,000 women and 22,000 children traveled to Canada between 1942 and 1947.[8]

Finding Fathers and Family

The attempts of white and biracial children, and some mothers, to learn the identity and whereabouts of American fathers started before the end of the war and has extended into the 21st century, often as the pursuit of grandchildren and other family members. Though economic support has been the motivation in some cases, it can be said that for most the search has been a genuine and inevitable need to know who the father was and more about him, hopefully to connect with him. In many cases it has been a quiet search, or one reluctantly pursued, with the desire to protect the father in whatever became of his American life.

The research has met two significant American barriers.

In 1973, the National Personnel Records Center in suburban St. Louis, Missouri, was partially destroyed by a fire that has confounded researchers into the 21st century, especially in research of military personnel records. Most records of Army personnel between 1912 and 1960 were lost, as well as three-quarters of Air Force records between 1947 and 1964, along with a limited number of Navy, Coast Guard and Marine Corps losses.

In the following year, the U.S. Department of Justice began to administer the Privacy Act of 1974. Though with some statutory exceptions, the Act regulated the government's management of information about individual citizens and the release of information about an individual without his or her permission.

In Canada, the Privacy Act of 1983 restricted access to information about an individual other than the individual seeking the information. There are exceptions for family members, but they do not apply to illegitimate children. Library and Archives Canada Military Heritage holds extensive records of Canadians who have served in armed forces. They are open and accessible under varying conditions. Information about World War I veterans can be found online by name.

Nonprofit and Social Organizations

Since the war, a number of non-governmental organizations have operated to assist children in search of their wartime fathers. Some have come and gone, and others have persisted through changes in the nature of the need to know and the evolution of information resources.

This is a survey of assistance still available in the year 2020. Internet addresses are not given because of their perishability, but search terms should lead to an organization, or information about it, whether it is current or in the past.

- GI Trace is a widely used organization with a website and forum devoted to research and discussion about American fathers of World War II children. It has absorbed some of the predecessor and since closed organizations devoted to finding American fathers of children in the United Kingdom, and offers links to other resources.

- Bow International Network, or Bow I.N., The European Associations of War Children, was formed in 2007 and meets annually in Berlin. It works with children of all wars up to the present day, with representation in Denmark, Norway, Germany, Finland, France, Bosnia, and the former Dutch Indonesia in relation to Japanese fathers.
- Children of American fathers and Vietnamese mothers are supported by Amerasians Without Borders, and the search term *Amerasian* will lead to similar organizations.
- Stichting Werkgroep Herkenning assists Dutch children of Dutch women and German occupying forces in World War II.
- International Soundex Reunion Registry attempts to effect reunions between consenting family members.
- The Black German Cultural Society offers support and information for Black people of German heritage.
- The American World War II Orphans Network (awon.org) on the internet includes a forum for those searching for fathers of the war.
- Two France-based organizations, Amicale Nationale des Enfants de la Guerre (1939–1945) and Cœurs Sans Frontières/Herzen ohne Grenzen (Hearts without Frontiers), work with children of the fathers of both nations involved in the occupations of both nations during the war.

Other organizations in Germany include the Deutsche Dienstelle, which holds records of German soldiers in the war, and the German Federal Archives—Military Archives, which contains personal documents and troop movement records which can help to determine location during certain dates in time.

Chapter Notes

Preface

1. The exact number of current burials in each of the cemeteries of the American Battle Monuments Commission is rarely a definite figure. It changes up and down with continuing dis-interments and interments that result from continuing efforts to identify unknown burials, and other factors.

Chapter One

1. By law and military policy, it would have been difficult for the two to become legally married, but it is believed that they were assisted in a municipal, non-church, marriage by a bureaucrat in the Wetzel family. Twenty years later it would be necessary for Lenie to seek a legal end to the marriage (Chapter 12). See Appendices: Legal Status of War Babies.

2. Military Children Born Abroad https://military.findlaw.com/family-employment-housing/, military-children-born-abroad.html, accessed 10/19/2019.

3. At the outset of World War I, the Netherlands had presented a neutral face to the rest of Western Europe since the late 19th century and declared its neutrality in the conflict that was to follow. It's position between Germany and Belgium placed it in a precarious position, and its airspace would be occasionally violated, but it held to its resolve, in part, by creating a standing force at its borders to defend the country if necessary. Its position in the center of warring countries, however, led to sometimes very difficult problems with food supplies and refugee populations. Though officially neutral the population was not

fully so, starting in the royal family. Queen Wilhelmina, was personally sympathetic to Belgium and France, but her husband, who was of German origin, was sympathetic to Germany. In the general population, similar family differences led to the enlistment of numbers of Dutch citizens in the various national armies of all sides. In the view of history, Dutch neutrality in World War I offered a measure of stability in a continent at war and continued that influence in the aftermath of war.

4. Donald L. Niewyk, *The Columbia Guide to the Holocaust* (New York, Columbia University Press, 2000), 422. Also, United States Holocaust Memorial Museum on-line Encyclopedia, https://encyclopedia.ushmm.org/content/en/article/documentation-on-the-persecution-of-roma, accessed 10/19/2019.

5. In 2007, then Argentinian-born Princess, now Queen, Maxima, wife of then Prince, now King, Willem-Alexander offered her view of Dutch identity to the Scientific Council for Government Policy, excerpted:

A difficult job because there are so many dimensions to it. It has been seven years since I started my personal search for the Dutch identity. I received help from numerous experts. I had the privilege to meet many people, to see, hear and taste a lot from the Netherlands. It was a beautiful, rich experience for which I am enormously grateful. But the Dutch identity, no I did not find that. The Netherlands are: large windows without curtains so that everyone can look inside, but also valuing privacy and cosiness. The Netherlands are: only one cookie with coffee, but enormous hospitality and warmth. The Netherlands are: sobriety and moderation, pragmatism, but also experiencing intense emotions together. So the Netherlands is much too many-sided to be capture in a single cliché. The Dutchman *does not exist.*

Maykel Verkuyten, *Identity and Cultural Diversity* (United Kingdom, Routledge 2013), 1.

6. Sabine Lee, "A Forgotten Legacy of the Second World War: GI children in post-war Britain and Germany," *Contemporary European History*, vol. 20, no. 2, 163.

7. "Negro Children Studied," *New York Times*, July 23, 1952, 5.

8. Philip Rohrbach and Niko Wahl, "Black Austria: The Children of African American Soldiers of the Occupation," exhibit of the Vienna Museum of Folk Life and Folk Art, 2016.

9. L. de Jong, *Het Koninrijk der Nederlanden in de Tweede Wereldoorlog*, vol. 5, pt. 1 (Leiden, Martinus Nijhoff, 1972), 246.

10. https://www.expatica.com/de/german-soldiers-fathered-50000-dutch-children/, accessed 11/15/2019.

Chapter Two

1. Mieke Kirkels, *Van Alabama naar Margraten* (Netherlands: Self-Published, 2014), 3.

2. *Ibid.*, 6.

3. *Ibid.*

4. Department of Defense. Department of the Army. Office of the Chief Signal Officer. *Training of Colored Troops.* Script. U.S. National Archives RG 111, https://catalog.archives.gov/id/24716.

5. Neil A. Wynn, *The African American Experience During World War II* (Lanham, MD: Rowman & Littlefield, 2010), 2.

6. *Ibid.*

7. Col. West A. Hamilton "The Negroes' Historical and Contemporary Role in National Defense" (speech, Hampton, Virginia, November 25, 1940), U.S. National Archives, RG 220, https://catalog.archives.gov/id/40019879.

8. Neil A. Wynn, *The African American*

Experience During World War II (Lanham, MD: Rowman & Littlefield, 2010), 3.

9. University of Missouri-Kansas City School of Law, "Lynchings by State and Race, 1882–1968," from the Archives at Tuskegee Institute. https://web.archive.org/web/20100629081241/http:/www.law.umkc.edu/faculty/projects/ftrials/shipp/lynchingsstate.html, accessed 10/30/2019.

10. "Our Special Grievances," *The Crisis*, vol. 16, no. September 5, 1918, 216. https://books.google.com/books?id=Y4ETAAAAYAAJ&printsec=frontcover#v=onepage&q&f=false.

11. *Ibid.*, 217.

12. Jack D. Foner *Blacks and the Military in American History* (Santa Barbara: Praeger, 1974), 111.

13. Neil A. Wynn, *The African American Experience During World War II* (Lanham, MD: Rowman & Littlefield, 2010), 5.

14. Graham Smith, *When Jim Crow met John Bull* (New York: St, Martin's Press, 1987), 7.

15. Neil A. Wynn, *The African American Experience During World War II* (Lanham, MD: Rowman & Littlefield, 2010), 7.

16. Graham Smith, *When Jim Crow met John Bull* (New York: St, Martin's Press, 1987), 9.

17. Vive La France!, *The Crisis*, vol. 17, no. 5, March 1919, 215. https://books.google.com/books?id=Y4ETAAAAYAAJ&printsec=frontcover#v=onepage&q=france&f=false.

18. List of African American Medal of Honor Recipients, https://en.wikipedia.org/wiki/List_of_African-American_Medal_of_Honor_recipients#World_War_I, accessed 11/16/2019.

19. "Promise Armory to Negro Fighters," *New York Times*, February 24, 1919, 3.

20. "The Negro and the South After the War," *Kansas City Sun*, February 1, 1919, 1.

21. "A White Mob Once Destroyed a Black Neighborhood in Tulsa," *New York Times*, October 5, 2018, A20.

22. "Senate Unanimously Passes a Bill Making Lynching a Federal Crime," *New York Times*, December 20, 2018.

23. Ulysses Lee, *The Employment of Negro Troops* (Washington: Center of Military History United States Army, 1966), Ch. 2, 22. https://history.army.mil/books/wwii/11-4/chapter2.htm, accessed 11/3/2019.

24. *Ibid.*, 28.

25. *Ibid.*, 27.

26. *Ibid.*

27. Maggi M. Morehouse, *Fighting in the Jim Crow Army* (Lanham, MD: Rowman & Littlefield, 2000), 26.

28. Ulysses Lee, *The Employment of Negro Troops* (Washington: Center of Military History United States Army, 1966), 43. https://history.army.mil/books/wwii/11-4/chapter2.htm, accessed 11/3/2019.

29. *Ibid.*, 45.

Chapter Three

1. Undated writing by Henry van Landingham, held by his grandson Marcus Geijselaers, Berg en Terblijt, Netherlands.

2. The Bombing of Rotterdam, https://www.brandgrens.nl/en/the-bombing-of-rotterdam, accessed 11/2/2019.

3. A documentary film about the human effects of the occupation can be found at the "New to the Netherlands" website: https://www.netinnederland.nl/en/artikelen/dossiers/overzicht/tweede-wereldoorlog2/bezetting.html

4. In Amsterdam, the Hollandsche Schouwburg had been a theatre of the Jewish Quarter of the city since 1892. With Nazi occupation of the city, it became the collection point for Jews that had been taken from their homes to be sent to the camps. Each night city trams were used to take the day's collection of Jews to state railroads, which took them on to the Westerbork concentration camp, 100 miles to the northeast. From there they were eventually moved to the harsher concentration camps of Europe. In the 21st century, the Hollandsche Schouwburg is a museum and memorial to Amsterdam's Jews lost in the war and sits across Plantage Middenlaan from the nation's Holocaust Museum.

5. Erroll Morris, "Bamboozling Ourselves," *New York Times* online blog, June 3, 2009. https://opinionator.blogs.nytimes.com//2009/06/03/bamboozling-ourselves-part-6/, accessed 10/31/2019.

6. "Amsterdam marks Anniversary if 1941 mass strike in support of Jews," http://www.worldjewishcongress.org/en/news/amsterdam-marks-anniversary-of-1941-general-strike-in-support-of-jews-2-4-2016, accessed 11/1/2019.

7. The Netherlands Historical Background, https://www.yadvashem.org/righteous/stories/netherlands-historical-background.html, accessed 11/1/2019.

8. "Rescue and Righteous Among the Nations in Holland," https://www.yadvashem.org/righteous/resources/rescue-and-righteous-among-the-nations-in-holland.html, accessed 11/1/2019.

9. Diane Wolf, *Beyond Anne Frank: Hidden Children and Postwar Families in Holland* (Berkeley, CA: University of California Press, 2007), 56.

10. Henri A. van der Zee, *The Hunger Winter: Occupied Holland 1944–1945* (Lincoln: University of Nebraska Press, 1998), 304,

11. "The Famine Ended 70 Years Ago. But Dutch Genes Still Bear Scars," *New York Times*, January 31, 2018.

12. Harry L. Coles and Albert K. Weinberg, "Slow Progress in Liberated Area Bodes Ill for Unliberated Holland," *The United States Army in World War II* (Washington, D.C.: Government Printing Office, 1986), 827.

13. Linda M. Woolf, "Survival and Resistance: The Netherlands Under Nazi Occupation," paper given to the United States Holocaust Memorial Museum, Washington, April 6, 1999. http://faculty.webster.edu/woolflm/netherlands.html, accessed 11/2/2019.

14. The Dutch royal family derives from the House of Orange in the medieval principality of Orange in the Provence region of southern France.

15. Linda M. Woolf, "Survival and Resistance: The Netherlands Under Nazi Occupation," paper given to the United States Holocaust Memorial Museum, Washington, April 6, 1999. http://faculty.webster.edu/woolflm/netherlands.html, accessed 11/2/2019.

16. Stewart Bentley, The Central Intelligence Agency, Center for the Study of Intelligence, "The Dutch Resistance and the OSS," https://www.cia.gov/library/center-for-the-study-of-intelligence/csi-publications/csi-studies/studies/spring98/Dutch.html, accessed 12/2/2019.

17. "Dutch Ask Germans Not to Deport Jews." *New York Times*, September 23, 1942, 10.

18. "For Some Dutch Jews, Limburg Was Refuge in Storm of Holocaust," *Forward*, https://forward.com/news/198437/for-some-dutch-jews-limburg-province-was-refuge-in/?p=all, accessed 11/2/2019.

19. E.R. O'Callaghan, *Laws and Ordinances of New Netherland 1638–1674* (Albany, NY: Weed Parsons & Co., 1807), 86.

20. Hans Krabbendam, Cornelis A. van Minnen, Giles Scott-Smith, eds., *Four Centuries of Dutch American Relations* (Albany: State University of New York Press, 2009), 197.

21. *Ibid.*, 86.

22. *Ibid.*, 353.

23. *Ibid.*, 326.

24. "Whole Netherland City Joins in Thanking U.S. for Liberation," *New York Times*, October 5, 1944, 4.

Chapter Four

1. United States War Department, *Command of Negro Troops*, War Department Pamphlet 20–6, February 29, 1944, 1. https://fdrlibrary.org/documents/356632/390886/tusk_doc_e.pdf/e52c54b7-3c64-4ef5-a1d1-052029d8c909, accessed 11/3/2019.

2. *Ibid.*, 3.

3. *Ibid.*, 4.

4. *Ibid.*, 13.

5. Headquarters, Army Service Forces, *Leadership and the Negro Soldier*, Army Services Force Manual, October 1944, Chapter Two. https://books.google.com/books?id=sUHiGAAACAAJ&printsec=frontcover#v=onepage&q&f=false, accessed 11/3/2019.

6. United States War Department, *Command of Negro Troops*, War Department Pamphlet 20–6, February 29, 1944, 13. https://fdrlibrary.org/documents/356632/390886/tusk_doc_e.pdf/e52c54b7-3c64-4ef5-a1d1-052029d8c909, accessed 11/3/2019.

7. *Ibid.*, 14.

8. Chester J. Pach, Jr., *Dwight D. Eisenhower: Domestic Affairs*, University of Virginia—Miller Center, https://millercenter.org/president/eisenhower/domestic-affairs, accessed 11/3/2019.

9. Ulysses Lee, *The Employment of Negro Troops* (Washington: Center of Military History United States Army, 1966), Ch. 15, 428. https://history.army.mil/books/wwii/11-4/chapter15.htm#b1, accessed 11/3/2019.

10. The full story is told in: Ann S. Reilly, *Man O' War and Will Harbut* (Self-Published, 2017).

Chapter Five

1. Mieke Kirkels, *Van Alabama naar Margraten* (Netherlands: Self-Published, 2014), 44.

2. At the instigation of Mieke Kirkels, the relationship between Jefferson Wiggins and Mrs. Merrill became the subject of research by New York Public Library historian Matthew Boylan in 2014. Wiggins had never known, or been able to recall, her full name, and Boylan found it to be Mrs. Anne Marie Merrill, though he could learn no more about her identity. He did find, however, information about the Stapleton branch's efforts with African American soldiers stationed at the Fox Hills Cantonment written by the library director in 1945, excerpted:

> [T]he Branch felt keenly the demand as long as troops were stationed here... At the same time, several members of the WAC, stationed at Fox Hills, were working on a more elementary level with barely literate colored troops who were stationed there. In addition, we were able to provide several books on adult elementary education for one staff member who wanted to provide an even broader background than she found in any of the elementary materials and worked particularly closely with these men.

Mr. Boylan's history can be found on the NYPL Blog, https://www.nypl.org/blog/2014/02/24/one-mans-education-double-v .

3. Mieke Kirkels, *Van Alabama naar Margraten* (Netherlands: Self-Published, 2014), 38.

4. *Ibid.*

5. *Ibid.*, 41.

6. *Ibid.*, 54.

7. William F. Ross and Charles F. Romanus, *The Quartermaster Corps: Operations in the War Against Germany* (Washington: Center of Military History, United States Army, 1991), 364. https://history.army.mil/html/books/010/10-15/CMH_Pub_10-15.pdf

8. *Ibid.*, 386.

9. *Ibid.*,171.

10. *Ibid.*

11. Joseph James Shomon, *Crosses in the Wind* (New York: Stratford House, 1947), 50.

12. Chris Dickon, *The Foreign Burial of American War Dead* (Jefferson, NC: McFarland, 2011), 113.

13. Mieke Kirkels, *Van Alabama naar Margraten* (Netherlands: Self-Published, 2014), source materials.

14. Mieke Kirkels and Jo Purnot, *From Farmland to Soldier's Cemetery* (Netherlands: Stichting Akkers von Margraten, 2009), 46.

15. *Ibid.*, 28.

16. *Ibid.*, 110.

17. Joseph James Shomon, *Crosses in the Wind* (New York: Stratford House, 1947), 87.

18. *Ibid.*, 107.

19. Mieke Kirkels and Jo Purnot, *From Farmland to Soldier's Cemetery* (Netherlands: Stichting Akkers von Margraten, 2009), 46.

Chapter Six

1. Undated writing by Henry van Landingham, held by his grandson Marcus Geijselaers, Berg en Terblijt, Netherlands.

2. "The Red Ball Express Information Page," http://skylighters.org/redball/, accessed 11/5/2019.

3. "Capital Transit Tire Reserve Cut to 500," *The Evening Star* (Washington, D.C.), December 18, 1944, B-11.

4. *Red Ball Express*, film, Universal Pictures, 1952, https://www.youtube.com/watch?v=p71VZ_UqYFo, quote at 47:45, accessed 11/9/2019.

5. Carlo D'Este, *Patton: A Genius for War* (New York: Harper Collins, 1995), 171.

6. *Ibid.*, 216.

7. Stanley Hirshson, *General Patton: A Soldier's Life* (New York: Harper Collins, 2002), 264.

8. "How Harry Truman went from being a racist to desegregating the military," *The Washington Post*, July 26, 2018.

9. Erich Lichtblau, *The Nazis Next Door* (Boston: Houghton Mifflin Harcourt, 2014), 5.

10. Howard Morley Safer, *A History of the Jews in America* (New York: Vintage Books, 1992), 554.

11. Martin Blumenson, *The Patton Papers: 1940–1945* (Boston: Houghton Mifflin, 1972), 751.

12. Erich Lichtblau, "Surviving the Nazis, Only to be Jailed by America," *New York Times*, February 7, 2015.

13. Saul Jay Singer, "Gen. Patton's Appalling Anti-Semitism," *The Jewish Press*, online, https://www.jewishpress.com/indepth/gen-pattons-appalling-anti-semitism/2017/12/20/

14. Robert Wilcox, *Target Patton: The Plot to Assassinate General George S. Patton* (Regnery Publishing, 2014), 342.

15. Jefferson Wiggins, *Another Generation Almost Forgotten* (Bloomington, IN: Xlibris Corporation, 2003), 128.

16. Mieke Kirkels, *Van Alabama naar Margraten* (Netherlands: Self-Published, 2014), 76.

17. Jefferson Wiggins, *Another Generation Almost Forgotten* (Bloomington, IN: Xlibris Corporation, 2003), 130.

18. Ulysses Lee, *The Employment of Negro Troops* (Washington: Center of Military History United States Army, 1966), 688. https://history.army.mil/books/wwii/11-4/chapter15.htm#b1, accessed 11/3/2019.

19. *Ibid.*

20. *Ibid.*, 689.

21. *Ibid.*

22. "Now is the Time Not to be Silent," *The Crisis*, vol. 49, no. 1, January 1942, 7.

23. Neil A. Wynn, *The African American Experience During World War II* (Lanham, MD: Rowman & Littlefield, 2010), 40.

24. Ulysses Lee, *The Employment of Negro Troops* (Washington: Center of Military History United States Army, 1966), 690. https://history.army.mil/books/wwii/11-4/chapter15.htm#b1, accessed 11/3/2019.

25. *Ibid.*, 693.

26. Neil A. Wynn, *The African American Experience During World War II* (Lanham, MD: Rowman & Littlefield, 2010), 55.

27. Joe W. Wilson, *The 761st "Black Panther" Tank Battalion in World War II.* (Jefferson, NC: McFarland & Company, 1999), 53.

28. George S. Patton, Paul Donal Harkins, *War As I Knew It* (Boston: Houghton Mifflin Harcourt, 1995), 160.

29. The citation would derive in part from an event in 1994 that had drawn the attention of then U.S. president Bill Clinton, the first reunion of The Association of the 2221 [sic] Negro Volunteers. The association had been formed by a former driver of the Red Ball Express who had been one of the 2,221 mostly quartermaster troops who had been converted to fighting troops under Eisenhower's plan. Its mission was to finally bring them the same kind of military recognition that had gone to white troops after the war. Remarkably, the combat records of most of them had been deleted after their return home, and, with that, certain benefits and awards for valor. It had taken the intervention of a black Chairman of the Joint Chiefs, Gen. Colin Powell, to bring about the restoration of those records and eventually to work toward a presidential message. See Matt Schudel, "J. Cameron Wade, World War II veteran and advocate for forgotten black soldiers, dies at age 87, *Washington Post*, February 25, 2012.

30. Widely available through Internet search, see https://en.wikipedia.org/wiki/George_S._Patton%27s_speech_to_the_Third_Army.

Chapter Seven

1. Albert de Booy, "Trees heeft een Canadees," on YouTube, https://www.youtube.com/watch?v=eWxxoxJFK_Q, accessed 11/7/2019.

2. "Voices of the Left Behind," http://www.voicesoftheleftbehind.com/who.shtml, accessed 11/6/2019.

3. "Dutch Girls Discouraged from 'Vamping' our GIs," *New York Times*, December 15, 1944, 6.

4. September 16, 1944 Archbishop's letter found in the Katholiek Documen-

tatiecentrum (Katholiek Documentation Center), Nijmegen, Netherlands.

5. Juul Dresen, "Unique Encounters in Liberated Limburg. A research on the interactions between African American soldiers and Dutch Women in the period 1944–1945." Source document is Archive of the Militair Gezag, 2.13.25 inv.nr. 307, 3 April, 1944, National Archives in the Hague.

6. "Wooden-shooed Away," *Stars and Stripes*, U.S. War Department, December 19, 1944, 1.

7. Lt. Col. Burner, writing in undated newspaper, Heerlen, NL. Referred to in Mieke Kirkels, *Kinderen van zwarte bevrijders*, 96.

8. The Conference of Bishops and The Dutch Religious Conference, The Deetman Commission Report, December 2011, Summary, 3. http://www.bishop-accountability.org/news2011/11_12/2011_12_26_DeetmanCommission_Deetman Commission_2.htm, accessed 11/7/2019.

9. *Ibid.*, 5.

10. *Ibid.*, 14.

11. Weblog "Bierenbroodspot," http://www.bierenbroodspot.info/summon-english.html, accessed 11/7/2019.

12. *Ibid.*

Chapter Eight

1. Army Service Forces, *A Welcome to Britain*, 1943, on YouTube, https://www.youtube.com/watch?v=SyYSBBE1DFw, @ 2:10.

2. *Ibid.*, @ 25:40.

3. *Ibid.*, @ 23:35.

4. Sabine Lee, *A Forgotten Legacy of the Second World War: GI children in postwar Britain and Germany*, Contemporary European History, vol. 20, issue 02, May 2011, 163. http://pure-oai.bham.ac.uk/ws/files/17367744/LeeS096077731100004Xa.pdf, accessed 11/7/2019.

5. Margaret Mead, "A GI View of Britain," *New York Times Magazine*, March 19, 1944, 18.

6. David Reynolds, *Rich Relations: The American Occupation of Britain* (New York: Harper Collins, 1995), 267.

7. *Ibid.*, 217.

8. *Ibid.*

9. John Belchem, *Before the Windrush:*

Race Relations in 20th Century Liverpool (Oxford: Oxford University Press, 2014), 92.

10. David Reynolds, *Rich Relations: The American Occupation of Britain* (New York: Harper Collins, 1995), 219.

11. John Virtue, *The Black Soldiers Who Built the Alaska Highway* (Jefferson, NC: McFarland, 2012), 173.

12. Ulysses Lee, *The Employment of Negro Troops* (Washington: Center of Military History United States Army, 1966), 624. https://history.army.mil/html/books/011/11-4/CMH_Pub_11-4-1.pdf, accessed 11/3/2019.

13. Graham Smith, *When Jim Crow met John Bull* (New York: St, Martin's Press, 1987), 104.

14. Ulysses Lee, *The Employment of Negro Troops* (Washington: Center of Military History United States Army, 1966), 625. https://history.army.mil/html/books/011/11-4/CMH_Pub_11-4-1.pdf, accessed 11/3/2019.

15. *Ibid.*, 423.

16. Paul B. Rich, *Race and Empire in British Politics* (Cambridge: Cambridge University Press, 1986), 152.

17. *Ibid.*

18. "Jim Crow in Britain in the 1840s and 1940s," quoting *Sunday Pictorial*, September 6, 1942, https://www.bulldozia.com/jim-crow/jim-crow-in-britain/, accessed 11/8/2019.

19. Graham Smith, *When Jim Crow met John Bull* (New York: St, Martin's Press, 1987), 90.

20. *Ibid.*, 195.

21. *Ibid.*, 196.

Chapter Nine

1. "Windrush: who exactly was on board?" BBC News, June 21, 2019, https://www.bbc.com/news/uk-43808007, accessed 11/8/2019.

2. Bob Carter, Clive Harris, Shirley Joshi, *The 1951–55 Conservative Government and the Racialisation of Black Immigratiom*, Centre for Research in Ethnic Relations, University of Warwick, Coventry, October 1987, Introduction.

3. The National Archives (UK), Letter from Prime Minister Clement Atlee to M.P. about immigration, July 5, 1948. Ho-213–715–12341, https://www.national archives.gov.uk/education/resources/attlees-britain/empire-windrush/, accessed 11/8/2019.

4. Linda McDowell, "How Caribbean Migrants Helped to Rebuild Britain," British Library Windrush Stories, October 4, 2018, https://www.bl.uk/windrush/articles/how-caribbean-migrants-rebuilt-britain, accessed 11/8/2019.

5. Amelia Hill, "'Hostile Environment': The Hardline Home Office Policy Tearing Families Apart," *The Guardian*, November 29, 2017, https://www.theguardian.com/uk-news/2017/nov/28/hostile-environment-the-hardline-home-office-policy-tearing-families-apart, accessed 11/8/2019.

6. Nick Hopkins, Heather Stewart, "Amber Rudd was Sent Targets for Migrant Removal, Lead Reveals," *The Guardian*, April 28, 2018, https://www.theguardian.com/politics/2018/apr/27/amber-rudd-was-told-about-migrant-removal-targets-leak-reveals, accessed 11/8/2019.

7. Graham Smith, *When Jim Crow met John Bull* (New York: St, Martin's Press, 1987), 204.

8. The National Archives (UK), folder: "Report of conference on the position of the illegitimate child who whose father is alleged to be a coloured American," December 19, 1944, MH55/1656, http://www.nationalarchives.gov.uk/documents/mh-55-1656.pdf, letter from The League of Colored People to Aneurin Bevan, M.P., 1, accessed 11/8/2019.

9. *Ibid.*, 2.

10. *Ibid.*, 3.

11. The National Archives (UK), folder: "Report of conference on the position of the illegitimate child who whose father is alleged to be a coloured American," December 19, 1944, MH55/1656, http://www.nationalarchives.gov.uk/documents/mh-55-1656.pdf, Report, 3.

12. *Ibid.*, 5.

13. *Ibid.*

14. *Ibid.*, 3.

15. *Ibid.*, 6.

16. *Ibid.*, 3.

17. *Ibid.*, 4.

18. Graham Smith, *When Jim Crow met John Bull* (New York: St, Martin's Press, 1987), 210.

19. *Ibid.*, 211.

20. Sabine Lee, *A Forgotten Legacy of the*

Second World War: GI children in postwar Britain and Germany, Contemporary European History, vol. 20, issue 02, May 2011, 163. http://pure-oai.bham.ac.uk/ws/files/17367744/LeeS096077731100004Xa.pdf, accessed 11/7/2019.

21. "England's Brown Babies in Trouble," the *Hartford Chronicle*, December 21, 1946, 2.

22. "Britain's Brown Babies Lack Fare to U.S.," the *Detroit Tribune*, June 7, 1947, 3.

23. "The Babies They Left Behind Them," *Life*, August 23, 1948, 41.

24. *Ibid.*

Chapter Ten

1. Geisel, Theodore, *Your Job in Germany*, film, Frank Capra, Army Services Force, 1946, https://www.youtube.com/watch?v=1v5QCGqDYGo, accessed 11/9/2019.

2. Sabine Lee, *A Forgotten Legacy of the Second World War: GI children in postwar Britain and Germany*, Contemporary European History, vol. 20, issue 02, May 2011, 168. http://pure-oai.bham.ac.uk/ws/files/17367744/LeeS096077731100004Xa.pdf, accessed 11/7/2019.

3. 12th Army Group, *Don't Be a Sucker in Germany*, pamphlet, undated. http://www.3ad.com/history/wwll/feature.pages/occupation.booklet.htm#anchor645243, accessed 11/9/2019.

4. Drew Middleton, "Officers Oppose Fraternizing Ban," *New York Times*, June 25, 1945, 1.

5. *Ibid.*

6. Sabine Lee, *A Forgotten Legacy of the Second World War: GI children in postwar Britain and Germany*, Contemporary European History, vol. 20, issue 02, May 2011, 169. http://pure-oai.bham.ac.uk/ws/files/17367744/LeeS096077731100004Xa.pdf, accessed 11/7/2019.

7. J. Robert Lilly, *Taken by Force* (London: Palgrave MacMillan, 2007), 12.

8. *Ibid.*, 118, 154–160.

9. Heide Fehrenbach, *Race After Hitler* (Princeton, NJ: Princeton University Press, 2005), 2.

10. May Opitz, May Ayim, Katharina Oguntoye, Dagmar Schultz, eds., *Showing Our Colors* (Amherst: University of Massachusetts Press, 1992), 44.

11. Richard J. Evans, *The Third Reich in Power* (New York: Penguin Books, 2005), 527.

12. Adolf Hitler, *Mein Kampf*, 1939 (Project Gutenberg of Australia), vol. 1, ch. 11.

13. Kjersti Ericsson, Eva Simonsen, *Children of World War II: The Hidden Enemy Legacy* (Oxford, Berg, 2005), 260.

14. Heide Fehrenbach, *Black Occupation Children and the Devolution of the Nazi Racial State*, The University of Michigan Press, 2009, 34. https://www.press.umich.edu/pdf/9780472116867-ch1.pdf, accessed 11/9/2019.

15. Heide Fehrenbach, *Race After Hitler* (Princeton, NJ: Princeton University Press, 2005), 65.

16. *Ibid.*, 67.

17. Sabine Lee, *A Forgotten Legacy of the Second World War: GI children in postwar Britain and Germany*, Contemporary European History, vol. 20, issue 02, May 2011, 173. http://pure-oai.bham.ac.uk/ws/files/17367744/LeeS096077731100004Xa.pdf, accessed 11/7/2019.

18. "Negro Children Studied," *New York Times*, July 23, 1952, 5.

19. Heide Fehrenbach, *Race After Hitler* (Princeton, NJ: Princeton University Press, 2005), 77.

20. Kjersti Ericsson, Eva Simonsen, *Children of World War II: The Hidden Enemy Legacy* (Oxford, Berg, 2005), 257.

21. "Forgotten Children of War," *Der Standard*, September 27, 2012, https://derstandard.at/1348283996693/Vergessene-Kinder-des-Krieges, accessed 11/9/2019.

22. "CROSS-POST: Exhibit Review: Thurman on 'Black Austria: The Children of African American Occupation Soldiers,'" https://networks.h-net.org/node/19384/discussions/135747/cross-post-exhibit-review-thurman-black-austria-children-african, accessed 11/9/2019.

23. Mariana Smetana, "Neger-Christl haben s' zu mir gesagt," *Salzburger Nachrichten*, July 30, 2013, https://www.sn.at/politik/weltpolitik/neger-christl-haben-s-zu-mir-gesagt-4630354, accessed 11/9/2019.

24. The film can be found in its entirety in various versions on YouTube, internet.

25. Heide Fehrenbach, *Race After Hit-*

ler (Princeton: Princeton University Press, 2005), 107.

26. *Ibid.*, 113.

27. William G. Nunn, "Brown Babies Turned into Sideshow Attractions," Pittsburgh *Courier*, July 17, 1948, 3.

28. *Ibid.*

29. "German Brown Babies Really Need Your Help," Pittsburgh *Courier*, April 30, 1949, 5.

30. Albert Schweitzer, *On the Edge of the Primeval Forest* (London: A&C Black, Ltd., 1924), 130.

31. Heide Fehrenbach, *Race After Hitler* (Princeton, NJ: Princeton University Press, 2005), 159.

32. Pittsburgh *Courier*, February 20, 1954, 13.

33. Heide Fehrenbach, *Race After Hitler* (Princeton, NJ: Princeton University Press, 2005), 101.

34. "Brown Babies Go to Work," *Ebony*, November 1960, 97.

35. *Ibid.*, 98.

Chapter Eleven

1. Dell de Chant, *The Sacred Santa: Religious Dimensions of Consumer Culture* (Eugene, OR: Wipf & Stock, 2008), 189.

2. Allison Blakely, *Blacks in the Dutch World* (Bloomington: Indiana University Press, 2001), 77.

3. Emma Thomas, "Outrage in Netherlands over calls to abolish 'Black Pete' clowns which march in Christmas parade dressed in blackface," *The Daily Mail*, October 24, 2013, https://www.dailymail.co.uk/news/article-2474693/Zwarte-Piet-abolished-Outrage-Netherlands-Black-Pete-Christmas-tradition.html, accessed 11/9/2019.

4. Gijs Beukers, "NTR replaces all Zwarte Pieten for soot wags," *de Volksrant*, September 17, 2019.

5. Allison Lalor, "Rutte Has Changed His Opinion on Zwarte Piet," *Dutch Review*, June 5, 2020, https://dutchreview.com/news/rutte-has-changed-his-opinion-on-zwarte-piet-agrees-institutional-racism-is-present-in-the-netherlands/.

6. Mieke Kirkels, *Van Alabama naar Margraten* (Netherlands: Self-Published, 2014), 72.

7. Steven White, *World War II and*

American Racial Politics (Cambridge: Cambridge University Press, 2019), 90.

8. Executive Order 9981, July 26, 1948; General Records of the United States Government; Record Group 11; National Archives.

9. Mieke Kirkels, *Van Alabama naar Margraten* (Netherlands: Self-Published, 2014), 89.

Chapter Twelve

1. Chris Dickon, *The Foreign Burial of American War Dead* (Jefferson, NC: McFarland, 2011), 118.

2. Mieke Kirkels, *Van Alabama naar Margraten* (Netherlands: Self-Published, 2014), 97.

3. Joseph James Shomon, *Crosses in the Wind* (New York: Stratford House, 1947), 67.

4. Jefferson Wiggins, speech given in Centre Céramique, Maastricht, September 11, 2009.

5. Letter from president Barack Obama to Jefferson Wiggins August 10, 2009, Mieke Kirkels, *Van Alabama naar Margraten* (Netherlands: Self-Published, 2014), 103.

6. Rob Gollin, "The Battered Life of a Deliverance Child," de Volksrant, April 24, 2015, https://www.volkskrant.nl/mensen/het-gehavende-leven-van-een-bevrijdingskind~b8e97b9e/, accessed 11/10/2019.

7. Paul van der Steen, "The Black Friend of the House Daughter," *NRC Handelsblad*, January 30, 2016. https://www.nrc.nl/nieuws/2016/01/30/de-zwarte-vriend-van-de-dochter-des-huizes-1582687-a423982, accessed 11/10/2019.

Chapter Thirteen

1. "Small Portrait: Liberation Child," *Libelle*, Netherlands, May 3, 1996, p 18.

2. *Ibid.*

3. Letter from Els Geijselaers-Nols to Henry van Landingham, August 18, 1994, held by her son Marcus Geijselaers, Bergit en Terblijt, Netherlands.

4. Letter from Henry van Landingham to Els Geijselaers-Nols, September 24, 1994, held by his grandson Marcus Geijselaers, Bergit en Terblijt, Netherlands.

5. *Ibid.*

Appendix

1. Bettie Morden, *The Women's Army Corps 1945–1978* (Washington, Center of Military History United States Army, 1990), 15.

2. Duncan Barrett, "British was brides faced own battles during 1940s," Los Angeles Times, October 20, 2014. https://www.latimes.com/nation/la-oe-barrett-war-brides-immigration-20141021-story.html, accessed 12/22/19.

3. Lynne Taylor, *In the Children's Best Interests* (University of Toronto Press, 2017), 165.

4. Fehrenbach, Heide, *Black Occupation Children and the Devolution of the Nazi Racial State*, The University of Michigan Press, 2009, 37. https://www.press.umich.edu/pdf/9780472116867-ch1.pdf, accessed 11/9/2019.

5. Public Law 203, August 7, 1953, https://www.govinfo.gov/content/pkg/STATUTE-67/pdf/STATUTE-67-Pg400.pdf, accessed 12/22/2019.

6. "Thousands of mixed-race British babies were born in World War II—and adoption by their black American fathers was blocked," The Conversation, https://theconversation.com/thousands-of-mixed-race-british-babies-were-born-in-world-war-ii-and-adoption-by-their-black-american-fathers-was-blocked-116790, accessed 12/22/2019.

7. Brenda Wilt, "War Brides," America in WW II, http://www.americainwwii.com/articles/war-brides/, accessed 12/22/2019.

8. "Canadian War Brides," Veterans Affairs Canada, https://www.veterans.gc.ca/eng/remembrance/history/second-world-war/canadian-war-brides, accessed 12/22/2019.

Bibliography

"Amsterdam Marks Anniversary of 1941 Mass Strike in Support of Jews," http://www.worldjewishcongress.org/en/news/amsterdam-marks-anniversary-of-1941-general-strike-in-support-of-jews-2-4-2016, viewed 11/1/2019.

Army Service Forces, *A Welcome to Britain*, 1943, on YouTube, https://www.youtube.com/watch?v=SyYSBBE1DFw.

"The Babies They Left Behind Them," *Life*, August 23, 1948.

Belchem, John, *Before the Windrush: Race Relations in 20th Century Liverpool* (Oxford: Oxford University Press, 2014).

Bentley, Stewart, The Central Intelligence Agency, Center for the Study of Intelligence, "The Dutch Resistance and the OSS," https://www.cia.gov/library/center-for-the-study-of-intelligence/csi-publications/csi-studies/studies/spring98/Dutch.html, viewed 12/2/2019.

Beukers, Gijs, "NTR replaces all Zwarte Pieten for soot wags," *de Volksrant*, September 17, 2019.

Black, William R., "How Watermelons Became a Racist Trope," *The Atlantic*, December 8, 2014.

Blakely, Allison, Blacks in the Dutch World (Bloomington: Indiana University Press, 2001).

Bland, Lucy, video *Professor Lucy Bland—inaugural lecture*, https://www.youtube.com/watch?v=nhfxNsJlNaA.

Blumenson, Martin, *The Patton Papers: 1940–1945* (Boston: Houghton Mifflin, 1972).

"The Bombing of Rotterdam," https://www.brandgrens.nl/en/the-bombing-of-rotterdam, viewed 11/2/2019.

"Britain's Brown Babies Lack Fare to U.S.," the *Detroit Tribune*, June 7, 1947.

"Brown Babies Go to Work," *Ebony*, November 1960.

"Capital Transit Tire Reserve Cut to 500," *The Evening Star* (Washington, D.C.), December 18, 1944.

Carter, Bob, et al, *The 1951–55 Conservative Government and the Racialisation of Black Immigratiom*,

Centre for Research in Ethnic Relations, University of Warwick, Coventry, October 1987.

Coles, Harry L., and Albert K. Weinberg, "Slow Progress in Liberated Area Bodes Ill for Unliberated Holland," *The United States Army in World War II* (Washington, Government Printing Office, 1986.

The Conference of Bishops and The Dutch Religious Conference, The Deetman Commission Report, December 2011, Summary, 3. http://www.bishop-accountability.org/news2011/11_12/2011_12_26_DeetmanCommission_DeetmanCommission_2.htm, viewed 11/7/2019.

"CROSS-POST: Exhibit Review: Thurman on 'Black Austria: The Children of African American Occupation Soldiers,'" https://networks.h-net.org/node/19384/discussions/135747/cross-post-exhibit-review-thurman-black-austria-children-african, viewed 11/9/2019.

de Booy, Hans, "Trees heeft een Canadees," on YouTube, https://www.youtube.com/watch?v=eWxxoxJFK_Q, viewed 11/7/2019.

de Chant, Dell, *The Sacred Santa: Religious Dimensions of Consumer Culture* (Eugene, OR: Wipf and Stock, 2008).

de Jong, L., *Het Koninrijk der Nederlanden in de Tweede Wereldoorlog*, vol. 5, pt. 1 (Leiden, Martinus Nijhoff, 1972).

Department of Defense, Department of the Army. Office of the Chief Signal Officer. *Training of Colored Troops*. Script. U.S. National Archives RG 111, https://catalog.archives.gov/id/24716.

D'Este, Carlo, *Patton: A Genius for War* (New York: HarperCollins, 1995).

Dickon, Chris, *The Foreign Burial of American War Dead* (Jefferson, NC: McFarland, 2011).

Dresen, Juul, "Unique Encounters in Liberated Limburg. A Research on the Interactions Between African American Soldiers and Dutch Women in the Period 1944–1945." Source document is Archive of the Militair Gezag, 2.13.25 inv.nr. 307, April 3, 1944, National Archives in the Hague.

"Dutch Ask Germans Not to Deport Jews," *New York Times*, September 23, 1942.

"Dutch Girls Discouraged from 'Vamping' our GIs," *New York Times*, December 15, 1944.

"England's Brown Babies in Trouble," the *Hartford Chronicle*, December 21, 1946.

Ericsson, Kjersti, and Eva Simonsen, *Children of World War II: The Hidden Enemy Legacy* (Oxford, Berg, 2005).

Evans, Richard J., *The Third Reich in Power* (New York: Penguin Books, 2005).

Executive Order 9981, July 26, 1948; General Records of the United States Government; Record Group 11; National Archives.

"The Famine Ended 70 Years Ago but Dutch Genes Still Bear Scars," *New York Times*, January 31, 2018.

Fehrenbach, Heide, *Black Occupation Children and the Devolution of the Nazi Racial State*, Ann Arbor: University of Michigan Press, 2009. https://www.press.umich.edu/pdf/9780472116867-ch1.pdf, viewed 11/9/2019.

Fehrenbach, Heide, *Race After Hitler* (Princeton, NJ: Princeton University Press, 2005).

Foner, Jack D., *Blacks and the Military in American History* (Santa Barbara, CA: Praeger, 1974).

"For Some Dutch Jews, Limburg Was Refuge in Storm of Holocaust," *Forward*, https://forward.com/news/198437/for-some-dutch-jews-limburg-province-was-refuge-in/?p=all, viewed 11/2/2019.

"Forgotten Children of War," *Der Standard*, September 27, 2012, https://derstandard.at/1348283996693/Vergessene-Kinder-des-Krieges, viewed 11/9/2019.

Gebhardt, Miriam, *Crimes Unspoken: The Rape of German Women at the End of the Second World War*, (Hoboken: Wiley, 2017).

Geisel, Theodore, *Your Job in Germany*, film, Frank Capra, Army Services Force, 1946, https://www.youtube.com/watch?v=1v5QCGqDYGo, viewed 11/9/2019.

"German Brown Babies Really Need Your Help," Pittsburgh *Courier*, April 30, 1949.

German soldiers fathered 50,000 Dutch children, https://www.expatica.com/de/german-soldiers-fathered-50000-dutch-children/, viewed 11/15/2019.

Gollin, Rob, "The Battered Life of a Deliverance Child," *de Volksrant*, April 24, 2015, https://www.volkskrant.nl/mensen/het-gehavende-leven-van-een-bevrijdingskind~b8e97b9e/, viewed 11/10/2019.

Hamilton, Col. West A. "The Negroes' Historical and Contemporary Role in National Defense" (speech, Hampton, Virginia, November 25, 1940), U.S. National Archives, RG 220, https://catalog.archives.gov/id/40019879.

Headquarters, Army Service Forces, *Leadership and the Negro Soldier*, Army Services Force Manual, October 1944, Chapter Two. https://books.google.com/books?id=sUHiGAAACAAJ&printsec=frontcover#v=onepage&q&f=false, viewed 11/3/2019.

Heijnen, Hans, prod., *Zwarte Limburgers* (Black Limburgers), 2017, 11nl Limburg (television), https://l1.nl/l1-docu-zwarte-limburgers-in-premiere-op-docfest-131664/.

Hill, Amelia, "'Hostile Environment': The Hardline Home Office Policy Tearing Families Apart," *The Guardian*, November 29, 2017, https://www.theguardian.com/uk-news/2017/

nov/28/hostile-environment-the-hardline-home-office-policy-tearing-families-apart, viewed 11/8/2019.

Hirshson, Stanley, *General Patton: A Soldier's Life* (New York: HarperCollins, 2002).

Hitler, Adolf, *Mein Kampf*, 1939 (Project Gutenberg of Australia).

Hopkins, Nick, and Heather Stewart, "Amber Rudd Was Sent Targets for Migrant Removal, Lead Reveals," *The Guardian*, April 28, 2018, https://www.theguardian.com/politics/2018/apr/27/amber-rudd-was-told-about-migrant-removal-targets-leak-reveals, viewed 11/8/2019.

"How Harry Truman Went from Being a Racist to Desegregating the Military," *The Washington Post*, July 26, 2018.

"Jim Crow in Britain in the 1840s and 1940s," quoting *Sunday Pictorial*, September 6, 1942, https://www.bulldozia.com/jim-crow/jim-crow-in-britain/, viewed 11/8/2019.

Kirkels, Mieke, *Van Alabama naar Margraten* (Netherlands: Self-Published, 2014).

Kirkels, Mieke, and Jo Purnot, *From Farmland to Soldier's Cemetery* (Netherlands: Stichting Akkers von Margraten, 2009).

Krabbendam, Hans, et al., eds., *Four Centuries of Dutch American Relations* (Albany: State University of New York Press, 2009).

Lee, Sabine, "A Forgotten Legacy of the Second World War: GI Children in Postwar Britain and Germany," *Contemporary European History*, vol. 20, no. 2.

Lee, Ulysses, *The Employment of Negro Troops* (Washington: Center of Military History United States Army, 1966). https://history.army.mil/books/wwii/11-4/chapter2.htm, viewed 11/3/2019.

Letter from President Barack Obama to Jefferson Wiggins, August 10, 2009, Mieke Kirkels, *Van Alabama nar Margraten* (Netherlands: Self-Published, 2014).

Lichtblau, Erich, *The Nazis Next Door* (Boston: Houghton Mifflin Harcourt, 2014).

Lilly, J. Robert, *Taken by Force* (London: Palgrave Mac Millan, 2007).

List of African American Medal of Honor Recipients, https://en.wikipedia.org/wiki/List_of_African-American_Medal_of_Honor_recipients#World_War_I, viewed 11/16/2019.

McDowell, Linda, "How Caribbean Migrants Helped to Rebuild Britain," British Library Windrush Stories, October 4, 2018, https://www.bl.uk/windrush/articles/how-caribbean-migrants-rebuilt-britain, viewed 11/8/2019.

Mead, Margaret, "A GI View of Britain," *New York Times Magazine*, March 19, 1944.

Middleton, Drew, "Officers Oppose Fraternizing Ban," *New York Times*, June 25, 1945.

Military Children Born Abroad https://military.findlaw.com/family-employment-housing/, military-children-born-abroad.html, viewed 10/19/2019

Morris, Erroll, "Bamboozling Ourselves," *New York Times* online blog, June 3, 2009. https://opinionator.blogs.nytimes.com//2009/06/03/bamboozling-ourselves-part-6/ viewed 10/31/2019.

The National Archives (UK), folder: "Report of conference on the position wo the illegitimate child who whose father is alleged to be a coloured American," December 19, 1944, MH55/1656, http://www.nationalarchives.gov.uk/documents/mh-55-1656.pdf, letter from The League of Colored People to Aneurin Bevan, M.P., 1, viewed 11/8/2019.

The National Archives (UK), Letter from Prime Minister Clement Atlee to M.P. about immigration, July 5, 1948. Ho-213–715–12341, https://www.nationalarchives.gov.uk/education/resources/attlees-britain/empire-windrush/, viewed 11/8/2019.

"The Negro and the South After the War," *Kansas City Sun*, February 1, 1919.

"Negro Children Studied," *New York Times*, July 23, 1952.

"The Netherlands Historical Background," https://www.yadvashem.org/righteous/stories/netherlands-historical-background.html, viewed 11/1/2019.

Niewyk, Donald L., *The Columbia Guide to the Holocaust* (New York: Columbia University Press, 2000).

"Now is the Time Not to be Silent," *The Crisis*, vol. 49, no. 1, January 1942.

Nunn, William G., "Brown Babies Turned into Sideshow Attractions," Pittsburgh *Courier*, July 17, 1948.

O'Callaghan, E.R., *Laws and Ordinances of New Netherland 1638–1674* (Albany: Weed Parsons & Co., 1807).

Olson, Lynne, *Last Hope Island* (New York: Random House, 2017).

Opitz, May, et al., eds., *Showing Our Colors* (Amherst: University of Massachusetts Press, 1992).

"Our Special Grievances," *The Crisis*, vol. 16, no. 5, September 1918, 216. https://books.google.com/books?id=Y4ETAAAAYAAJ&printsec=frontcover#v=onepage&q&f=false

Pach, Chester J., Jr., *Dwight D. Eisenhower: Domestic Affairs*, University of Virginia— Miller Center, https://millercenter.org/president/eisenhower/domestic-affairs, viewed 11/3/2019.

Patton, Gen. George S., and Paul Donal Harkins, *War as I Knew It* (Boston: Houghton Mifflin Harcourt, 1995).

Patton, Tracy Owens, "That Was the Worst Day of My Life," Communications and Journalism Department, University of Wyoming, June 9, 2017.

"Promise Armory to Negro Fighters," *New York Times*, February 24, 1919.

Red Ball Express, film, Universal Pictures, 1952, https://www.youtube.com/watch?v=p71VZ_UqYFo, viewed 11/9/2019.

"The Red Ball Express Information Page," http://skylighters.org/redball/, viewed 11/5/2019.

"Rescue and Righteous Among the Nations in Holland," https://www.yadvashem.org/righteous/resources/rescue-and-righteous-among-the-nations-in-holland.html, viewed 11/1/2019

Reynolds, David, *Rich Relations: The American Occupation of Britain* (New York: HarperCollins, 1995).

Rich, Paul B., *Race and Empire in British Politics* (Cambridge: Cambridge University Press, 1986).

Rohrbach, Philip, and Niko Wahl, "Black Austria: The Children of African American Soldiers of the Occupation," exhibit of the Vienna Museum of Folk Life and Folk Art, 2016.

Ross, William F., and Charles F. Romanus, *The Quartermaster Corps: Operations in the War Against Germany* (Washington, D.C.: Center of Military History, United States Army, 1991). https://history.army.mil/html/books/010/10-15/CMH_Pub_10-15.pdf.

Safer, Howard Morley, *A History of the Jews in America* (New York: Vintage Books, 1992).

Schweitzer, Albert, *On the Edge of the Primeval Forest* (London: A&C Black, Ltd., 1924).

"Senate Unanimously Passes a Bill Making Lynching a Federal Crime," *New York Times*, December 20, 2018.

September 16, 1944 Archbishop's letter Found in the Katholiek documentatiecentrum (Catholic Documentation Center), Nijmegen, Netherlands.

Shomon, Joseph James, *Crosses in the Wind* (New York: Stratford House, 1947).

Singer, Saul Jay, "Gen. Patton's Appalling Anti-Semitism," *The Jewish Press*, online, https://www.jewishpress.com/indepth/gen-pattons-appalling-anti-semitism/2017/12/20/

"Small Portrait: Liberation Child," *Libelle*, Netherlands, May 3, 1996

Smetana, Mariana, "Neger-Christl haben s' zu mir gesagt," *Salzburger Nachtridden*, July 30, 2013, https://www.sn.at/politik/weltpolitik/neger-christl-haben-s-zu-mir-gesagt-4630354, viewed 11/9/2019.

Thomas, Emma, "Outrage in Netherlands over Calls to Abolish 'Black Pete' Clowns Which March in Christmas Parade Dressed in Blackface," *The Daily Mail*, October 24, 2013, https://www.dailymail.co.uk/news/article-2474693/Zwarte-Piet-abolished-Outrage-Netherlands-Black-Pete-Christmas-tradition.html, viewed 11/9/2019.

12th Army Group, *Don't Be a Sucker in Germany*, pamphlet, undated. http://www.3ad.com/history/wwll/feature.pages/occupation.booklet.htm#anchor645243, viewed 11/9/2019.

United States Embassy, The Hague, Netherlands, *Alabama to Margraten*, 2013, on YouTube. https://www.youtube.com/watch?v=QE0QszXRg3k.

United States War Department, *Command of Negro Troops*, War Department Pamphlet 20–6, February 29, 1944. https://fdrlibrary.org/documents/356632/390886/tusk_doc_e.pdf/e52c54b7-3c64-4ef5-a1d1-052029d8c909, viewed 11/3/2019.

United States War Department, *Command of Negro Troops*, War Department Pamphlet 20-6, February 29, 1944. https://fdrlibrary.org/documents/356632/390886/tusk_doc_e.pdf/e52c54b7-3c64-4ef5-a1d1-052029d8c909, viewed 11/3/2019.

University of Missouri–Kansas City School of Law, "Lynchings by State and Race, 1882–1968," from the Archives at Tuskegee Institute. https://web.archive.org/web/20100629081241/ http:/www.law.umkc.edu/faculty/projects/ftrials/shipp/lynchingsstate.html, viewed 10/30/2019.

van der Steen, Paul, "The Black Friend of the House Daughter," *NRC Handelsblad*, January 30, 2016. https://www.nrc.nl/nieuws/2016/01/30/de-zwarte-vriend-van-de-dochter-des-huizes-1582687-a423982, viewed 11/10/2019.

van der Zee, Henri A., *The Hunger Winter: Occupied Holland 1944–1945* (Lincoln, NE: University of Nebraska Press, 1998),

Verkuyten, Maykel, *Identity and Cultural Diversity* (United Kingdom: Routledge 2013).

Virtue, John, *The Black Soldiers Who Built the Alaska Highway* (Jefferson, NC: McFarland, 2012).

"Vive La France!" *The Crisis*, vol. 17, no. 5, March 1919, 215. https://books.google.com/books?id=Y4ETAAAAYAAJ&printsec=frontcover#v=onepage&q=france&f=false.

"Voices of the Left Behind," http://www.voicesoftheleftbehind.com/who.shtml, viewed 11/6/2019.

Weblog "Bierenbroodspot," http://www.bierenbroodspot.info/summon-english.html, viewed 11/7/2019.

"A White Mob Once Destroyed a Black Neighborhood in Tulsa," *New York Times*, October 5, 2018.

"Whole Netherland City Joins in Thanking U.S. for Liberation," *New York Times*, October 5, 1944.

Wiggins, Jefferson, *Another Generation Almost Forgotten* (Bloomington, IN: Xlibris Corporation, 2003.

Wiggins, Jefferson, speech at Centre Céramique Maastricht, September 9, 2009.

Wilcox, Robert, *Target Patton: The Plot to Assassinate General George S. Patton* (Regnery Publishing, 2014).

Wilson, Joe W., *The 761st "Black Panther" Tank Battalion in World War II.* (Jefferson, NC: McFarland, 1999).

"Windrush: Who Exactly Was on Board?" BBC News, June 21, 2019, https://www.bbc.com/news/uk-43808007, viewed 11/8/2019.

Wolf, Diane, *Beyond Anne Frank: Hidden Children and Postwar Families in Holland* (Berkeley, CA: University of California Press, 2007).

"Wooden-shooed Away," *Stars and Stripes*, U.S. War Department, December 19, 1944.

Woolf, Linda M., "Survival and Resistance: The Netherlands Under Nazi Occupation," paper given to the United States Holocaust Memorial Museum, Washington, April 6, 1999. http://faculty.webster.edu/woolflm/netherlands.html, viewed 11/2/2019.

Wynn, Neil A., *The African American Experience During World War II* (Lanham, MD: Rowman & Littlefield Publishers, 2010).

Index

Numbers in **bold italics** indicate pages with illustrations